THE HARMONY GUIDES

450 Knitting STITCHES

VOLUME 2

includes knit and purl patterns, rib
patterns, basic cables, edging patterns

COLLINS & BROWN

First published by Lyric Books in 1986 as
The Harmony Guide to Knitting Stitches
Reissued in 1998

This edition published in 2007 by
Collins & Brown Limited
151 Freston Road
London
W10 6TH

An imprint of Anova Books Company Ltd

ISBN 978 1 85585 629 5

A CIP catalogue record for this book is available from the British Library.

10 9 8 7 6 5 4 3

Printed by SNP Leefung, China

This book can be ordered direct from the publisher.
Contact the marketing department, but try your bookshop first.

www.anovabooks.com

Contents

Introduction 4

Abbreviations 16

Knit and Purl Patterns 18

Patterns for Texture and Colour 31

All-over Lace Patterns 49

Lace Panel Stitches 62

Rib Patterns 68

Cables 74

Edging Patterns 95

Introduction

Knitting needles

Knitting needles are used in pairs to produce a flat knitted fabric. They are pointed at one end to form the stitches and have a knob at the other end to retain the stitches. They may be made in plastic, wood, steel or alloy and range in size from 2mm to 17mm in diameter. In England needles used to be sized by numbers — the higher the number, the smaller the needle. Metric sizing has now been internationally adopted. Needles are also made in different lengths. Choose a length that will comfortably hold the stitches required for each project.

It is useful to have a range of sizes so that tension swatches can be knitted up and compared. Discard any needles that become bent. Points should be fairly sharp, blunt needles reduce the speed and ease of working.

Circular and double-pointed needles are used to produce a tubular fabric or flat rounds. Many traditional fisherman's sweaters are knitted in the round. Double-pointed needles are sold in sets of four or six. Circular needles consist of two needles joined by a flexible length of plastic. The plastic varies in length. Use the shorter lengths for knitting sleeves, neckbands etc, and the longer lengths for larger pieces such as sweaters and skirts.

Cable needles are short needles used to hold the stitches of a cable to the back or front of the main body of the knitting.

Needle gauges are punched with holes corresponding to needle sizes and are marked with both the old numerical sizing and the metric sizing so you can easily check the size of any needle.

Stitch holders resemble large safety pins and are used to hold stitches while they are not being worked, for example, around a neckline when the neckband stitches will be picked up and worked after back and front have been joined. As an alternative, thread a blunt-pointed sewing needle with a generous length of contrast-coloured yarn, thread it through the stitches to be held while they are still on the needle, then slip the stitches off the needle and knot both ends of the contrast yarn.

Wool sewing needles are used to sew completed pieces of knitting together. They are large with a broad eye for easy threading and a blunt point that will slip between the knitted stitches without splitting and fraying the yarn. Do not use sharp pointed sewing needles to sew up knitting. A tapestry needle is also suitable.

A row counter is used to count the number of rows that have been knitted. It is a cylinder with a numbered dial that is pushed onto the needle and the dial is turned at the completion of each row.

A tape measure is essential for checking tension swatches and for measuring the length and width of completed knitting. For an accurate result, always smooth knitting out (without stretching) on a firm flat surface before measuring it.

A crochet hook is useful for picking up dropped stitches.

Knitting yarn

Yarn is the term used for strands of spun fibre which are twisted together into a continuous thread of the required thickness. Yarn can be of animal origin (wool, angora, mohair, silk, alpaca), vegetable origin (cotton, linen) or man-made (nylon, acrylic, rayon). Knitting yarn may be made up from a combination of different fibres.

Each single strand of yarn is known as a ply. A number of plys are twisted together to form the yarn. The texture and characteristics of the yarn may be varied by the combination of fibres and by the way in which the yarn is spun. Wool and other natural fibres are often combined with man-made fibres to make a yarn that is more economical and hard-wearing. Wool can also be treated to make it machine washable. The twist of the yarn can be varied too. A tightly twisted yarn is firm and smooth and knits up into a hard-wearing fabric. Loosely twisted yarn has a softer finish when knitted.

Buying yarn

Yarn is most commonly sold ready wound into balls of specific weight measured in grams or ounces. Some yarn, particularly very thick yarn, is also sold in a coiled hank or skein and must be wound up into a ball before you begin knitting.

Yarn manufacturers (called spinners) wrap each ball with a paper band on which is printed a lot of necessary information. The ball band states the weight of the yarn and its composition. It will give instructions for washing and ironing and will state the ideal range of needle sizes to be used with the yarn. The ball band also carries the shade number and dye lot number. It is important that you use yarn of the same dye lot for a single project. Different dye lots vary subtly in shading which may not be apparent when you are holding two balls, but which will show as a variation in shade on the finished piece of knitting.

Always keep the ball band as a reference. The best way is to pin it to the tension swatch (see page 9) and keep them together with any left over yarn and spare buttons or other trimmings. That way you can always check the washing instructions and also have materials for repairs.

Holding the needles 1

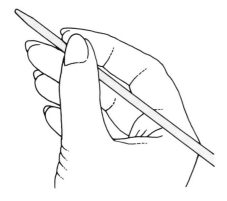

The right needle is held in the same position as holding a pencil. For casting on and working the first few rows the knitted piece passes over the hand, between the thumb and the index finger. As work progresses let the thumb slide under the knitted piece, grasping the needle from below.

Holding the needles 2

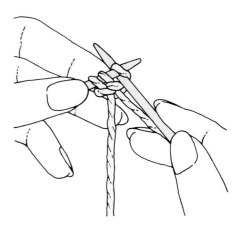

The left needle is held lightly over the top, using the thumb and index finger to control the tip of the needle.

Holding the yarn method 1

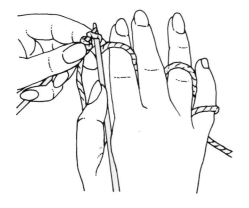

Holding yarn in right hand, pass yarn under the little finger, then around same finger, over third finger, under centre finger and over index finger. The index finger is used to pass the yarn around needle tip. The yarn circled around the little finger creates the necessary tension for knitting evenly.

Holding the yarn method 2

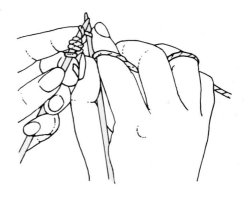

Holding yarn in right hand, pass under the little finger, over third finger, under centre finger and over index finger. The index finger is used to pass the yarn around the needle tip. The tension on the yarn is controlled by gripping the yarn in the crook of the little finger.

For North American Readers

**English terms are used throughout this book.
Please note equivalent American terms:-**

**Tension – Gauge
Cast Off – Bind Off
Stocking Stitch – Stockinette Stitch**

Casting On

There are two 'best ways' of casting on, each serving a rather different purpose. The Thumb Method is used whenever a very elastic edge is required or when the rows immediately after the cast-on edge are to be worked in garter stitch or stocking stitch. The second method is the Cable or 'between needles' method. This gives a very firm neat finish and is best for use before ribbing or any other firm type of stitch.

Both these methods commence with a slip knot and this is the starting-off point for almost everything you do in knitting.

Slip knot

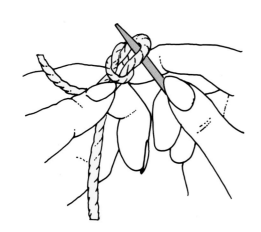

(a)

(b)

(c)

a) Wind the yarn around two fingers and over the two fingers again to the back of the first thread.
b) Using a knitting needle pull the back thread through the front one to form a loop.
c) Pull end to tighten the loop.

Thumb method

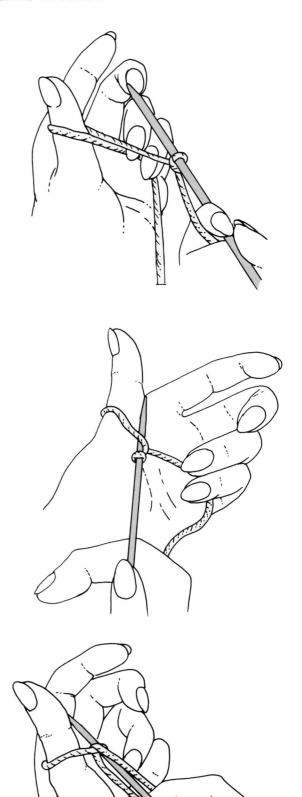

(a)

(b)

(c)

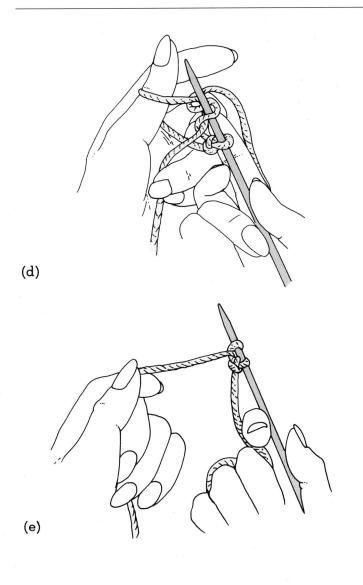

(d)

(e)

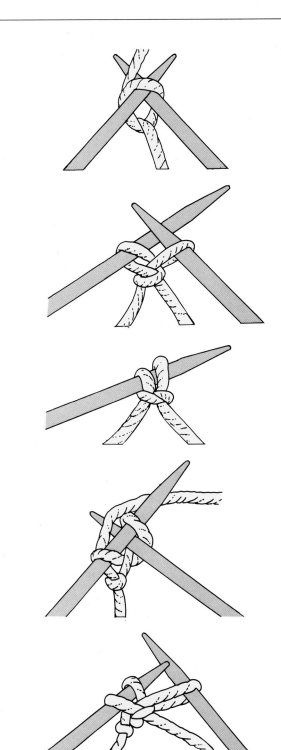

(b)

(c)

(d)

(e)

(f)

(a) Make a slip knot about 1m from the end of the yarn. Place the slip knot on a needle and hold the needle in the right hand with the ball end of the yarn over your first firnger. *Wind the loose end of the yarn around the left thumb from front to back.

(b) Insert the needle through the yarn on the thumb.

(c) Take the yarn with your right forefinger over the point of the needle, (diagram c).

(d) Pull a loop through to form the first stitch.

(e) Remove your left thumb from the yarn and pull the loose end to secure the stitch.

Repeat from * until the required number of stitches has been cast on.

Cable method

(a)

This method requires the use of two needles.

(a) Make a slip knot and place on left hand needle.

(b) Insert right hand needle through the slip knot and pass the yarn over the right needle.

(c) Pull a loop through.

(d) Place this loop on the left hand needle.

(e) Insert right hand needle between the two stitches on the left hand needle. Wind yarn round point of right hand needle.

(f) Draw a loop through, place this loop on left hand needle.

Repeat steps e) and f) until the required number of stitches are on the needle.

The Basic Stitches

Knit stitch

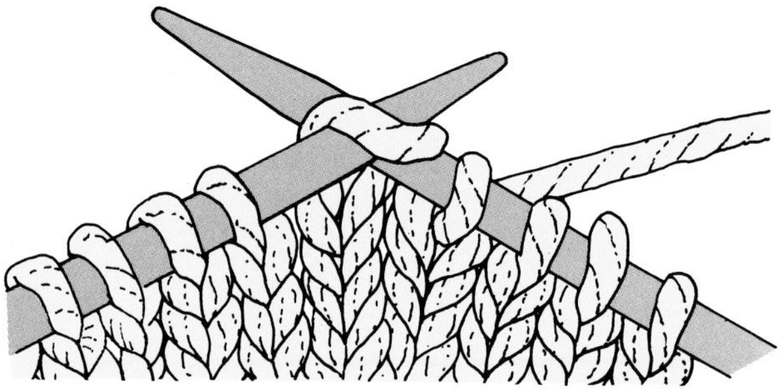

a)

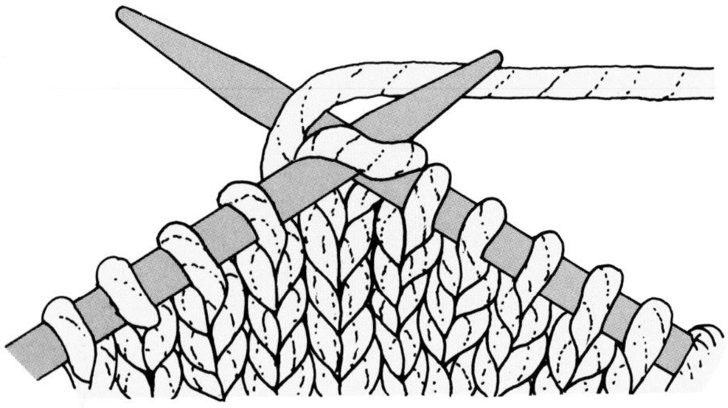

b)

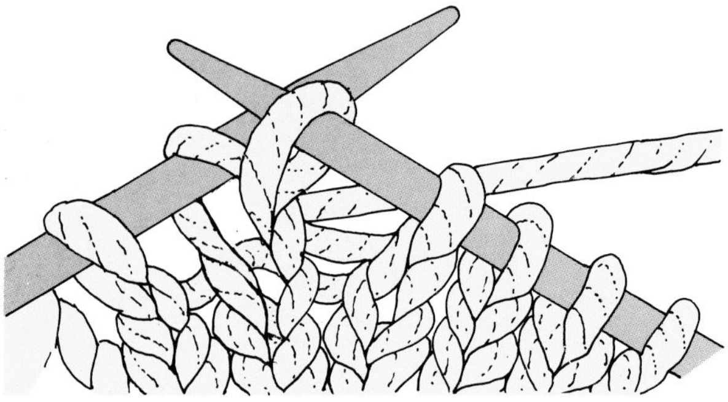

c)

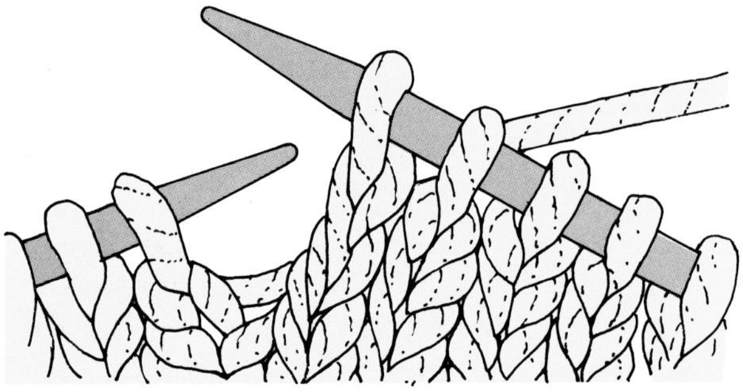

d)

Purl stitch

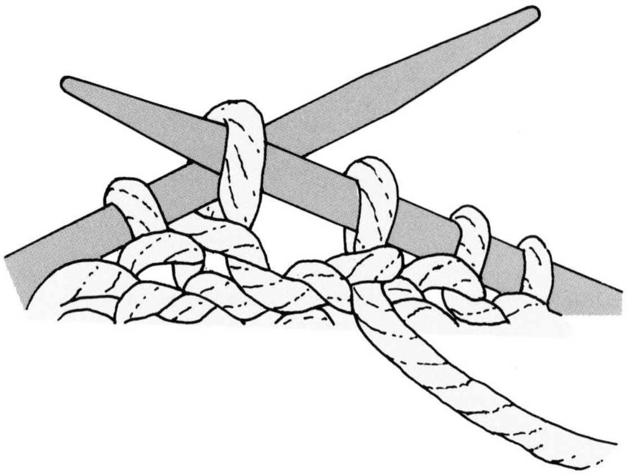

a)

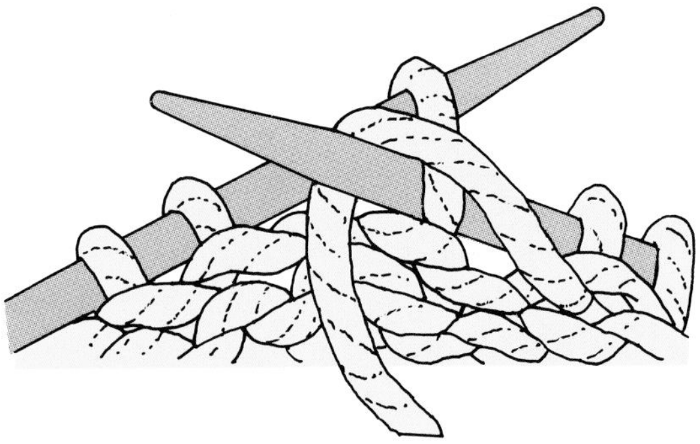

b)

c)

d)

a) With the yarn at the back of the work insert the right hand needle from left to right through the front of the first stitch on the left hand needle; b) wind the yarn over the right hand needle; c) pull through a loop; d) slip the original stitch off the left hand needle. Repeat this until all stitches have been transferred from left needle to right needle.

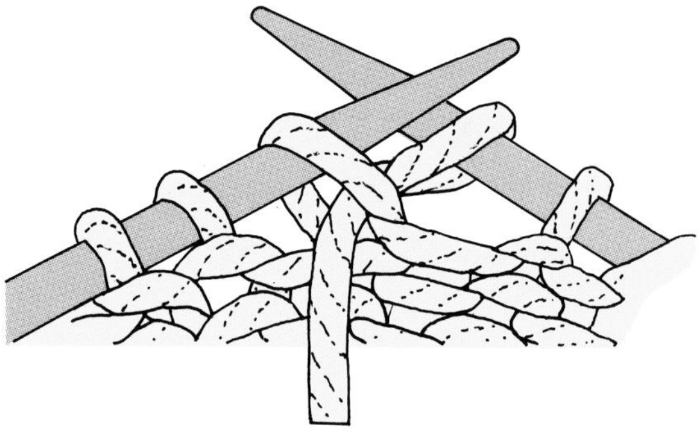

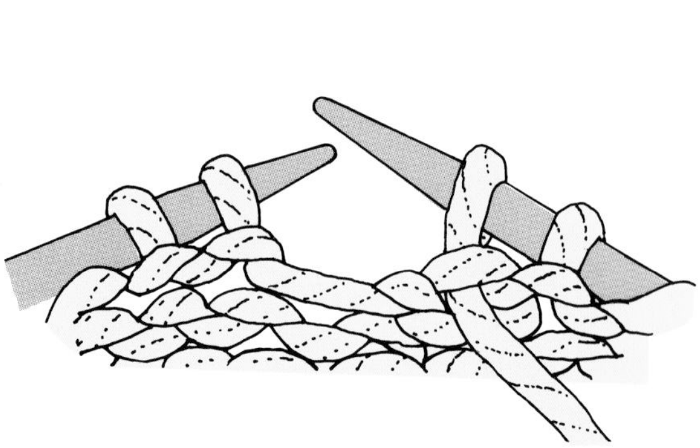

a) With the yarn at the front of the work insert the right hand needle from right to left through the front of the first stitch on the left hand needle; b) wind the yarn round the right hand needle; c) draw a loop through to the back; d) slip the original stitch off the left hand needle. Repeat this until all stitches are transferred to right hand needle.

Casting off

Always cast off in pattern. This means that in stocking stitch you cast off knitwise (see below) on a knit row and purlwise on a purl row. Casting off ribbing should always be done as if you were continuing to rib and most pattern stitches can also be followed during the course of the casting off.

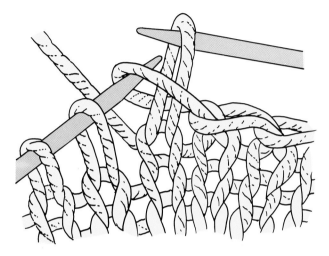

1) Knitwise
Knit the first two stitches.* Using the left hand needle lift the first stitch over the second and drop it off the needle. Knit the next stitch and repeat from the *.

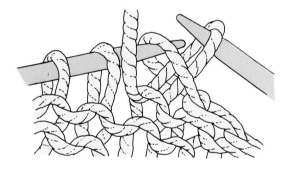

2) Purlwise
Purl the first two stitches, then * using the left hand needle lift the first stitch over the second and drop it off the needle. Purl the next stitch and repeat from the *.

Using a crochet hook to cast off can be extremely time saving. Treat the crochet hook as if it were the right hand needle and knit or purl the first two stitches in the usual way.* Pull the second stitch through the first, knit or purl the next stitch and repeat from the *. This method is extremely useful when a loose elastic cast off edge is required as you can gently loosen the stitch still on the crochet hook to ensure that the elasticity is retained.

Tension or gauge

The correct tension (or gauge) is the most important contribution to the successful knitting of a garment. The informaton under this heading given at the beginning of all patterns refers to the number of stitches required to fill a particular area; for example a frequent tension indication would be '22 sts and 30 rows = 10 cms square measured over stocking stitch on 4 mm needles'. This means that it is necessary to produce fabric made up of the proportion of stitches and rows as given in the tension paragraph in order to obtain the correct measurements for the garment you intend to knit, regardless of the needles **you** use. The needle size indicated in the pattern is the one which **most** knitters will use to achieve this tension but it is the tension that is important, not needle size.

The way to ensure that you do achieve a correct tension is to work a tension sample or swatch before starting the main part of the knitting. Although this may seem to be time wasting and a nuisance it can save the enormous amount of time and aggravation that would result from having knitted a garment to the wrong size.

Tension swatch

The instructions given in the tension paragraph of a knitting pattern are either for working in stocking stitch or in pattern stitch. If they are given in pattern stitch it is necessary to work a multiple of stitches the same as the multiple required in the pattern. If in stocking stitch any number can be cast on but whichever method is used this should always be enough to give at least 12 cms in width. Work in pattern or stocking stitch according to the wording of the tension paragraph until the piece measures at least 10 cms in depth. Break the yarn about 15 cms from the work and thread this end through the stitches, then remove the knitting needle. Place a pin vertically into the fabric a few stitches from the side edge. Measure 10 cms carefully and insert a second pin. Count the stitches. If the number of stitches between the pins is less than that specified in the pattern (even by half a stitch) your garment will be too large. Use smaller needles and knit another tension sample. If your sample has more stitches over 10 cms, the garment will be too small. Change to larger needles. Check the number of rows against the given tension also.

It is most important to get the width measurement correct before starting to knit. Length measurements can usually be adjusted during the course of knitting by adjusting the measurements to underarm or sleeve length, which is frequently given as a measurement and not in rows.

Increasing and Decreasing

There are various methods of increasing and decreasing and they serve two purposes. The first is to make the knitting wider or narrower, to shape it. The second purpose is to create the decorative effects in lacy or in textured patterns.

Using increasing and decreasing to shape

When knitting the various parts of a garment, increases or decreases are worked in pairs at each end of the row on the symmetrical pieces — (back, sleeves etc) to give a balanced shape. The fronts of a cardigan however are shaped differently on each side to give the correct shape for the armhole on one side and the neck shaping at the other.

It is very important to follow the instructions given in the knitting pattern very carefully. The designer will have worked out the various shapings to give the best possible results for each piece of material, and to ensure that the pieces fit together correctly when made up.

Slip stitch decrease

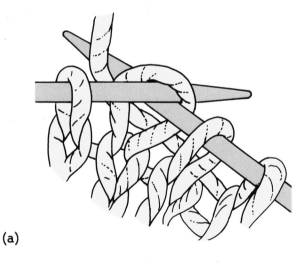

(a)

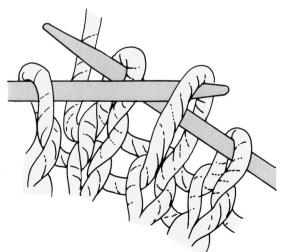

(b)

(a) Slip next stitch onto the right-hand needle without knitting it then knit the next stitch.

(b) Lift the slipped stitch over the knitted stitch and drop it off the needle. The abbreviation is **sl 1, k1, psso** (slip 1, knit 1, pass slipped stitch over). On a purl row the abbreviation is **sl 1, p1, psso**.

Working two stitches together

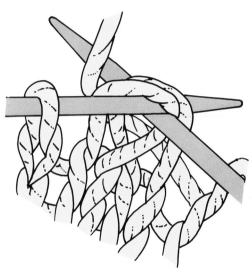

This decrease is worked simply by inserting the right-hand needle through two stitches instead of one and then knitting them together as one stitch. On a purl row, insert the needle purlwise through the two stitches and purl in the usual way. The abbreviation is **k2tog** or **p2tog**.

Yarn forward increase

knit row

To make the yarn forward increase in a knit row, bring the yarn to the front, take it over the right hand needle and knit the stitch. The completed increase creates a visible hole and is often used in lace patterns. The increase is abbreviated in knitting patterns as **yf** (yarn forward) or as **yfwd**.

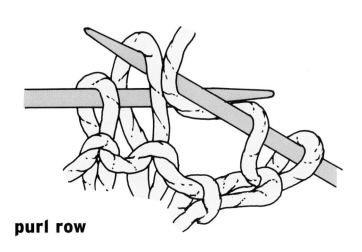

purl row

In a purl row, take the yarn over the right hand needle to the back of the work, then under the needle to the front. The abbreviation is **yrn** (yarn round needle).

Sometimes the abbreviation **yo** (yarn over) is used as a general term on knit or purl rows to indicate that a stitch has to be increased at that position by the method of winding the yarn round the needle, as opposed to the 'front and back' method described below. In this case it is necessary to ensure that you wind the yarn correctly; after you have worked the next stitch check to see that you have actually made an extra stitch and not just carried the yarn from front to back or vice versa!

Working into the front and back of a stitch

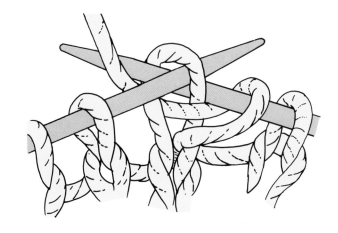

knit row

Knit into the stitch and before slipping it off the needle, knit again into the back of the loop. This is abbreviated in patterns as **Inc 1,** or inc in next st.

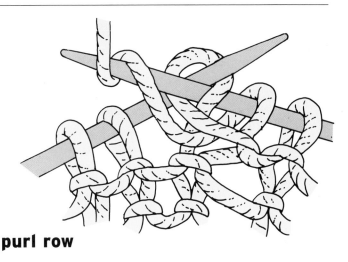

purl row

The method on a purl row is similar. Purl into the front of the stitch then purl into the back of it before slipping it off the needle.

Make 1

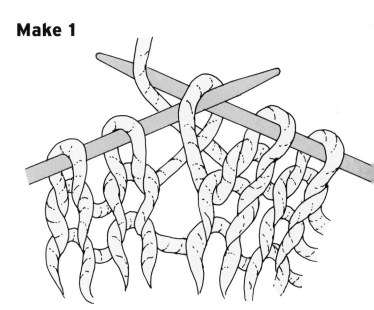

Lift the yarn lying between the stitch just worked and the next stitch and place it on left hand needle, then knit (or purl) into back of this loop. This increase is abbreviated as **M 1** (make 1).

Joining and Finishing

Picking up dropped stitches

If a stitch drops off the needle it is usually easy to pick it up immediately, even if it has slipped through to the row below. Simply pick up the stitch and the strand above it on the right hand needle. Then insert the left hand needle through the stitch and pull the strand through the stitch using the right hand needle to form the stitch once more in its correct place.

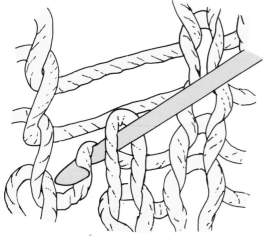

However, if a stitch drops un-noticed it can easily form a ladder running down a number of rows. In this case the stitch must be re-formed all the way up the ladder using a crochet hook. Always work from the front or knit side of the work. Pick up a strand and pull it through the stitch below to form a new stitch. Continue all the way up the ladder.

If more than one stitch has dropped, secure the others with a safety pin until you are ready to pick them up.

Grafting

Grafting invisibly joins two pieces of knitting. The edges are not cast off, and the knitting can be joined either while it is still on the needles or after it has been taken off.

Knitting on the needles

Thread a wool or tapestry needle with a length of knitting yarn. Place the two pieces to be joined with right side facing and hold the knitting needles in the left hand. *Pass the wool needle knitwise through the first stitch on the front needle and slip the stitch off the knitting needle. Pass the wool needle purlwise through the second stitch on the same needle, leaving the stitch on the needle. Pass purlwise through the first stitch on the back knitting needle and slip the stitch off, then pass knitwise through the second stitch on the same needle, leaving the stitch on the needle. Repeat from *. Pull the yarn through so as to form stitches of the same size as the knitted ones. To finish, darn in loose ends at the back of the work.

Knitting taken off the needles

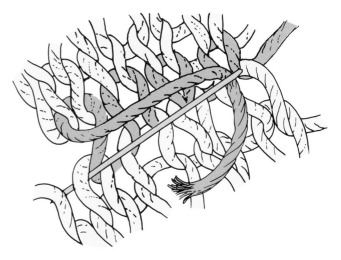

Carefully lay the pieces to be joined close together, with the stitches on each side corresponding to those opposite. Thread a wool or tapestry needle with the knitting yarn. Beginning on the right hand side, bring the needle up through the first stitch of the upper piece, bring it down through the first stitch of the lower piece and bring it up again through the next stitch to the left. *On the upper piece, pass the needle down through the same stitch it came up through before and bring it up through the next stitch to the left. On the lower piece, take the needle down through the stitch it came up through before and bring it up through the next stitch on the left. Repeat from *

Backstitch seam

Thread a wool or tapestry needle with the knitting yarn. Place the pieces to be joined right sides together. Ensure that they match pattern for pattern and row for row. Work backstitch along the seam close to the edge.

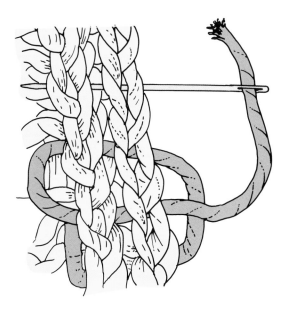

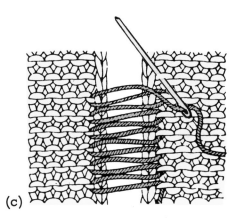

This method of sewing is the most commonly used but to give a really professional finish to your garments you should use a Mattress Stitch for sewing all the seams.

Mattress stitch seam

You will see in the diagrams below visual descriptions of the mattress stitch that we use for almost every seam in the garments we make as this gives the neatest, most professional finish.

Mattress stitch can be worked either one stitch in from the edge (diagram a) or half a stitch in from the edge (diagram b) according to how neat the edge of the fabric is, and how thick the yarn is. Where the knit side of the work is the right side work under two rows at a time (as shown in diagrams a and b); where purl is used as the right side it is better to work under only one row at a time (diagram c) although experience will tell you what is actually required.

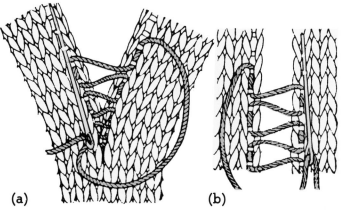

(a)   (b)

The secret of good mattress stitching is to keep the seam elastic without allowing it to stretch too much. The best way to do this is to work the mattress stitch loosely for 1 or 2 centimetres and then pull the thread very firmly so that the stitches are held together quite

(c)

tightly. Now stretch this seam slightly to give the required amount of elasticity, then continue with the next section of the seam.

If you are used to sewing your knitting together by other means it may take a little while to get used to using mattress stitch. However — practise makes perfect and the professional finish you will achieve will make it worth while. One advantage of mattress stitch is that it can be used to sew shaped edges together quite easily; because you are working on the right side of the work all the time it is much easier to see where you are and to keep the seam neat.

Picking up stitches along an edge

Once the main body of the knitting is complete, it is often necessary to add some extra rows to finish the work, to make a border or an edging. Sometimes these sections are knitted separately and sewn on, but it is quicker and neater to pick up stitches along the edge and knit directly onto these.

To pick up stitches along a cast on or cast off edge, for example to add a border or to work a collar, insert the point of the knitting needle under the first stitch, pass the yarn around the needle and draw a loop through to form a stitch. Continue for as many stitches as are required.

To pick up stitches along side edges, for example, to work the button band on a cardigan, insert the point of the needle between the first and second rows 1 stitch or ½ stitch in from the edge, pass the yarn over the needle and draw a loop through. Often, the number of stitches that must be picked up are not the same as the number along the edge or the number of rows. It is easier to pick up the stitches evenly if you divide the length of the edge in half, then in half again and again, so the edge is divided into eighths. Mark each division with a pin. Divide the number of stitches to be picked up by eight and pick up approximately that number of stitches in each section.

13

Working with Colour

Joining in a new colour

It is better to join new yarn in at the beginning of a row. If it is not possible to do this and the yarn has to be joined in the middle of a row simply pick up the new yarn and continue knitting. After you have knitted a few more rows darn in the ends of the old and new yarns neatly at the back of the work.

Stranding colours

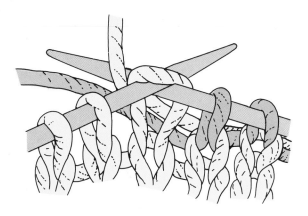

Use this method for colour patterns with small repeats. Hold the second colour in the left hand and carry it loosely across the wrong side of the work. To change colours exchange the position of the two yarns and insert the needle into the next stitch. Lift the old yarn over the right hand needle with your left hand and bring the new yarn over ready to work the stitch. Before pulling the loop through take the old yarn back again then complete the stitch in the usual way. The old and new colours will thus be twisted together; this is necessary at the joining point to avoid making a hole. The secret of working good 2-colour knitting is to carry the colour not in use **loosely** across the wrong side of the work and take care not to pull it tight when changing the colours over.

Weaving

It is possible to work every alternate stitch of a fairisle pattern as given above for Stranding. This gives a neat appearance at the back of the work but distorts the shape of the stitches and alters the tension. Unless the pattern specifically calls for this method it is not recommended.

Colour patterns

Where colours are used in large blocks or over large areas at a time, it is best to use a separate ball of yarn for each section.

When using separate balls of yarn, the yarns must be twisted over each other otherwise a hole will be formed between the colours. When the colour change is in a vertical line, cross the yarns on both knit and purl rows.

When the colour change is on a slanting line, the yarns need be crossed only on alternate rows.

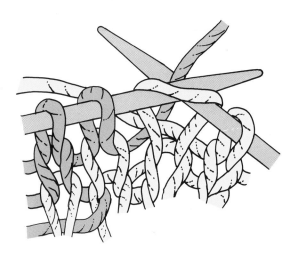

(a) When the colour change slants to the right, cross the yarns on the knit row. Take the first colour in front of the second colour, drop it, then pick up and knit with the second colour. On the purl row the diagonal slants in such a way that the yarns automatically cross.

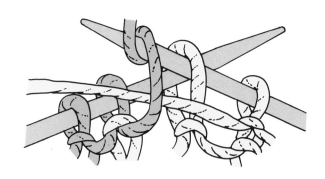

(b) When the colour change slants to the left, the yarns must be crossed on the purl row. On the knit row the diagonal slant causes the yarns to cross automatically.

Swiss darning

Swiss darning is a form of embroidery on knitting that exactly covers the knitted stitches so that the finished embroidery looks as if it had been knitted in. It is a useful and versatile technique. When a pattern calls for very small or widely spaced colour motifs, or for a very thin vertical stripe as in many plaids, it is often much easier to darn in afterwards than to knit it in.

To exactly duplicate the knitted stitches, use yarn of the same type as the knitting. For more obviously decorative effects, any suitable knitting or embroidery yarn can be used.

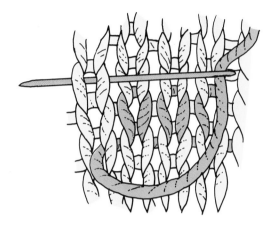 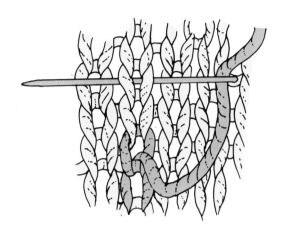

(a) To work Swiss darning horizontally, work from right to left. Darn in the yarn invisibly at the back. Bring the needle out in the centre of a stitch, take it up and around the head of the stitch, (under the stitch above), then take the needle back through the centre of the **same** stitch.

(b) To work the embroidery vertically, work from bottom to top. Bring the needle out in the centre of the stitch, then take it up and around the head of the stitch (under the stitch above). Take the needle back through the centre of the **same** stitch then up through the centre of the stitch above.

Following a Pattern and Abbreviations

Knitting patterns are written in a language all of their own. Abbreviations are used for many of the repetitive words which occur in the instructions and although all manufacturers do not use exactly the same abbreviations, an experienced knitter can follow the jargon.

Before starting to knit any pattern, always read it right through. Even if you are not experienced, this will give you an idea of how the pattern is structured and you will know what to expect. After knitting one or two patterns you will understand how the pattern works.

Multiples

A certain number of stitches are required to form one complete pattern, say a cable, a zigzag or a leaf shape. The number of stitches on the needle must be divisible by this number. The information is given at the beginning of a pattern. For example: multiple of 4 sts; multiple of 8 plus 1 sts. Some patterns also specify the number of rows required to complete the pattern.

Asterisks and Brackets

These are used to indicate repetition of a sequence of stitches. For example: *k3, p1; rep from * to end. This means knit 3 stitches and purl 1 stitch to the end of the row. The instructons within brackets are worked for the number of times required. For example: [k3, p1] 4 times. This means that the stitches within the brackets are worked 4 times in all.

Work Straight

This instruction means that you knit with the number of stitches on the needle for the required length or number of rows without increasing or decreasing.

Abbreviations

Below, the common pattern abbreviations are explained in detail. Opposite are some Special Abbreviations which usually occur in cable and other highly textured patterns.

Alt=Alternate This usually occurs during an instruction for shaping, for example: increase 1 stitch at end of next and every **alt** row until there are X sts. This means that, counting the next row as row 1, the increase is worked on rows 1, 3, 5, 7 etc., until the required number of stitches is reached. If the instruction reads 'increase 1 stitch at end of every **alt** row...' then the increases are worked on rows 2, 4, 6, 8 etc.

Beg=beginning   **Cms=centimetres**

Dec=decrease This is a shaping instruction. 1, 2 or even 3 stitches can be decreased in one go during knitting, but if more than this is required it is usually necessary to 'cast off' some stitches. See page 9 for this. For a description of the usual ways to work a decrease see page 10 .

Inc=increase This is a shaping instruction. 1 or 2 stitches can be increased in one place but if more than this is required it is usually necessary to 'cast on' some stitches. See page 10 for this and for a description of the usual ways to work an increase.

K=knit   P=purl These abbreviations describe all the detailed working of a pattern. Example: K1, p3, k1. This means that you knit 1 stitch, then you purl 3 stitches then you knit 1 stitch.

Psso=pass slipped stitch over This abbreviation occurs after a slip abbreviation. Example: K9, sl 1, k1, psso, k2. This means that you knit 9 stitches, slip the next stitch, knit 1 more stitch; then you lift the slipped stitch (using the point of the left hand needle) over the 1 knit stitch and drop it off the needle, then you knit the last 2 stitches. This is a frequently used method of decreasing.

Rep=repeat

Sl=slip Example: Sl 1, k1. This means that you slip the next stitch on to the right hand needle without knitting it , then you knit the next stitch.

St=stitch   Sts=stitches

St st=stocking stitch This consists of 1 row knit, 1 row purl, and gives a fabric which is smooth on one side and rough on the other. To facilitate sewing always keep the stitch at the beginning and end of each row in stocking stitch. Some knitters slip the first stitch of a knit row, or knit the first stitch of a purl row. If you use a mattress stitch seam (see page13) keep the edge stitches in true stocking stitch.

Tbl=through back of loop

Tog=together Usually used as a method of decreasing. For example: k2tog.

Yb=yarn back   Yf=yarn forward

Yfon=yarn forward and over needle Yarn forward, as if to purl. Used to make a stitch between two knit stitches.

Yfrn=yarn forward and round needle Used to make a stitch between a knit and purl stitch. Take the yarn right round the needle, finishing at the front.

Yon=yarn over needle Used to make a stitch between a purl and a knit stitch.

Yrn=yarn round needle Used to make a stitch between 2 purl stitches.

Alt = alternate; beg = beginning; cms = centimetres; dec = decrease; inc = increase; ins = inches; k = knit; m = metres; p = purl; psso = pass slipped stitch over; p2sso = pass 2 slipped sts over; rep = repeat; sl = slip; st = stitch; sts = stitches; st st = stocking stitch (1 row k, 1 row p); tbl = through back of loop; tog = together; yb = yarn back; yf = yarn forward; yfon = yarn forward and over needle; yfrn = yarn forward and round needle; yo = yarn over; yon = yarn over needle; yrn = yarn round needle.

M1 (Make 1 Stitch) = pick up horizontal strand of yarn lying between stitch just worked and next st and knit it.

MB (Make Bobble) = knit into front, back and front of next st, turn and k3, turn and p3, turn and k3, turn and sl 1, k2tog, psso (bobble completed).

K1B = insert needle through centre of st below next st on needle and knit this in the usual way, slipping the st above off needle at the same time.

Sl 2tog knitwise = insert needle into the next 2 sts on left hand needle as if to k2tog then slip both sts onto right hand needle without knitting them.

KB1 = knit into back of next stitch.

PB1 = purl into back of next stitch.

C2B or C2F (Cross 2 Back or Cross 2 Front) = knit into back (or front) of 2nd st on needle, then knit first st, slipping both sts off needle at the same time.

C2L (Cross 2 Left) = slip next st onto cable needle and hold at front of work, knit next st from left-hand needle, then knit st from cable needle.

C2R (Cross 2 Right) = slip next st onto cable needle and hold at back of work, knit next st from left-hand needle, then knit st from cable needle.

C2P (Cross 2 Purl) = purl into front of 2nd st on needle, then purl first st, slipping both sts off needle together.

T2 (Twist 2) = slip next st onto cable needle and hold at back of work, PB1 from left-hand needle then PB1 from cable needle.

T2L (Twist 2 Left) = slip next st onto a cable needle and hold at front of work, purl next st from left-hand needle, then KB1 from cable needle.

T2R (Twist 2 Right) = slip next st onto a cable needle and hold at back of work, KB1 from left-hand needle, then purl st from cable needle.

T2F (Twist 2 Front) = slip next st onto cable needle and hold at front of work, purl next st from left-hand needle, then knit st from cable needle.

T2B (Twist 2 Back) = slip next st onto cable needle and hold at back of work, knit next st from left-hand needle, then purl st from cable needle.

C3 (Cross 3) = knit into front of 3rd st on needle, then knit first st in usual way slipping this st off needle, now knit 2nd st in usual way, slipping 2nd and 3rd sts off needle together.

C3B (Cross 3 Back) = slip next st onto a cable needle and hold at back of work, knit next 2 sts from left-hand needle, then knit st from cable needle.

C3F (Cross 3 Front) = slip next 2 sts onto a cable needle and hold at front of work, knit next st from left-hand needle, then knit sts from cable needle.

C3L (Cable 3 Left) = slip next st onto cable needle and hold at front of work, knit next 2 sts from left-hand needle, then knit st from cable needle.

C3R (Cable 3 Right) = slip next 2 sts onto cable needle and hold at back of work, knit next st from left-hand needle, then knit sts from cable needle.

T3B (Twist 3 Back) = slip next st onto a cable needle and hold at back of work, knit next 2 sts from left-hand needle, then purl st from cable needle.

T3F (Twist 3 Front) = slip next 2 sts onto a cable needle and hold at front of work, purl next st from left-hand needle, then knit sts from cable needle.

T3L (Twist 3 Left) = slip next st onto a cable needle and hold at front of work, work [KB1, p1] from left-hand needle, then KB1 from cable needle.

T3R (Twist 3 Right) = slip next 2 sts onto a cable needle and hold at back of work, KB1 from left-hand needle, then [p1, KB1] from cable needle.

C4B or C4F (Cable 4 Back or Cable 4 Front) = slip next 2 sts onto a cable needle and hold at back (or front) of work, knit next 2 sts from left-hand needle, then knit sts from cable needle.

C4L (Cross 4 Left) = slip next st onto cable needle and leave at front of work, knit next 3 sts from left-hand needle then knit st from cable needle.

C4R (Cross 4 Right) = slip next 3 sts onto cable needle and leave at back of work, knit next st from left-hand needle then knit sts from cable needle.

T4B (Twist 4 Back) = slip next 2 sts onto cable needle and hold at back of work, knit next 2 sts from left-hand needle, then purl the 2 sts from cable needle.

T4F (Twist 4 Front) = slip next 2 sts onto cable needle and hold at front of work, purl next 2 sts from left-hand needle, then knit sts from cable needle.

T4L (Twist 4 Left) = slip next 2 sts onto cable needle and hold at front of work, k1, p1, from left-hand needle, then knit sts from cable needle.

T4R (Twist 4 Right) = slip next 2 sts onto cable needle and hold at back of work, knit next 2 sts from left-hand needle, then p1, k1, from cable needle.

C5 (Cable 5) = slip next 3 sts onto a cable needle and hold at back of work, knit next 2 sts from left-hand needle, then knit sts from cable needle.

C5B or C5F (Cross 5 Back or Cross 5 Front) = slip next 3 sts onto a cable needle and hold at back (or front) of work, knit next 2 sts from left-hand needle, slip the purl st from point of cable needle back onto left-hand needle, purl this st, then k2 from cable needle.

C5L (Cross 5 Left) = slip next 4 sts onto cable needle and hold at front of work, purl next st on left-hand needle, then knit sts on cable needle.

C5R (Cross 5 Right) = slip the next st onto a cable needle and hold at back of work, knit next 4 sts on left-hand needle, then purl the st on cable needle.

T5B (Twist 5 Back) = slip next 2 sts onto a cable needle and hold at back of work, knit next 3 sts from left-hand needle, then purl sts from cable needle.

T5F (Twist 5 Front) = slip next 3 sts onto a cable needle and hold at front of work, purl next 2 sts from left-hand needle, then knit sts from cable needle.

T5L (Twist 5 Left) = slip next 2 sts onto cable needle and hold at front of work, k2, p1 from left-hand needle then k2 from cable needle.

T5R (Twist 5 Right) = slip next 3 sts onto a cable needle and hold at back of work, knit next 2 sts from left-hand needle, then work [p1, k2] from cable needle.

T5FL (Twist 5 Front Left) = slip next 2 sts onto cable needle and hold at front of work, purl next 3 sts from left-hand needle, then knit the 2 sts from cable needle.

T5BR (Twist 5 Back Right) = slip next 3 sts onto cable needle and leave at back of work, knit next 2 sts from left-hand needle, then purl the 3 sts from cable needle.

C6 (Cross 6) = slip next 4 sts onto cable needle and hold at front of work, knit next 2 sts from left-hand needle, then slip the 2 purl sts from cable needle back to left-hand needle. Pass the cable needle with 2 remaining knit sts to back of work, purl 2 sts from left-hand needle, then knit the 2 sts from cable needle.

C6B or C6F (Cable 6 Back or Cable 6 Front) = slip next 3 sts onto cable needle and hold at back (or front) of work, knit next 3 sts from left-hand needle, then knit sts from cable needle.

T6B (Twist 6 Back) = slip next 3 sts onto a cable needle and hold at back of work, knit next 3 sts from left-hand needle, then purl sts from cable needle.

T6F (Twist 6 Front) = slip next 3 sts onto a cable needle and hold at front of work, purl next 3 sts from left-hand needle, then knit sts from cable needle.

T6L (Twist 6 Left) = slip next 2 sts onto cable needle and hold at front of work, work k2, p2 from left-hand needle, then knit the 2 sts from cable needle.

T6R (Twist 6 Right) = slip next 4 sts onto cable needle and hold at back of work, knit next 2 sts from left-hand needle, then work p2, k2 from cable needle.

C7F or C7B (Cable 7 Front or Cable 7 Back) = slip next 4 sts onto cable needle and hold at front (or back) of work, knit next 3 sts on left-hand needle, slip purl st from cable needle onto left-hand needle and purl it, then k3 from cable needle.

C8B or C8F (Cable 8 Back or Cable 8 Front) = slip next 4 sts onto cable needle and hold at back (or front) of work, knit next 4 sts from left-hand needle, then knit sts from cable needle.

C9B (Cable 9 Back) = slip next 4 sts onto cable needle and hold at back of work, knit next 5 sts from left-hand needle, then knit sts from cable needle.

C9F (Cable 9 Front) = slip next 5 sts onto cable needle and hold at front of work, knit next 4 sts from left-hand needle, then knit sts from cable needle.

C12B or C12F (Cable 12 Back or Cable 12 Front) = slip next 6 sts onto a cable needle and hold at back (or front) of work, knit next 6 sts from left-hand needle, then knit sts from cable needle.

Knit and Purl Patterns

Stocking Stitch Triangles

Multiple of 5
1st row (right side): Knit.
2nd row: *K1, p4; rep from * to end.
3rd row: *K3, p2; rep from * to end.
4th row: *K3, p2; rep from * to end.
5th row: *K1, p4; rep from * to end.
6th row: Knit.
Rep these 6 rows.

Dot Stitch

Multiple of 4 + 3
1st row (right side): K1, *p1, k3; rep from * to last 2 sts, p1, k1.
2nd row: Purl.
3rd row: *K3, p1; rep from * to last 3 sts, k3.
4th row: Purl.
Rep these 4 rows.

Box Stitch

Multiple of 4 + 2
1st row: K2, *p2, k2; rep from * to end.
2nd row: P2, *k2, p2; rep from * to end.
3rd row: As 2nd row.
4th row: As 1st row.
Rep these 4 rows.

Double Moss Stitch

Multiple of 2 + 1
1st row: K1, *p1, k1; rep from * to end.
2nd row: P1, *k1, p1; rep from * to end.
3rd row: As 2nd row.
4th row: As 1st row.
Rep these 4 rows.

Moss Stitch I

Multiple of 2 + 1
1st row: K1, *p1, k1; rep from * to end.
Rep this row.

Moss Stitch II

Worked as Moss Stitch I.
2 rows in colour A, 2 rows in B, 2 rows in A and 2 rows in C throughout.

Diagonal Garter Ribs

Multiple of 5 + 2
1st and every alt row (right side): Knit.
2nd row: *P2, k3; rep from * to last 2 sts, p2.
4th row: K1, *p2, k3; rep from * to last st, p1.
6th row: K2, *p2, k3; rep from * to end.
8th row: *K3, p2; rep from * to last 2 sts, k2.
10th row: P1, *k3, p2; rep from * to last st, k1.
Rep these 10 rows.

Garter Ribs

Panels of alternate knit and purl garter st are effective with any number of sts in each panel. Here we show a 2 st and a 4 st version.

2-Stitch Ribs I

Multiple of 4 + 2
1st row: K2, *p2, k2; rep from * to end.
Rep this row.

2-Stitch Ribs II

Worked as 2-Stitch Ribs I.
Worked in 1 row each in colours A, B and C throughout.

4-Stitch Ribs

Multiple of 8 + 4
1st row: K4, *p4, k4; rep from * to end.
Rep this row.

Fleck Stitch

Multiple of 2 + 1
1st row (right side): Knit.
2nd row: Purl.
3rd row: K1, *p1, k1; rep from * to end.
4th row: Purl.
Rep these 4 rows.

Double Fleck Stitch

Multiple of 6 + 4
1st and 3rd rows (right side): Knit.
2nd row P4, *k2, p4; rep from * to end.
4th row: P1, *k2, p4; rep from * to last 3 sts, k2, p1.
Rep these 4 rows.

Check Stitch

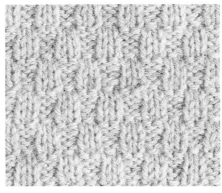

Multiple of 4 + 2
1st row: K2, *p2, k2; rep from * to end.
2nd row: P2, *k2, p2; rep from * to end.
Rep these last 2 rows once more.
5th row: As 2nd row.
6th row: As 1st row.
Rep these last 2 rows once more.
Rep these 8 rows.

Double Basket Weave

Multiple of 4 + 3
1st and every alt row (right side): Knit.
2nd row: *K3, p1; rep from * to last 3 sts, k3.
4th row: As 2nd row.
6th row: K1, *p1, k3; rep from * to last 2 sts, p1, k1.
8th row: As 6th row.
Rep these 8 rows.

Reverse Stocking Stitch Chevrons

Check Stitch

Multiple of 6 + 5
1st row (right side): K5, *p1, k5; rep from * to end.
2nd row: K1, *p3, k3; rep from * to last 4 sts, p3, k1.
3rd row: P2, *k1, p2; rep from * to end.
4th row: P1, *k3, p3; rep from * to last 4 sts, k3, p1.
5th row: K2, *p1, k5; rep from * to last 3 sts, p1, k2.
6th row: Purl.
Rep these 6 rows.

Ladder Stitch

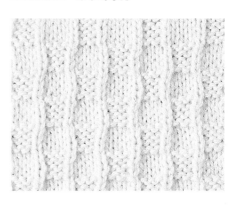

Multiple of 8 + 5
1st row (right side): K5, *p3, k5; rep from * to end.
2nd row: P5, *k3, p5; rep from * to end.
Rep the last 2 rows once more.
5th row: K1, *p3, k5; rep from * to last 4 sts, p3, k1.
6th row: P1, *k3, p5; rep from * to last 4 sts, k3, p1.
Rep these last 2 rows once more.
Rep these 8 rows.

Dotted Ladder Stitch

Multiple of 8 + 5
1st row (right side): K2, p1, k2, *p3, k2, p1, k2; rep from * to end.
2nd row: [P1, k1] twice, p1, *k3, [p1, k1] twice, p1; rep from * to end.
Rep the last 2 rows once more.
5th row: K1, *p3, k2, p1, k2; rep from * to last 4 sts, p3, k1.
6th row: P1, k3, p1, *[k1, p1] twice, k3, p1; rep from * to end.
Rep the last 2 rows once more.
Rep these 8 rows.

Knit and Purl Patterns

Interrupted Rib

Multiple of 2 + 1
1st row (right side): P1, *k1, p1; rep from * to end.
2nd row: K1, *p1, k1; rep from * to end.
3rd row: Purl.
4th row: Knit.
Rep these 4 rows.

Basket Weave

Multiple of 4 + 3
1st and 3rd rows (right side): Knit.
2nd row: *K3, p1; rep from * to last 3 sts, k3.
4th row: K1, *p1, k3; rep from * to last 2 sts, p1, k1.
Rep these 4 rows.

Ridged Rib

Multiple of 2 + 1
1st and 2nd rows: Knit.
3rd row (right side): P1, *k1, p1; rep from * to end.
4th row: K1, *p1, k1; rep from * to end.
Rep these 4 rows.

Double Ridged Rib

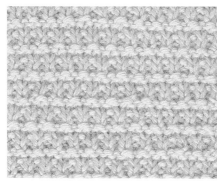

Multiple of 2 + 1
1st and 2nd rows: Knit.
3rd row (right side): P1, *k1, p1; rep from * to end.
4th row: K1, *p1, k1; rep from * to end.
5th and 6th rows: Knit.
7th row: As 4th row.
8th row: P1, *k1, p1; rep from * to end.
Rep these 8 rows.

Lattice Stitch

Multiple of 6 + 1
1st row (right side): K3, *p1, k5; rep from * to last 4 sts, p1, k3.
2nd row: P2, *k1, p1, k1, p3; rep from * to last 5 sts, k1, p1, k1, p2.
3rd row: K1, *p1, k3, p1, k1; rep from * to end.
4th row: K1, *p5, k1; rep from * to end.
5th row: As 3rd row.
6th row: As 2nd row.
Rep these 6 rows.

Alternating Triangles

Multiple of 5
1st row (right side): *P1, k4; rep from * to end.
2nd and 3rd rows: *P3, k2; rep from * to end.
4th row: *P1, k4; rep from * to end.
5th row: *K4, p1; rep from * to end.
6th and 7th rows: *K2, p3; rep from * to end.
8th row: As 5th row.
Rep these 8 rows.

Steps

Multiple of 8 + 2
1st row (right side): *K4, p4; rep from * to last 2 sts, k2.
2nd row: P2, *k4, p4, rep from * to end.
Rep the last 2 rows once more.
5th row: K2, *p4, k4; rep from * to end.
6th row: *P4, k4; rep from * to last 2 sts, p2.
7th row: As 5th row.
8th row: As 6th row.
9th row: *P4, k4; rep from * to last 2 sts, p2.
10th row: K2, *p4, k4; rep from * to end.
Rep the last 2 rows once more.
13th row: As 2nd row.
14th row: *K4, p4; rep from * to last 2 sts, k2.
Rep the last 2 rows once more.
Rep these 16 rows.

Diagonal Checks

Multiple of 5 sts.
1st row (right side): *P1, k4; rep from * to end.
2nd row: *P3, k2; rep from * to end.
3rd row: As 2nd row.
4th row: *P1, k4; rep from * to end.
5th row: *K1, p4; rep from * to end.
6th row: *K3, p2; rep from * to end.
7th row: As 6th row.
8th row: As 5th row.
Rep these 8 rows.

Garter Stitch Steps

Multiple of 8
1st and every alt row (right side): Knit.
2nd and 4th rows: *K4, p4; rep from * to end.
6th and 8th rows: K2, *p4, k4; rep from * to last 6 sts, p4, k2.
10th and 12th rows: *P4, k4; rep from * to end.
14th and 16th rows: P2, *k4, p4; rep from * to last 6 sts, k4, p2.
Rep these 16 rows.

Purled Ladder Stitch

Multiple of 4 + 2
1st and 2nd rows: Knit.
3rd row (right side): P2, *k2, p2; rep from * to end.
4th row: K2, *p2, k2; rep from * to end.
5th and 6th rows: Knit.
7th row: As 4th row.
8th row: P2, *k2, p2; rep from * to end.
Rep these 8 rows.

Tile Stitch

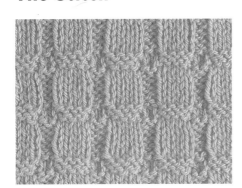

Multiple of 6 + 4
1st row (right side): K4, *p2, k4; rep from * to end.
2nd row: P4, *k2, p4; rep from * to end.
Rep the last 2 rows twice more.
7th row: As 2nd row.
8th row: K4, *p2, k4; rep from * to end.
Rep these 8 rows.

Moss Diamonds

Multiple of 10 + 7
1st row (right side): *[K3, p1] twice, k1, p1; rep from * to last 7 sts, k3, p1, k3.
2nd row: *[P3, k1] twice, p1, k1; rep from * to last 7 sts, p3, k1, p3.
3rd row: K2, p1, k1, p1, *[k3, p1] twice, k1, p1; rep from * to last 2 sts, k2.
4th row: P2, k1, p1, k1, *[p3, k1] twice, p1, k1; rep from * to last 2 sts, p2.
5th row: [K1, p1] 3 times, *[k2, p1] twice, [k1, p1] twice; rep from * to last st, k1.
6th row: [P1, k1] 3 times, *[p2, k1] twice, [p1, k1] twice; rep from * to last st, p1.
7th row: As 3rd row.
8th row: As 4th row.
9th row: As 1st row.
10th row: As 2nd row.
11th row: K3, p1, *k2 [p1, k1] twice, p1, k2, p1; rep from * to last 3 sts, k3.
12th row: P3, k1, *p2, [k1, p1] twice, k1, p2, k1; rep from * to last 3 sts, p3.
Rep these 12 rows.

Moss Panels

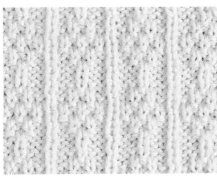

Multiple of 8 + 7
1st row (wrong side): K3, *p1, k3; rep from

* to end.
2nd row: P3, *k1, p3; rep from * to end.
3rd row: K2, p1, k1, *[p1, k2] twice, p1, k1; rep from * to last 3 sts, p1, k2.
4th row: P2, k1, p1, *[k1, p2] twice, k1, p1; rep from * to last 3 sts, k1, p2.
5th row: K1, *p1, k1; rep from * to end.
6th row: P1, *k1, p1; rep from * to end.
7th row: As 3rd row.
8th row: As 4th row.
9th row: As 1st row.
10th row: As 2nd row.
Rep these 10 rows.

Woven Stitch

Multiple of 4 + 2
1st row (right side): Knit.
2nd row: Purl.
3rd row: K2, *p2, k2; rep from * to end.
4th row: P2, *k2, p2; rep from * to end.
5th row: Knit.
6th row: Purl.
7th row: As 4th row.
8th row: As 3rd row.
Rep these 8 rows.

Diagonal Rib

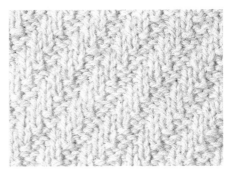

Multiple of 4
1st and 2nd rows: *K2, p2; rep from * to end.
3rd row (right side): K1, *p2, k2; rep from * to last 3 sts, p2, k1.
4th row: P1, *k2, p2; rep from * to last 3 sts, k2, p1.
5th and 6th rows: *P2, k2; rep from * to end.
7th row: As 4th row.
8th row: As 3rd row.
Rep these 8 rows.

Knit and Purl Patterns

Unusual Check Pattern

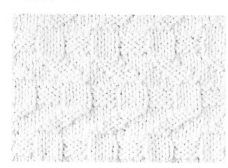

Multiple of 8 sts.
1st row (right side): Knit.
2nd row: *K4, p4; rep from * to end.
3rd row: P1, *k4, p4; rep from * to last 7 sts, k4, p3.
4th row: K2, *p4, k4; rep from * to last 6 sts, p4, k2.
5th row: P3, *k4, p4; rep from * to last 5 sts, k4, p1.
6th row: *P4, k4; rep from * to end.
7th row: Knit.
8th row: *K4, p4; rep from * to end.
Rep the last row 3 times more.
12th row: Purl.
13th row: As 6th row.
14th row: K1, *p4, k4; rep from * to last 7 sts, p4, k3.
15th row: P2, *k4, p4; rep from * to last 6 sts, k4, p2.
16th row: K3, *p4, k4; rep from * to last 5 sts, p4, k1.
17th row: As 2nd row.
18th row: Purl.
19th row: *P4, k4; rep from * to end.
Rep the last row 3 times more.
Rep these last 22 rows.

Horizontal Dash Stitch

Multiple of 10 + 6
1st row (right side): P6, *k4, p6; rep from * to end.
2nd and every alt row: Purl.
3rd row: Knit.
5th row: P1, *k4, p6; rep from * to last 5 sts, k4, p1.
7th row: Knit.
8th row: Purl.
Rep these 8 rows.

Diamond Panels

Multiple of 8 + 1
1st row (right side): Knit.
2nd row: K1, *p7, k1; rep from * to end.
3rd row: K4, *p1, k7; rep from * to last 5 sts, p1, k4.
4th row: K1, *p2, k1, p1, k1, p2, k1; rep from * to end.
5th row: K2, *[p1, k1] twice, p1, k3; rep from * to last 7 sts, [p1, k1] twice, p1, k2.
6th row: As 4th row.
7th row: As 3rd row.
8th row: As 2nd row.
Rep these 8 rows.

Enlarged Basket Stitch

Multiple of 18 + 10
1st row (right side): K11, *p2, k2, p2, k12; rep from * to last 17sts, p2, k2, p2, k11.
2nd row: P1, *k8, [p2, k2] twice, p2; rep from * to last 9 sts, k8, p1.
3rd row: K1, *p8, [k2, p2] twice, k2; rep from * to last 9 sts, p8, k1.
4th row: P11, *k2, p2, k2, p12; rep from * to last 17 sts, k2, p2, k2, p11.
Rep the last 4 rows once more.
9th row: Knit.
10th row: [P2, k2] twice, p12, *k2, p2, k2, p12; rep from * to last 8 sts, [k2, p2] twice.
11th row: [K2, p2] twice, k2, *p8, [k2, p2] twice, k2; rep from * to end.
12th row: [P2, k2] twice, p2, *k8, [p2, k2] twice, p2; rep from * to end.
13th row: [K2, p2] twice, k12, *p2, k2, p2, k12; rep from * to last 8 sts, [p2, k2] twice.
Rep the last 4 rows once more
18th row: Purl.
Rep these 18 rows.

Chevron

Multiple of 8 + 1
1st row (right side): K1, *p7, k1; rep from * to end.
2nd row: P1, *k7, p1; rep from * to end.
3rd row: K2, *p5, k3; rep from * to last 7 sts, p5, k2.
4th row: P2, *k5, p3; rep from * to last 7 sts, k5, p2.
5th row: K3, *p3, k5; rep from * to last 6 sts, p3, k3.
6th row: P3, *k3, p5; rep from * to last 6 sts, k3, p3.
7th row: K4, *p1, k7; rep from * to last 5 sts, p1, k4.
8th row: P4, *k1, p7; rep from * to last 5 sts, k1, p4.
9th row: As 2nd row.
10th row: As 1st row.
11th row: As 4th row.
12th row: As 3rd row.
13th row: As 6th row.
14th row: As 5th row.
15th row: As 8th row.
16th row: As 7th row.
Rep these 16 rows.

Large Basket Weave

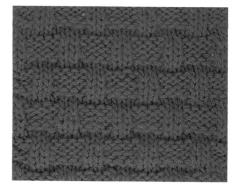

Multiple of 6 + 2
1st row (right side): Knit.
2nd row: Purl.
3rd row: K2, *p4, k2; rep from * to end.
4th row: P2, *k4, p2; rep from * to end.
Rep the last 2 rows once more.
7th row: Knit.
8th row: Purl.
9th row: P3, *k2, p4; rep from * to last 5 sts, k2, p3.

10th row: K3, *p2, k4; rep from * to last 5 sts, p2, k3.
Rep the last 2 rows once more.
Rep these 12 rows.

Tweed Pattern

Multiple of 6 + 3
1st row (right side): K3, *p3, k3; rep from * to end.
Rep the last row twice more.
4th row: Knit.
5th row: Purl.
6th row: Knit.
7th row: K3, *p3, k3; rep from * to end.
Rep the last row twice more.
10th row: Purl.
11th row: Knit.
12th row: Purl.
Rep these 12 rows.

Pyramids

Multiple of 8 + 1
1st row (wrong side): P1, *k1, p1; rep from * to end.
2nd row: K1, *p1, k1; rep from * to end.
Rep these 2 rows once more.
5th row: P2, *[k1, p1] twice, k1, p3; rep from * to last 7 sts, [k1, p1] twice, k1, p2.
6th row: K2, *[p1, k1] twice, p1, k3; rep from *.to last 7 sts, [p1, k1] twice, p1, k2.
Rep the last 2 rows once more.
9th row: P3, *k1, p1, k1, p5; rep from *

to last 6 sts, k1, p1, k1, p3.
10th row: K3, *p1, k1, p1, k5; rep from * to last 6 sts, p1, k1, p1, k3.
Rep the last 2 rows once more.
13th row: P4, *k1, p7; rep from * to last 5 sts, k1, p4.
14th row: K4, *p1, k7; rep from * to last 5 sts, p1, k4.
Rep the last 2 rows once more.
Rep these 16 rows.

Spaced Checks

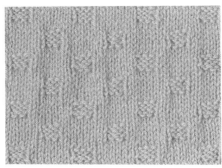

Multiple of 10 + 1
1st row (wrong side): Purl.
2nd row: K4, *p3, k7; rep from * to last 7 sts, p3, k4.
3rd row: P4, *k3, p7; rep from * to last 7 sts, k3, p4.
4th row: As 2nd row.
5th row: Purl.
6th row: Knit.
7th row: K2, *p7, k3; rep from * to last 9 sts, p7, k2.
8th row: P2, *k7, p3; rep from * to last 9 sts, k7, p2.
9th row: As 7th row.
10th row: Knit.
Rep these 10 rows.

Close Checks

Multiple of 6 + 3
1st row (right side): K3, *p3, k3; rep from * to end.
2nd row: P3, *k3, p3; rep from * to end.
Rep the last 2 rows once more.
5th row: As 2nd row.
6th row: As 1st row.
Rep the last 2 rows once more.
Rep these 8 rows.

Squares

Multiple of 10 + 2
1st row (right side): Knit.
2nd row: Purl.
3rd row: K2, *p8, k2; rep from * to end.
4th row: P2, *k8, p2; rep from * to end.
5th row: K2, *p2, k4, p2, k2; rep from * to end.
6th row: P2, *k2, p4, k2, p2; rep from * to end.
Rep the last 2 rows twice more.
11th row: As 3rd row.
12th row: As 4th row.
Rep these 12 rows.

Elongated Chevron

Multiple of 18 + 1
1st row (right side): P1, *[k2, p2] twice, k1, [p2, k2] twice, p1; rep from * to end.
2nd row: K1, *[p2, k2] twice, p1, [k2, p2] twice, k1; rep from * to end.
Rep the last 2 rows once more.
5th row: [P2, k2] twice, *p3, k2, p2, k2; rep from * to last 2 sts, p2.
6th row: [K2, p2] twice, *k3, p2, k2, p2; rep from * to last 2 sts, k2.
Rep the last 2 rows once more.
9th row: As 2nd row.
10th row: As 1st row.
11th row: As 2nd row.
12th row: As 1st row.
13th row: As 6th row.
14th row: As 5th row.
15th row: As 6th row.
16th row: As 5th row.
Rep these 16 rows.

Knit and Purl Patterns

Chequerboard

Multiple of 8 + 4
1st row: K4, *p4, k4; rep from * to end.
2nd row: P4, *k4, p4; rep from * to end.
Rep the last 2 rows once more.
5th row: As 2nd row.
6th row: As 1st row.
Rep the last 2 rows once more.
Rep these 8 rows.

Top Hat Pattern

Multiple of 6 + 4
1st row (right side): K4, *p2, k4; rep from * to end.
2nd row: P4, *k2, p4; rep from * to end.
Rep the last 2 rows once more.
5th row: P1, k2, *p4, k2; rep from * to last st, p1.
6th row: K1, p2, *k4, p2; rep from * to last st, k1.
Rep the last 2 rows once more.
9th row: Purl.
10th row: Knit.
Rep these 10 rows.

King Charles Brocade

Multiple of 12 + 1
1st row (right side): K1, *p1, k9, p1, k1; rep from * to end.
2nd row: K1, p1, k1, *p7, [k1, p1] twice, k1; rep from * to last 10 sts, p7, k1, p1, k1.
3rd row: [K1, p1] twice, *k5, [p1, k1] 3 times, p1; rep from * to last 9 sts, k5, [p1, k1] twice.
4th row: P2, *k1, p1, k1, p3; rep from * to last 5 sts, k1, p1, k1, p2.
5th row: K3, *[p1, k1] 3 times, p1, k5; rep from * to last 10 sts, [p1, k1] 3 times, p1, k3.
6th row: P4, *[k1, p1] twice, k1, p7; rep from * to last 9 sts, [k1, p1] twice, k1, p4.
7th row: K5, *p1, k1, p1, k9; rep from * to last 8 sts, p1, k1, p1, k5.
8th row: As 6th row.
9th row: As 5th row.
10th row: As 4th row.
11th row: As 3rd row.
12th row: As 2nd row.
Rep these 12 rows.

Fancy Chevron

Multiple of 22 + 1
1st row (right side): K1, *p3, [k1,p1] twice, k1, p5, k1, [p1, k1] twice, p3, k1; rep from * to end.
2nd row: P2, *k3, [p1, k1] twice, p1, k3, p1, [k1, p1] twice, k3, p3; rep from * to last 21 sts, k3, [p1, k1] twice, p1, k3, p1, [k1, p1] twice, k3, p2.
3rd row: K3, *p3, [k1, p1] 5 times, k1, p3, k5; rep from * to last 20 sts, p3, [k1, p1] 5 times, k1, p3, k3.
4th row: K1, *p3, k3, [p1, k1] 4 times, p1, k3, p3, k1; rep from * to end.
5th row: P2, *k3, p3, [k1, p1] 3 times, k1, p3, k3, p3; rep from * to last 21 sts, k3, p3, [k1, p1] 3 times, k1, p3, k3, p2.
6th row: K3, *p3, k3, [p1, k1] twice, p1, k3, p3, k5; rep from * to last 20 sts, p3, k3, [p1, k1] twice, p1, k3, p3, k3.
7th row: K1, *p3, k3, p3, k1, p1, k1, p3, k3, p3, k1; rep from * to end.
8th row: K1, *[p1, k3, p3, k3] twice, p1, k1; rep from * to end.
9th row: K1, *p1, k1, p3, k3, p5, k3, p3, k1, p1, k1; rep from * to end.
10th row: K1, *p1, k1, p1, [k3, p3] twice, k3, [p1, k1] twice; rep from * to end.
11th row: K1, [p1, k1] twice, p3, k3, p1, k3, p3, *[k1, p1] 4 times, k1, p3, k3, p1, k3, p3; rep from * to last 5 sts, [p1, k1] twice, k1.
12th row: K1, [p1, k1] twice, p1, k3, p5, k3, *[p1, k1] 5 times, p1, k3, p5, k3; rep from * to last 6 sts, [p1, k1] 3 times.

13th row: P2, *[k1, p1] twice, k1, p3, k3, p3, [k1, p1] twice, k1, p3; rep from * to last 21 sts, [k1, p1] twice, k1, p3, k3, p3, [k1, p1] twice, k1, p2.
14th row: K3, *[p1, k1] twice, [p1, k3] twice, [p1, k1] twice, p1, k5; rep from * to last 20 sts, [p1, k1] twice, [p1, k3] twice, [p1, k1] twice, p1, k3.
Rep these 14 rows.

Dotted Chevron

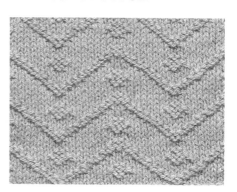

Multiple of 18 sts.
1st row (right side): K8, *p2, k16; rep from * to last 10 sts, p2, k8.
2nd row: P7, *k4, p14; rep from * to last 11 sts, k4, p7.
3rd row: P1, *k5, p2, k2, p2, k5, p2; rep from * to last 17 sts, k5, p2, k2, p2, k5, p1.
4th row: K2, *p3, k2, p4, k2, p3, k4; rep from * to last 16 sts, p3, k2, p4, k2, p3, k2.
5th row: P1, *k3, p2, k6, p2, k3, p2; rep from * to last 17 sts, k3, p2, k6, p2, k3, p1.
6th row: P3, *k2 [p3, k2] twice, p6; rep from * to last 15 sts, k2, [p3, k2] twice, p3.
7th row: K2, *p2, k3, p4, k3, p2, k4; rep from * to last 16 sts, p2, k3, p4, k3, p2, k2.
8th row: P1, *k2, [p5, k2] twice, p2; rep from * to last 17 sts, k2, [p5, k2] twice, p1.
9th row: P2, *k14, p4; rep from * to last 16 sts, k14, p2.
10th row: K1, *p16, k2; rep from * to last 17 sts, p16, k1.
Rep these 10 rows.

Zigzag Stitch

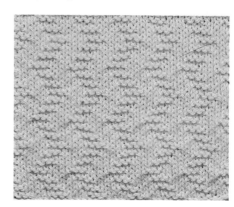

Multiple of 6 sts.

1st row (right side): *K3, p3; rep from * to end.

2nd and every alt row: Purl.

3rd row: P1, *k3, p3; rep from * to last 5 sts, k3, p2.

5th row: P2, *k3, p3; rep from * to last 4 sts, k3, p1.

7th row: *P3, k3; rep from * to end.

9th row: As 5th row.

11th row: As 3rd row.

12th row: Purl.

Rep these 12 rows.

Fancy Diamond Pattern

Multiple of 15 sts.

1st row (right side): K1, *p13, k2; rep from * to last 14 sts, p13, k1.

2nd row: P2, *k11, p4; rep from * to last 13 sts, k11, p2.

3rd row: K3, *p9, k6; rep from * to last 12 sts, p9, k3.

4th row: P4, *k7, p8; rep from * to last 11 sts, k7, p4.

5th row: K5, *p5, k10; rep from * to last 10 sts, p5, k5.

6th row: K1, *p5, k3, p5, k2; rep from * to last 14 sts, p5, k3, p5, k1.

7th row: P2, *k5, p1, k5, p4; rep from * to last 13 sts, k5, p1, k5, p2.

8th row: As 3rd row.

9th row: As 7th row.

10th row: As 6th row.

11th row: As 5th row.

12th row: As 4th row.

13th row: As 3rd row.

14th row: As 2nd row.

Rep these 14 rows.

Repeating Diamonds

Multiple of 22 + 1

1st row (right side): K2, *p2, k2, p1, k3, p1, k1, p1, k3, p1, k2, p2, k3; rep from * to last 21 sts, p2, k2, p1, k3, p1, k1, p1, k3, p1, k2, p2, k2.

2nd row: P2, *k2, p2, k5, p1, k5, p2, k2, p3; rep from * to last 21 sts, k2, p2, k5, p1, k5, p2, k2, p2.

Rep the last 2 rows once more.

5th row: K1, *p2, k2, [p1, k3] 3 times, p1, k2, p2, k1; rep from * to end.

6th row: P1, *k2, p2, k5, p3, k5, p2, k2, p1; rep from * to end.

Rep the last 2 rows once more.

9th row: P2, *k2, p1, k3, [p1, k2] twice, p1, k3, p1, k2, p3; rep from * to last 21 sts, k2, p1, k3, [p1, k2] twice, p1, k3, p1, k2, p2.

10th row: K2, *p2, k5, p2, k1, p2, k5, p2, k3; rep from * to last 21 sts, p2, k5, p2, k1, p2, k5, p2, k2.

Rep the last 2 rows once more.

13th row: P1, *k2, p1, k3, p1, k2, p3, k2, p1, k3, p1, k2, p1; rep from * to end.

14th row: K1, *p2, k5, p2, k3, p2, k5, p2, k1; rep from * to end.

Rep the last 2 rows once more.

17th row: K2, *p1, k3, p1, k2, p2, k1, p2, k2, p1, k3, p1, k3; rep from * to last 21 sts, p1, k3, p1, k2, p2, k1, p2, k2, p1, k3, p1, k2.

18th row: P2, *k5, p2, k2, p1, k2, p2, k5, p3; rep from * to last 21 sts, k5, p2, k2, p1, k2, p2, k5, p2.

Rep the last 2 rows once more.

21st row: K1, *p1, k3, p1, k2, p2, k3, p2, k2, p1, k3, p1, k1; rep from * to end.

22nd row: P1, *k5, p2, k2, p3, k2, p2, k5, p1; rep from * to end.

Rep the last 2 rows once more.

25th to 28th rows: Work 17th and 18th rows twice.

29th to 32nd rows: Work 13th and 14th rows twice.

33rd to 36th rows: Work 9th and 10th rows twice.

37th to 40th rows: Work 5th and 6th rows twice.

Rep these 40 rows.

Parallelogram Check

Multiple of 10 sts.

1st row (right side): *K5, p5; rep from * to end.

2nd row: K4, *p5, k5; rep from * to last 6 sts, p5, k1.

3rd row: P2, *k5, p5; rep from * to last 8 sts, k5, p3.

4th row: K2, *p5, k5; rep from * to last 8 sts, p5, k3.

5th row: P4, *k5, p5; rep from * to last 6 sts, k5, p1.

6th row: *P5, k5; rep from * to end.

Rep these 6 rows.

Wavy Rib

Multiple of 6 + 2

1st row (right side): P2, *k4, p2; rep from * to end.

2nd row: K2, *p4, k2; rep from * to end.

Rep the last 2 rows once more.

5th row: K3, p2, *k4, p2; rep from * to last 3 sts, k3.

6th row: P3, k2, *p4, k2; rep from * to last 3 sts, p3.

Rep the last 2 rows once more.

Rep these 8 rows.

Diamond Brocade

Multiple of 8 + 1

1st row (right side): K4, *p1, k7; rep from * to last 5 sts, p1, k4.

2nd row: P3, *k1, p1, k1, p5; rep from * to last 6 sts, k1, p1, k1, p3.

3rd row: K2, *p1, k3; rep from * to last 3 sts, p1, k2.

4th row: P1, *k1, p5, k1, p1; rep from * to end.

5th row: *P1, k7; rep from * to last st, p1.

6th row: As 4th row.

7th row: As 3rd row.

8th row: As 2nd row.

Rep these 8 rows.

Knit and Purl Patterns

Textured Stripe

Multiple of 3 sts.
1st row (right side): Knit.
2nd row: Purl.
Rep the last 2 rows once more.
5th row: K1, *p1, k2; rep from * to last 2 sts, p1, k1.
6th row: P1, *k1, p2; rep from * to last 2 sts, k1, p1.
Rep the last 2 rows once more.
9th row: *P2, k1; rep from * to end.
10th row: *P1, k2; rep from * to end.
Rep the last 2 rows once more.
Rep these 12 rows.

Check Pattern

Multiple of 3 + 1
1st row (right side): Knit.
2nd row: Purl.
3rd row: K1, *p2, k1; rep from * to end.
4th row: Purl.
Rep these 4 rows.

Banded Basket Stitch

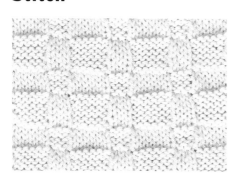

Multiple of 9 + 6
1st row (right side): P6, *k3, p6; rep from * to end.
2nd row: K6, *p3, k6; rep from * to end.
Rep the last 2 rows twice more.
7th row: As 2nd row.
8th row: P6, *k3, p6; rep from * to end.
Rep the last 2 rows once more.
Rep these 10 rows.

Chevron Rib

Multiple of 12 + 1
1st row (right side): P2, k2, p2, k1, p2, k2, *p3, k2, p2, k1, p2, k2; rep from * to last 2 sts, p2.
2nd row: K2, p2, k2, p1, k2, p2, *k3, p2, k2, p1, k2, p2; rep from * to last 2 sts, k2.
3rd row: P1, *k2, p2, k3, p2, k2, p1; rep from * to end.
4th row: K1, *p2, k2, p3, k2, p2, k1; rep from * to end.
5th row: As 2nd row.
6th row: P2, k2, p2, k1, p2, k2, *p3, k2, p2, k1, p2, k2; rep from * to last 2 sts, p2.
7th row: As 4th row.
8th row: As 3rd row.
Rep these 8 rows.

Broken Diagonal Check

Multiple of 8
1st row (right side): *K6, p2; rep from * to end.
2nd row: P1, * k2, p6; rep from * last 7 sts, k2, p5.
3rd row: K4, * p2, k6; rep from * to last 4 sts, p2, k2.
4th row: P3, *k2, p6; rep from * to last 5 sts, k2, p3.
5th row: K2, *p2, k6; rep from * to last 6 sts, p2, k4.
6th row: P5, *k2, p6; rep from * to last 3 sts, k2, p1. **7th row**: Purl.
8th row: K2, * p6, k2; rep from * to last 6 sts, p6

Pennant Stitch

Multiple of 5
1st row (right side): Knit.
2nd row: *K1, p4; rep from * to end.
3rd row: *K3, p2; rep from * to end.
4th row: As 3rd row.
5th row: As 2nd row.
Knit 2 rows.
8th row: *P4, k1; rep from * to end.
9th row: *P2, k3; rep from * to end.
10th row: As 9th row.
11th row: As 8th row.
12th row: Knit.
Rep these 12 rows.

9th row: As 3rd row.
10th row: As 4th row.
11th row: As 5th row.
12th row: As 6th row.
13th row: *P2, k6; rep from * to end.
14th row: Knit.
Rep these 14 rows.

Diagonal Seed Stitch

Multiple of 6
1st row (right side): *K5, p1; rep from * to end.
2nd row: P1, *k1, p5; rep from * to last 5 sts, k1, p4.
3rd row: K3, *p1, k5; rep from * to last 3 sts, p1, k2.
4th row: P3, *k1, p5; rep from * to last 3 sts, k1, p2.
5th row: K1, *p1, k5; rep from * to last 5 sts, p1, k4.
6th row: *P5, k1; rep from * to end.
Rep these 6 rows.

Piqué Triangles

Multiple of 5
1st row (right side): *P1, k4; rep from * to end.
2nd row: *P3, k2; rep from * to end.
3rd row: As 2nd row.
4th row: *P1, k4; rep from * to end.
Rep these 4 rows.

Mosaic Stitch

Multiple of 10 + 7
1st row (right side): P3, *k1, p3, k1, p1, k1, p3; rep from * to last 4 sts, k1, p3.
2nd row: K3, *p1, k3, p1, k1, p1, k3; rep from * to last 4 sts, p1, k3.
Rep the last 2 rows once more.
5th row: P2, *k1, p1, k1, p3, k1, p3; rep from * to last 5 sts, k1, p1, k1, p2.
6th row: K2, *p1, k1, p1, k3, p1, k3; rep from * to last 5 sts, p1, k1, p1, k2.
Rep the last 2 rows once more.
Rep these 8 rows.

Embossed Diamonds

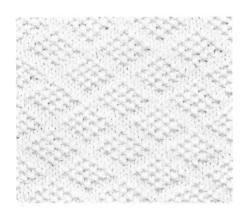

Multiple of 10 + 3
1st row (right side): P1, k1, p1, *[k3, p1] twice, k1, p1; rep from * to end.
2nd row: P1, k1, *p3, k1, p1, k1, p3, k1; rep from * to last st, p1.
3rd row: K4, *[p1, k1] twice, p1, k5; rep from * to last 9 sts, [p1, k1] twice, p1, k4.
4th row: P3, *[k1, p1] 3 times, k1, p3; rep from * to end
5th row: As 3rd row.
6th row: As 2nd row.
7th row: As 1st row.
8th row: P1, k1, p1, *k1, p5, [k1, p1] twice; rep from * to end.
9th row: [P1, k1] twice, *p1, k3, [p1, k1] 3 times; rep from * to last 9 sts, p1, k3, [p1, k1] twice, p1.
10th row: As 8th row.
Rep these 10 rows.

Moss Stitch Parallelograms

Multiple of 10
1st row (right side): *K5, [p1, k1] twice, p1; rep from * to end.
2nd row: [P1, k1] 3 times, *p5, [k1, p1] twice, k1; rep from * to last 4 sts, p4.
3rd row: K3, *[p1, k1] twice, p1, k5; rep from * to last 7 sts, [p1, k1] twice, p1, k2.
4th row: P3, *[k1, p1] twice, k1, p5; rep from * to last 7 sts, [k1, p1] twice, k1, p2.
5th row: [K1, p1] 3 times, *k5, [p1, k1] twice, p1; rep from * to last 4 sts, k4.
6th row: Purl.
Rep these 6 rows.

Plain Diamonds

Multiple of 9
1st row (right side): K4, *p1, k8; rep from * to last 5 sts, p1, k4.

2nd row: P3, *k3, p6; rep from * to last 6 sts, k3, p3.
3rd row: K2, *p5, k4; rep from * to last 7 sts, p5, k2.
4th row: P1, *k7, p2; rep from * to last 8 sts, k7, p1.
5th row: Purl.
6th row: As 4th row.
7th row: As 3rd row.
8th row: As 2nd row.
Rep these 8 rows.

Triangle Ribs

Multiple of 8
1st row (right side): *P2, k6; rep from * to end.
2nd row: *P6, k2; rep from * to end.
3rd row: *P3, k5; rep from * to end.
4th row: *P4, k4; rep from * to end.
5th row: *P5, k3; rep from * to end.
6th row: *P2, k6; rep from * to end.
7th row: *P7, k1; rep from * to end.
8th row: *P2, k6; rep from * to end.
9th row: As 5th row.
10th row: As 4th row.
11th row: As 3rd row.
12th row: As 2nd row.
Rep these 12 rows.

Garter Stitch Ridges

Any number of stitches
1st row (right side): Knit.
2nd row: Purl.
Rep the last 2 rows once more.
Purl 6 rows.
Rep these 10 rows.

Knit and Purl Patterns

Moss Stitch Zigzag

Multiple of 9
1st row (right side): *[K1, p1] twice, k4, p1; rep from * to end.
2nd row: *P4, [k1, p1] twice, k1; rep from * to end.
3rd row: [K1, p1] 3 times, *k4, [p1, k1] twice, p1; rep from * to last 3 sts, k3.
4th row: P2,*[k1, p1] twice, k1, p4; rep from * to last 7 sts, [k1, p1] twice, k1, p2.
5th row: K3, *[p1, k1] twice, p1, k4; rep from * to last 6 sts, [p1, k1] 3 times.
6th row: *[K1, p1] twice, k1, p4; rep from * to end.
7th row: As 5th row.
8th row: As 4th row.
9th row: As 3rd row.
10th row: As 2nd row.
Rep these 10 rows.

Moss Stitch Triangles

Multiple of 8
1st row (right side): *P1, k7; rep from * to end.
2nd row: P6, *k1, p7; rep from * to last 2 sts, k1, p1.
3rd row: *P1, k1, p1, k5; rep from * to end
4th row: P4, *k1, p1, k1, p5; rep from * to last 4 sts, [k1, p1] twice.
5th row: *[P1, k1] twice, p1, k3; rep from * to end.
6th row: P2, *[k1, p1] twice, k1, p3; rep from * to last 6 sts, [k1, p1] 3 times.
7th row: *P1, k1; rep from * to end.
8th row: As 6th row.
9th row: As 5th row.
10th row: As 4th row.
11th row: As 3rd row.
12th row: As 2nd row.
Rep these 12 rows.

Hexagon Stitch

Multiple of 10 + 1
1st row (right side): Knit.
2nd row: Purl.
3rd row: K4, *p1, k1, p1, k7; rep from * to last 7 sts, p1, k1, p1, k4.
4th row: P3, *[k1, p1] twice, k1, p5; rep from * to last 8 sts, [k1, p1] twice, k1, p3.
5th row: K2, *[p1, k1] 3 times, p1, k3; rep from * to last 9 sts, [p1, k1] 3 times, p1, k2.
Rep the last 2 rows once more.
8th row: As 4th row.
9th row: As 3rd row.
10th row: Purl.
11th row: Knit.
12th row: Purl.
13th row: K1, p1, *k7, p1, k1, p1; rep from * to last 9 sts, k7, p1, k1.
14th row: K1, p1, k1, *p5, [k1, p1] twice, k1; rep from * to last 8 sts, p5, k1, p1, k1.
15th row: [K1, p1] twice, *k3, [p1, k1] 3 times, p1; rep from * to last 7 sts, k3, [p1, k1] twice.
Rep the last 2 rows once more.
18th row: As 14th row.
19th row: As 13th row.
20th row: Purl.
Rep these 20 rows.

Chevron Stripes

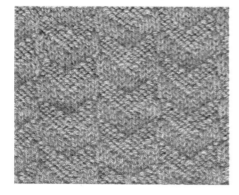

Multiple of 18 + 9
1st row (right side): P4, k1, p4, *k4, p1, k4, p4, k1, p4; rep from * to end.
2nd row: K3, *p3, k3; rep from * to end.
3rd row: P2, k5, p2, *k2, p5, k2, p2, k5, p2; rep from * to end.
4th row: K1, p7, k1, *p1, k7, p1, k1, p7, k1; rep from * to end.
5th row: K4, p1, k4, *p4, k1, p4, k4, p1, k4; rep from * to end.
6th row: P3, *k3, p3; rep from * to end.
7th row: K2, p5, k2, *p2, k5, p2, k2, p5, k2; rep from * to end.
8th row: P1, k7, p1, *k1, p7, k1, p1, k7, p1; rep from * to end.
Rep these 8 rows.

Moss Stitch Squares

Multiple of 12 + 3
1st row (right side): Knit.
2nd row: Purl.
3rd row: K4, *[p1, k1] 3 times, p1, k5; rep from * to last 11 sts, [p1, k1] 3 times, p1, k4.
4th row: P3, *[k1, p1] 4 times, k1, p3; rep from * to end.
5th row: K4, *p1, k5; rep from * to last 5 sts, p1, k4.
6th row: P3, *k1, p7, k1, p3; rep from * to end.
Rep the last 2 rows twice more, then the 5th row again.
12th row: As 4th row.
13th row: As 3rd row.
14th row: Purl.
Rep these 14 rows.

Moss Stitch Panes

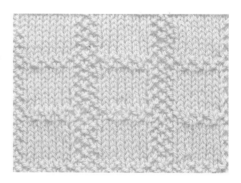

Multiple of 10 + 3
1st row (right side): P1, *k1, p1; rep from * to end.
2nd row: P1, *k1, p1; rep from * to end.
3rd row: P1, k1, p1, *k7, p1, k1, p1; rep from * to end.
4th row: P1, k1, p9, *k1, p9; rep from * to last 2 sts, k1, p1.
Rep the last 2 rows 3 times more.
Rep these 10 rows.

Moss Stitch Diagonal

Multiple of 8 + 3

1st row (right side): K4, *p1, k1, p1, k5; rep from * to last 7 sts, p1, k1, p1, k4.
2nd row: P3, *[k1, p1] twice, k1, p3; rep from * to end.
3rd row: K2, *p1, k1, p1, k5; rep from * to last st, p1.
4th row: P1, k1, *p3, [k1, p1] twice, k1; rep from * to last st, p1.
5th row: *P1, k1, p1, k5; rep from * to last 3 sts, p1, k1, p1.
6th row: *[P1, k1] twice, p3, k1; rep from * to last 3 sts, p1, k1, p1.
7th row: P1, *k5, p1, k1, p1; rep from * to last 2 sts, k2.
8th row: [P1, k1] 3 times, *p3, [k1, p1] twice, k1; rep from * to last 5 sts, p3, k1, p1.
Rep these 8 rows.

Garter Stitch Triangles

Multiple of 8 + 1

1st row (right side): P1, *k7, p1; rep from * to end.
2nd row and every alt row: Purl.
3rd row: P2, *k5, p3; rep from * to last 7 sts, k5, p2.
5th row: P3, *k3, p5; rep from * to last 6 sts, k3, p3.
7th row: P4, *k1, p7; rep from * to last 5 sts, k1, p4.
9th row: K4, *p1, k7; rep from * to last 5 sts, p1, k4.
11th row: K3, *p3, k5; rep from * to last 6 sts, p3, k3.
13th row: K2, *p5, k3; rep from * to last 7 sts, p5, k2.
15th row: K1, *p7, k1; rep from * to end.
16th row: Purl.
Rep these 16 rows.

Seed Stitch Checks

Multiple of 10 + 5

1st row (right side): K5, *[p1, k1] twice, p1, k5; rep from * to end.
2nd row: P6, *k1, p1, k1, p7; rep from * to last 9 sts, k1, p1, k1, p6.
Rep the last 2 rows once more then the 1st row again.
6th row: *[K1, p1] twice, k1, p5; rep from * to last 5 sts, [k1, p1] twice, k1.
7th row: [K1, p1] twice, *k7, p1, k1, p1; rep from * to last st, k1.
Rep the last 2 rows once more then the 6th row again.
Rep these 10 rows.

Purl Triangles

Multiple of 8 + 1

1st row (right side): K1, *p7, k1; rep from * to end.
2nd row: P1, *k7, p1; rep from * to end.
3rd row: K2, *p5, k3; rep from * to last 7 sts, p5, k2.
4th row: P2, *k5, p3; rep from * to last 7 sts, k5, p2.
5th row: K3, *p3, k5; rep from * to last 6 sts, p3, k3.
6th row: P3, *k3, p5; rep from * to last 6 sts, k3, p3.
7th row: K4, *p1, k7; rep from * to last 5 sts, p1, k4.
8th row: P4, *k1, p7; rep from * to last 5 sts, k1, p4.
9th row: As 8th row.
10th row: As 7th row.
11th row: As 6th row.
12th row: As 5th row.
13th row: As 4th row.
14th row: As 3rd row.
15th row: As 2nd row.
16th row: K1, *p7, k1; rep from * to end.
Rep these 16 rows.

Double Parallelogram Stitch

Multiple of 10

1st row (right side): *P5, k5; rep from * to end.
2nd row: K1, *p5, k5; rep from * to last 9 sts, p5, k4.
3rd row: P3, *k5, p5; rep from * to last 7 sts, k5, p2.
4th row: K3, *p5, k5; rep from * to last 7 sts, p5, k2.
5th row: P1, *k5, p5; rep from * to last 9 sts, k5, p4.
6th row: P4, *k5, p5; rep from * to last 6 sts, k5, p1.
7th row: K2, *p5, k5; rep from * to last 8 sts, p5, k3.
8th row: P2, *k5, p5; rep from * to last 8 sts, k5, p3.
9th row: K4, *p5, k5; rep from * to last 6 sts, p5, k1.
10th row: *K5, p5; rep from * to end.
Rep these 10 rows.

Moss Stitch Diamonds

Multiple of 10 + 9

1st row (right side): K4, *p1, k9; rep from * to last 5 sts, p1, k4.
2nd row: P3, *k1, p1, k1, p7; rep from * to last 6 sts, k1, p1, k1, p3.
3rd row: K2, *[p1, k1] twice, p1, k5; rep from * to last 7 sts, [p1, k1] twice, p1, k2.
4th row: [P1, k1] 4 times, *p3, [k1, p1] 3 times, k1; rep from * to last st, p1.
5th row: P1, *k1, p1; rep from * to end.
6th row: As 4th row.
7th row: As 3rd row.
8th row: As 2nd row.
9th row: As 1st row.
10th row: Purl.
Rep these 10 rows.

Knit and Purl Patterns

Moss Stitch Double Parallelograms

Multiple of 10
1st row (right side): *K5, [p1, k1] twice, p1; rep from * to end.
2nd row: P1, *[k1, p1] twice, k1, p5; rep from *to last 9 sts, [k1, p1] twice, k1, p4.
3rd row: K3, *[p1, k1] twice, p1, k5; rep from * to last 7 sts, [p1, k1] twice, p1, k2.
4th row: P3, *[k1, p1] twice, k1, p5; rep from * to last 7 sts, [k1, p1] twice, k1, p2.
5th row: K1, *[p1, k1] twice, p1, k5; rep from * to last 9 sts, [p1, k1] twice, p1, k4.
6th row: *[P1, k1] twice, p5, k1; rep from * to end.
7th row: K1, p1, *k5, [p1, k1] twice, p1; rep from * to last 8 sts, k5, p1, k1, p1.
8th row: P1, k1, *p5, [k1, p1] twice, k1; rep from * to last 8 sts, p5, k1, p1, k1.
9th row: *[K1, p1] twice, k5, p1; rep from * to end.
10th row: *P5, [k1, p1] twice, k1; rep form * to end.
Rep these 10 rows.

Garter Stitch Checks

Multiple of 10+5
1st row (right side): K5, *p5, k5; rep from * to end.
2nd row: Purl.
Rep the last 2 rows once more then the 1st row again.
6th row: K5, *p5, k5; rep from * to end.
7th row: Knit.
Rep the last 2 rows once more then the 6th row again.
Rep these 10 rows.

Double Signal Check

Multiple of 18+9
1st row (right side): K1, p7, k1, *p1, k7, p1, k1, p7, k1; rep from * to end.
2nd row: P2, k5, p2, *k2, p5, k2, p2, k5, p2; rep from * to end.
3rd row: K3, *p3, k3; rep from * to end.
4th row: P4, k1, p4, *k4, p1, k4, p4, k1, p4; rep from * to end.
5th row: P1, k7, p1, *k1, p7, k1, p1, k7, p1; rep from * to end.
6th row: K2, p5, k2, *p2, k5, p2, k2, p5, k2; rep from * to end.
7th row: P3, *k3, p3; rep from * to end.
8th row: K4, p1, k4, *p4, k1, p4, k4, p1, k4; rep from * to end.
Rep these 8 rows.

Stocking Stitch Checks

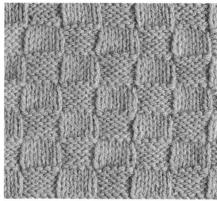

Multiple of 10+5
1st row (right side): K5, *p5, k5; rep from * to end.
2nd row: P5, *k5, p5; rep from * to end.
Rep the last 2 rows once more then 1st row again.
6th row: K5, *p5, k5; rep from * to end.
7th row: As 2nd row.
Rep the last 2 rows once more then 6th row again.
Rep these 10 rows.

Small Basket Stitch

Multiple of 10+5
1st row (right side): [K1, p1] twice, *k7, p1, k1, p1; rep from * to last st, k1.
2nd row: P1, [k1, p1] twice, *k5, [p1, k1] twice, p1; rep from * to end.
Rep the last 2 rows once more.
5th row: K6, *p1, k1, p1, k7; rep from * to last 9 sts, p1, k1, p1, k6.
6th row: *K5, [p1, k1] twice, p1; rep from * to last 5 sts, k5.
Rep the last 2 rows once more.
Rep these 8 rows.

Double Moss Stitch Triangles

Multiple of 8+1
1st row (right side): *K1, p7; rep from * to last st, k1.
2nd row: *P1, k7; rep from * to last st, p1.
3rd row: *P1, k1, p5, k1; rep from * to last st, p1.
4th row: *K1, p1, k5, p1; rep from * to last st, k1.
5th row: K1, p1, *k1, p3, [k1, p1] twice; rep from * to last 7 sts, k1, p3, k1, p1, k1.
6th row: P1, k1, *p1, k3, [p1, k1] twice; rep from * to last 7 sts, p1, k3, p1, k1, p1.
7th row: *P1, k1; rep from*to last st, p1.
8th row: *K1, p1; rep from*to last st, k1.
9th row: P4, *k1, p7; rep from * to last 5 sts, k1, p4.
10th row: K4, *p1, k7; rep from * to last 5 sts, p1, k4.
11th row: P3, *k1, p1, k1, p5; rep from * to last 6 sts, k1, p1, k1, p3.
12th row: K3, *p1, k1, p1, k5; rep from * to last 6 sts, p1, k1, p1, k3.
13th row: P2, *[k1, p1] twice, k1, p3; rep from * to last 7 sts, [k1, p1] twice, k1, p2.
14th row: K2, *[p1, k1] twice, p1, k3; rep from * to last 7 sts, [p1, k1] twice, p1, k2.
15th row: As 7th row.
16th row: As 8th row.
Rep these 16 rows.

Many of these surface textures are very attractive knitted in stripes of more than one colour. We have given examples of these, where applicable, throughout this section.

Knot Pattern

Multiple of 6 + 5

Special Abbreviation

Make knot = p3 tog leaving sts on left-hand needle, now knit them tog, then purl them tog again, slipping sts off needle at end.

Commence Pattern

Work 2 rows in st st, starting knit.

3rd row (right side): K1, *make knot (see Special Abbreviation), k3; rep from * to last 4 sts, make knot, k1.

Work 3 rows in st st, starting purl.

7th row: K4, *make knot, k3; rep from * to last st, k1.

8th row: Purl.

Rep these 8 rows.

Honeycomb Cable Stitch

Mutliple of 4 + 2

1st row (right side): Knit.

2nd row: K2, *p2, k2; rep from * to end.

Rep the last 2 rows once more.

5th row: K1, *C2F, C2B; rep from * to last st, k1.

6th row: P2, *k2, p2; rep from * to end.

7th row: Knit.

8th row: As 6th row.

Rep the last 2 rows once more.

11th row: K1, *C2B, C2F; rep from * to last st, k1.

12th row: As 2nd row.

Rep these 12 rows.

Rice Stitch I

Multiple of 2 + 1

1st row (right side): P1, *KB1, p1; rep from * to end.

2nd row: Knit.

Rep these 2 rows.

Rice Stitch II

Worked as Rice Stitch I.

Beginning with the 1st row, worked in stripes of 2 rows in colour A, 2 rows in B and 2 rows in C.

Garter Slip Stitch I

Multiple of 2 + 1

1st row (right side): Knit.

2nd row: Knit.

3rd row: K1, *sl 1 purlwise, k1; rep from * to end.

4th row: K1, *yf, sl 1 purlwise, yb, k1; rep from * to end.

Rep these 4 rows.

Garter Slip Stitch II

Worked as Garter Slip Stitch I.

1st and 2nd pattern rows worked in A, 3rd and 4th rows in B, throughout.

Garter Slip Stitch III

Worked as Garter Slip Stitch I.

Beginning with the 1st row, 2 rows worked in colour A, 2 rows in B and 2 rows in C throughout.

Garter Slip Stitch IV

Worked as Garter Slip Stitch I.

Worked in 1 row each in colours A, B and C throughout.

Patterns for Texture and Colour

Garter Slip Stitch V

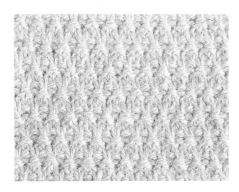

Multiple of 2 + 1
1st row (right side): Knit.
2nd row: Knit.
3rd row: K1, *sl 1 purlwise, k1; rep from * to end.
4th row: K1, *yf, sl 1 purlwise, yb, k1; rep from * to end.
Knit 2 rows.
7th row: K2, *sl 1 purlwise, k1; rep from * to last st, k1.
8th row: K2, *yf, sl 1 purlwise, yb, k1; rep from * to last st, k1.
Rep these 8 rows.

Garter Slip Stitch VI

Worked as Garter Slip Stitch V.
1st, 2nd, 5th and 6th pattern rows worked in A, 3rd, 4th, 7th and 8th rows worked in B throughout.

Garter Slip Stitch VII

Worked as Garter Slip Stitch V.
Beginning with the 1st row 2 rows worked in colour A, 2 rows in colour B and 2 rows in colour C throughout.

Garter Slip Stitch VIII

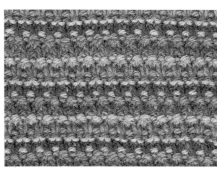

Worked as Garter Slip Stitch V.
Worked in 1 row each in colours A, B and C throughout.

Bramble Stitch I

Multiple of 4 + 2
1st row (right side): Purl.
2nd row: K1, *(k1, p1, k1) into next st, p3tog; rep from * to last st, k1.
3rd row: Purl.
4th row: K1, *p3tog, (k1, p1, k1) into next st; rep from * to last st, k1.
Rep these 4 rows.

Bramble Stitch II

Worked as Bramble Stitch I.
Beginning with the 2nd row, 2 rows worked in colour A, 2 rows in B, 2 rows in A and 2 rows in C throughout.

Bramble Stitch III

Worked as Bramble Stitch I.
Beginning with the 2nd row, 2 rows worked in colour A, 2 rows in B and 2 rows in C throughout.

Mini Bobble Stitch I

Multiple of 2 + 1
Special Abbreviation
MB (Make Bobble) = work (p1, k1, p1, k1) all into next st, pass 2nd, 3rd and 4th sts over first st.
1st row (right side): Knit.
2nd row: K1, *MB (see Special Abbreviation), k1; rep from * to end.
3rd row: Knit.
4th row: K2, *MB, k1; rep from * to last st, k1.
Rep these 4 rows.

Mini Bobble Stitch II

Worked as Mini Bobble Stitch I.
1st and 2nd pattern rows worked in A, 3rd and 4th rows worked in B throughout.

Mini Bobble Stitch III

Worked as Mini Bobble Stitch I.
Beginning with the 1st row, 2 rows worked in colour A, 2 rows in B and 2 rows in C throughout.

Basket Rib I

Multiple of 2 + 1
1st row (right side): Knit.
2nd row: Purl.
3rd row: K1, *sl 1 purlwise, k1; rep from * to end.
4th row: K1, *yf, sl 1 purlwise, yb, k1; rep from * to end.
Rep these 4 rows.

Basket Rib II

Worked as Basket Rib I
1st and 2nd pattern rows worked in A, 3rd and 4th rows worked in B throughout.

Basket Rib III

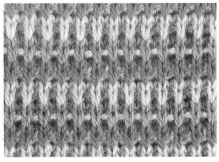

Worked as Basket Rib I.
Worked in 1 row each in colours A, B and C throughout.

Woven Cable Stitch I

Multiple of 4
1st row (right side): *C4F; rep from * to end.
2nd row: Purl.
3rd row: K2, *C4B; rep from * to last 2 sts, k2.
4th row: Purl.
Rep these 4 rows.

Woven Cable Stitch II

Multiple of 4
Special Abbreviation
C4 Back or Front (Cable 4 Back or Front) = slip next 2 sts onto a cable needle and hold at back or front of work, knit next 2 sts from left-hand needle using B, then knit sts from cable needle using A.
1st Foundation row: Knit *2A, 2B; rep from * to end.
2nd Foundation row: Purl *2B, 2A; rep

from * to end.
1st Pattern row: *C4 Front (see Special Abbreviation); rep from * to end.
2nd row: Purl *2A, 2B; rep from * to end.
3rd row: K2A, *C4 Back; rep from * to last 2 sts, k2B.
4th row: Purl *2B, 2A; rep from * to end.
Rep these 4 rows.

Candle Flame Stitch

Multiple of 4 + 2
1st row (right side): K2, *p2, k2; rep from * to end.
2nd row: P2, *k2, p2; rep from * to end.
3rd row: K2, *p2, C2F; rep from * to last 4 sts, p2, k2.
4th and 5th rows: As 2nd row.
6th row: As 1st row.
7th row: P2, *C2F, p2; rep from * to end.
8th row: As 1st row.
Rep these 8 rows.

Honeycomb Stitch

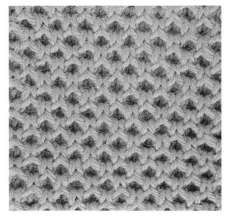

Multiple of 4
1st row (right side): *C2F, C2B; rep from * to end.
2nd row: Purl.
3rd row: *C2B, C2F; rep from * to end.
4th row: Purl.
Rep these 4 rows.

Patterns for Texture and Colour

Orchard Stitch

Multiple of 6+5
(**Note**: Stitches should only be counted after the 6th or 12th rows of this pattern.)
1st row (right side): P2, *k into front, back, front and back of next st, p2, k1, p2; rep from * to last 3 sts, k into front, back, front and back of next st, p2.
2nd row: *K2, [k1 winding yarn round needle twice] 4 times, k2, p1; rep from * to last 8 sts, k2, [k1 winding yarn round needle twice] 4 times, k2.
3rd row: P2, *k4 (dropping extra loops), p2, k1, p2; rep from * to last 6 sts, k4 (dropping extra loops), p2.
Rep the last 2 rows once more.
6th row: *K2, p4tog, k2, p1; rep from * to last 8 sts, k2, p4tog, k2.
7th row: P2, *k1, p2, k into front, back, front and back of next st, p2; rep from * to last 3 sts, k1, p2.
8th row: *K2, p1, k2, [k1 winding yarn round needle twice] 4 times; rep from * to last 5 sts, k2, p1, k2.
9th row: *P2, k1, p2, k4 (dropping extra loops); rep from * to last 5 sts, p2, k1, p2.
Rep the last 2 rows once more.
12th row: *K2, p1, k2, p4tog; rep from * to last 5 sts, k2, p1, k2.
Rep these 12 rows.

Trellis Stitch I

Multiple of 6+5
1st row (right side): K1, p3, *keeping yarn at front of work sl 3 purlwise, p3; rep from * to last st, k1.
2nd row: P1, k3, *keeping yarn at back of work sl 3 purlwise, k3; rep from * to last st, p1.
3rd row: K1, p3, *k3, p3; rep from * to last st, k1.
4th row: P1, k3, *p3, k3; rep from * to last st, p1.

5th row: K5, *insert point of right-hand needle upwards under the 2 strands in front of the sl sts and knit the next st, then lift the 2 strands off over the point of the right-hand needle (called pull up loop), k5; rep from * to end.
6th row: As 3rd row.
7th row: P1, *keeping yarn at front sl 3 purlwise, p3; rep from * to last 4 sts, sl 3 purlwise, p1.
8th row: K1, *keeping yarn at back sl 3 purlwise, k3; rep from * to last 4 sts, sl 3 purlwise, k1.
9th row: As 4th row.
10th row: As 3rd row.
11th row: K2, *pull up loop, k5; rep from * to last 3 sts, pull up loop, k2.
12th row: As 4th row.
Rep these 12 rows.

Trellis Stitch II

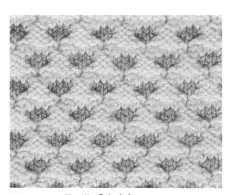

Worked as Trellis Stitch I.

1st and 2nd rows and 7th and 8th rows of pattern worked in contrast colour. Wrong side of fabric becomes the right side.

Speckle Rib I

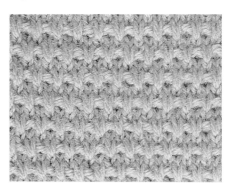

Multiple of 2+1
1st row (right side): Knit.
2nd row: Purl.
3rd row: K1, *sl 1 purlwise, k1; rep from * to end.
4th row: K1, *yf, sl 1 purlwise, yb, k1; rep from * to end.
5th row: Knit.
6th row: Purl.
7th row: K2, *sl 1 purlwise, k1; rep from * to last st, k1.
8th row: K2, *yf, sl 1 purlwise, yb, k1; rep from * to last st, k1.
Rep these 8 rows.

Speckle Rib II

Worked as Speckle Rib I.

1st, 2nd, 5th and 6th pattern rows worked in A, 3rd, 4th, 7th and 8th rows worked in B throughout.

Speckle Rib III

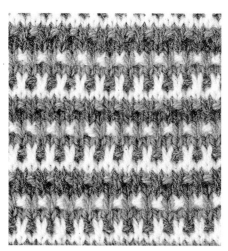

Worked as Speckle Rib I.
Beginning with the 1st row, 2 rows worked in colour A, 2 rows in B and 2 rows in C throughout.

Speckle Rib IV

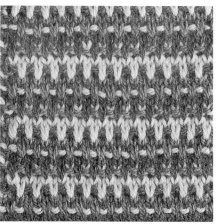

Worked as Speckle Rib I.
Worked in 1 row each in colours A, B and C throughout.

Moss Slip Stitch I

Multiple of 2 + 1

1st row (right side): K1, *sl 1 purlwise, k1; rep from * to end.

2nd row: K1, *yf, sl 1 purlwise, yb, k1; rep from * to end.

3rd row: K2, *sl 1 purlwise, k1; rep from * to last st, k1.

4th row: K2, *yf, sl 1 purlwise, yb, k1; rep from * to last st, k1.

Rep these 4 rows.

Moss Slip Stitch II

Worked as Moss Slip Stitch I.

1st and 2nd pattern rows worked in colour A, 3rd and 4th rows worked in B throughout.

Moss Slip Stitch III

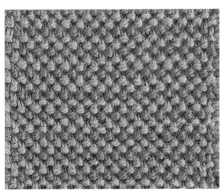

Worked as Moss Slip Stitch I.

Beginning with the 1st row, 2 rows worked in colour A, 2 rows in B and 2 rows in C throughout.

Moss Slip Stitch IV

Worked as Moss Slip Stitch I.

Worked in 1 row each in colours A, B and C throughout.

Twisted Moss I

Multiple of 2 + 1

1st row (wrong side): Knit.

2nd row: K1, *K1B, k1; rep from * to end.

3rd row: Knit.

4th row: K1B, *k1, K1B; rep from * to end.

Rep these 4 rows.

Twisted Moss II

Worked as Twisted Moss I.

Beginning with the 1st row, 2 rows worked in colour A, and 4 rows in colour B throughout.

Twisted Moss III

Worked as Twisted Moss I.

1st and 2nd pattern rows worked in A, 3rd and 4th rows in B throughout.

Garter Stitch Chevron

Multiple of 11

Knit 5 rows in colour A.

6th row (right side): Using colour B, *k2tog, k2, knit into front and back of each of the next 2 sts, k3, sl 1, k1, psso; rep from * to end.

7th row: Using colour B, purl.

Rep the last 2 rows twice more. Work 6th row again using A instead of B.

Rep these 12 rows.

Tweed Stitch

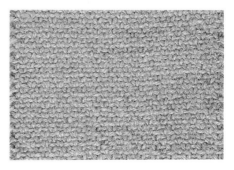

Multiple of 2 + 1

1st row (right side): K1, *yf, sl 1 purlwise, yb, k1; rep from * to end.

2nd row: P2, *yb, sl 1 purlwise, yf, p1; rep from * to last st, p1.

Rep these 2 rows.

Patterns for Texture and Colour

Pillar Stitch I

Multiple of 2
1st row (wrong side): Purl.
2nd row: K1, *yf, k2, pass yf over k2; rep from * to last st, k1.
Rep these 2 rows.

Pillar Stitch II

Worked as Pillar Stitch I.

1st row worked in colour C, then, beginning with 2nd row, 2 rows worked in colour A, 2 rows in B and 2 rows in C throughout.

Eiffel Tower Stitch

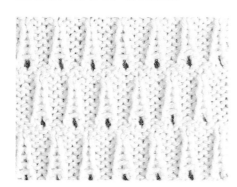

Multiple of 4 + 1
1st row (right side): P4, *yrn, p2tog, p2; rep from * to last st, p1.
2nd row: K4, *p1, k3; rep from * to last st, k1.
3rd row: P4, *k1, p3; rep from * to last st, p1.
Rep these last 2 rows twice more.
8th row: Knit.

9th row: P2, *yrn, p2tog, p2; rep from * to last 3 sts, yrn, p2tog, p1.
10th row: K2, *p1, k3; rep from * to last 3 sts, p1, k2.
11th row: P2, *k1, p3; rep from * to last 3 sts, k1, p2.
Rep the last 2 rows twice more.
16th row: Knit.
Rep these 16 rows.

Cob Nut Stitch

Multiple of 4 + 3
Note: Stitches should only be counted after the 4th, 5th, 6th, 10th, 11th or 12th rows of this pattern.
Special Abbreviation
CN1 (Make 1 Cob Nut) = knit 1 without slipping st off left-hand needle, yf, then k1 once more into same st.
Commence Pattern
1st row (right side): P3, *CN1 (see Special Abbreviation), p3; rep from * to end.
2nd row: K3, *p3, k3; rep from * to end.
3rd row: P3, *k3, p3; rep from * to end.
4th row: K3, *p3tog, k3; rep from * to end.
5th row: Purl.
6th row: Knit.
7th row: P1, *CN1, p3; rep from * to last 2 sts, CN1, p1.
8th row: K1, *p3, k3; rep from * to last 4 sts, p3, k1.
9th row: P1, *k3, p3; rep from * to last 4 sts, k3, p1.
10th row: K1, *p3tog, k3; rep from * to last 4 sts, p3tog, k1.
11th row: Purl.
12th row: Knit.
Rep these 12 rows.

Slip Stitch Rib

Multiple of 2 + 1
1st row (wrong side): Purl.
2nd row: K1, *yf, sl 1 purlwise, yb, k1; rep from * to end.
Rep these 2 rows.

Garter and Slip Stitch

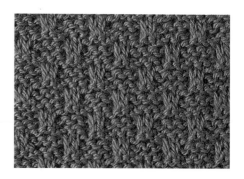

Multiple of 6 + 4
1st row (right side): Knit.
2nd row: K1, *yf, sl 2 purlwise, yb, k4; rep from * to last 3 sts, yf, sl 2 purlwise, yb, k1.
3rd row: K1, *keeping yarn at back sl 2 purlwise, k4; rep from * to last 3 sts, sl 2 purlwise, k1.
Rep the last 2 rows once more.
6th row: As 2nd row.
7th row: Knit.
8th row: K4, *yf, sl 2 purlwise, yb, k4; rep from * to end.
9th row: K4, *keeping yarn at back sl 2 purlwise, k4; rep from * to end.
Rep the last 2 rows once more.
12th row: As 8th row.
Rep these 12 rows.

Garter Stitch Diamonds

Multiple of 8 + 2
1st row (right side): Knit.
2nd row: P4, *keeping yarn at front sl 2 purlwise, p6; rep from * to last 6 sts, sl 2 purlwise, p4.
3rd row: K3, *C2F, C2B, k4; rep from * to last 7 sts, C2F, C2B, k3.
4th row: P3, *keeping yarn at front sl 1 purlwise, yb, k2, yf, sl 1 purlwise, p4; rep from * to last 7 sts, sl 1 purlwise, yb, k2,

yf, sl 1 purlwise, p3.

5th row: K2, *C2F, k2, C2B, k2; rep from * to end.

6th row: P2, *keeping yarn at front sl 1 purlwise, yb, k4, yf, sl 1 purlwise, p2; rep from * to end.

7th row: K1, *C2F, k4, C2B; rep from * to last st, k1.

8th row: P1, keeping yarn at front sl 1 purlwise, yb, *k6, yf, sl 2 purlwise, yb; rep from * to last 8 sts, k6, yf, sl 1 purlwise, p1.

9th row: Knit.

10th row: As 8th row.

11th row: K1, *C2B, k4, C2F; rep from * to last st, k1.

12th row: As 6th row.

13th row: K2, *C2B, k2, C2F, k2; rep from * to end.

14th row: As 4th row.

15th row: K3, *C2B, C2F, k4; rep from * to last 7 sts, C2B, C2F, k3.

16th row: As 2nd row.

Rep these 16 rows.

Stocking Stitch Ridge I

Multiple of 2

Note: Stitches should not be counted after the 2nd row.

1st row (right side): Knit.

2nd row: P1, *k2tog; rep from * to last st, p1.

3rd row: K1, *knit into front and back of next st; rep from * to last st, k1.

4th row: Purl.

Rep these 4 rows.

Stocking Stitch Ridge II

Worked as Stocking Stitch Ridge I.

Worked in stripes of 4 rows in colour A, 4 rows in B and 4 rows in C throughout.

Knot Stitch I

Multiple of 2 + 1

1st row (right side): Knit.

2nd row: K1, *p2tog without slipping sts off needle, then k tog the same 2 sts; rep from * to end.

3rd row: Knit.

4th row: *P2tog without slipping sts off needle, then k tog the same 2 sts; rep from * to last st, k1.

Rep these 4 rows.

Knot Stitch II

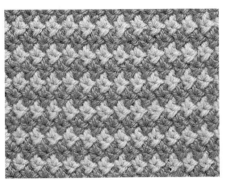

Worked as Knot Stitch I.

1st and 2nd pattern rows worked in A, 3rd and 4th rows in B throughout.

Brick Stitch I

Multiple of 4 + 1

1st row (right side): K4, *k1 winding yarn twice round needle, k3; rep from * to last st, k1.

2nd row: P4, *sl 1 purlwise dropping extra loop, p3; rep from * to last st, p1.

3rd row: K4, *sl 1 purlwise, k3; rep from * to last st, k1.

4th row: K4, *yf, sl 1 purlwise, yb, k3; rep from * to last st, k1.

5th row: K2, *k1 winding yarn twice round needle, k3; rep from * to last 3 sts, k1 winding yarn twice round needle, k2.

6th row: P2, *sl 1 purlwise dropping extra loop, p3; rep from * to last 3 sts, sl 1 purlwise, p2.

7th row: K2, *sl 1 purlwise, k3; rep from * to last 3 sts, sl 1 purlwise, k2.

8th row: K2, *yf, sl 1 purlwise, yb, k3; rep from * to last 3 sts, yf, sl 1 purlwise, yb, k2.

Rep these 8 rows.

Brick Stitch II

Multiple of 4 + 1

1st row (right side): K4, *k1 winding yarn twice round needle, k3; rep from * to last st, k1.

2nd row: P4, *sl 1 purlwise dropping extra loop, p3; rep from * to last st, p1.

3rd row: K4, *sl 1 purlwise, k3; rep from * to last st, k1.

4th row: K4, *yf, sl 1 purlwise, yb, k3; rep from * to last st, k1.

Rep the last 4 rows once more.

9th row: K2, *k1 winding yarn twice round needle, k3; rep from * to last 3 sts, k1 winding yarn twice round needle, k2.

10th row: P2, *sl 1 purlwise dropping extra loop, p3; rep from * to last 3 sts, sl 1 purlwise, p2.

11th row: K2, *sl 1 purlwise, k3; rep from * to last 3 sts, sl 1 purlwise, k2.

12th row: K2, *yf, sl 1 purlwise, yb, k3; rep from * to last 3 sts, yf, sl 1 purlwise, yb, k2.

Rep the last 4 rows once more.

Rep these 16 rows.

Brick Stitch III

Worked as Brick Stitch II.

1st row worked in colour B then 4 rows in A and 4 rows in B throughout.

Patterns for Texture and Colour

Wheatsheaf Pattern

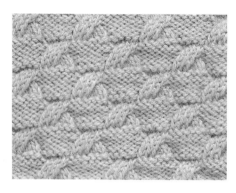

Multiple of 12 + 8

Special Abbreviation

CB6 = slip next 3 sts onto a cable needle and leave at back of work, [KB1] 3 times from left-hand needle, then k3 sts from cable needle.

1st row (right side): P7, *k3, [KB1] 3 times, p6; rep from * to last st, p1.

2nd row: K7, *[PB1] 3 times, p3, k6; rep from * to last st, k1.

Rep the last 2 rows once more.

5th row: P7, *CB6 (see Special Abbreviation), p6; rep from * to last st, p1.

6th row: K7, *p3, [PB1] 3 times, k6; rep from * to last st, k1.

7th row: P1, *k3 [KB1] 3 times, p6; rep from * to last 7 sts, k3, [KB1] 3 times, p1.

8th row: K1, *[PB1] 3 times, p3, k6; rep from * to last 7 sts, [PB1] 3 times, p3, k1.

Rep the last 2 rows once more.

11th row: P1, *CB6, p6; rep from * to last 7 sts, CB6, p1.

12th row: K1, *p3, [PB1] 3 times, k6; rep from * to last 7 sts, p3, [PB1] 3 times, k1.

Rep these 12 rows.

Pull Up Stitch I

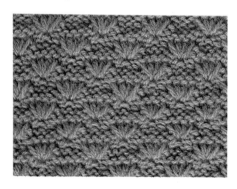

Multiple of 6 + 5

Note: Stitches should *not* be counted after the 3rd or 7th rows of this pattern.

Special Abbreviation

Make cluster = k1, insert needle through centre of st 3 rows below next st on needle, yo and pull up a loop, knit st above in the usual way, pull up another loop as before through *same* hole, knit next st from needle, pull up another loop through same hole.

Foundation row (do not repeat this row): Knit.

1st row (right side): Purl.

2nd row: Knit.

3rd row: P1, *make cluster (see Special Abbreviation), p3; rep from * to last 4 sts, make cluster, p1.

4th row: K1, *[p2tog] 3 times, k3; rep from * to last 7 sts, [p2tog] 3 times, k1.

5th row: Purl.

6th row: Knit.

7th row: P4, *make cluster, p3; rep from * to last st, p1.

8th row: K4, *[p2tog] 3 times, k3; rep from * to last st, k1.

Rep these 8 rows.

Pull Up Stitch II

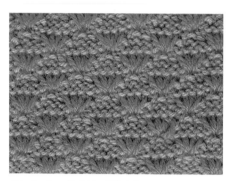

Worked as Pull Up Stitch I.

1st, 2nd, 5th and 6th pattern rows worked in A, 3rd, 4th, 7th and 8th rows worked in B throughout.

Stairway Check

Multiple of 8 + 4

1st row (right side): *KB1; rep from * to end.

2nd row: [PB1] 4 times, *k4, [PB1] 4 times; rep from * to end.

3rd row: P1, *[KB1] 4 times, p4; rep from * to last 3 sts, [KB1] 3 times.

4th row: [PB1] twice, *k4, [PB1] 4 times; rep from * to last 2 sts, k2.

5th row: P3, *[KB1] 4 times, p4; rep from * to last st, KB1.

6th row: K4, *[PB1] 4 times, k4; rep from * to end.

7th row: As 1st row.

8th row: [PB1] 4 times, *k4, [PB1] 4 times; rep from * to end.

9th row: [KB1] 4 times, *p4, [KB1] 4 times; rep from * to end.

Rep the last 2 rows once more.

12th row: *PB1; rep from * to end.

13th row: P4, *[KB1] 4 times, p4; rep from * to end.

14th row: PB1, *k4, [PB1] 4 times; rep from * to last 3 sts, k3.

15th row: P2, *[KB1] 4 times, p4; rep from * to last 2 sts, [KB1] twice.

16th row: [PB1] 3 times, *k4, [PB1] 4 times; rep from * to last st, k1.

17th row: As 9th row.

18th row: As 12th row.

19th row: P4, *[KB1] 4 times, p4; rep from * to end.

20th row: K4, *[PB1] 4 times, k4; rep from * to end.

Rep the last 2 rows once more.

Rep these 22 rows.

Garter Drop Stitch

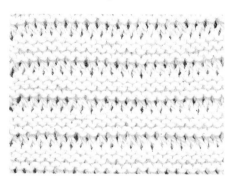

Any number of stitches

Work 4 rows in garter stitch (every row knit).

5th row: *K1 winding yarn twice round needle; rep from * to end.

6th row: K to end, dropping the extra loops.

Rep these 6 rows.

Ridged Knot Stitch I

Multiple of 3 + 2

1st row (right side): Knit.

2nd row: K1, *p3tog leaving sts on needle, yrn, then p same 3 sts together again; rep from * to last st, k1.

3rd and 4th rows: Knit.

Rep these 4 rows.

Ridged Knot Stitch II

Worked as Ridged Knot Stitch I.
1st and 2nd pattern rows worked in A, 3rd and 4th rows in B throughout.

Twisted Check Pattern

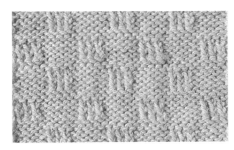

Multiple of 8+5
1st row (right side): Purl.
2nd row: K1, *[PB1] 3 times, k5; rep from * to last 4 sts, [PB1] 3 times, k1.
3rd row: P1, *[KB1] 3 times, p5; rep from * to last 4 sts, [KB1] 3 times, p1.
4th row: As 2nd row.
5th row: Purl.
6th row: Knit.
7th row: P5, *[KB1] 3 times, p5; rep from * to end.
8th row: K5, *[PB1] 3 times, k5; rep from * to end.
9th row: As 7th row.
10th row: Knit.
Rep these 10 rows.

Diagonal Knot Stitch I

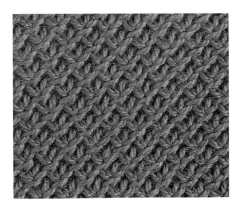

Multiple of 3+1
Special Abbreviation
Make Knot = P3tog leaving sts on needle, yrn, then purl same 3 sts together again.
1st and every alt row (right side): Knit.
2nd row: *Make Knot (see Special Abbreviation); rep from * to last st, p1.
4th row: P2, *Make Knot; rep from * to last 2 sts, p2.
6th row: P1, *Make Knot; rep from * to end.
Rep these 6 rows.

Diagonal Knot Stitch II

Worked as Diagonal Knot Stitch I.
Beginning with the 1st row, 2 rows worked in A and 2 rows in B throughout.

Cable Fabric

Multiple of 6
1st row: Knit.
2nd and every alt row: Purl.
3rd row: *K2, C4B; rep from * to end.
5th row: Knit.
7th row: *C4F, k2; rep from * to end.
8th row: Purl.
Rep these 8 rows.

Twisted Basket Weave

Multiple of 8+5
1st row (right side): P5, *C3, p5; rep from * to end.
2nd row: K5, *p3, k5; rep from * to end.
Rep the last 2 rows once more.
5th row: P1, *C3, p5; rep from * to last 4 sts, C3, p1.
6th row: K1, *p3, k5; rep from * to last 4 sts, p3, k1.
Rep the last 2 rows once more.
Rep these 8 rows.

Lichen Twist

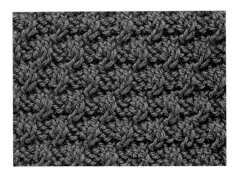

Multiple of 4+2
1st row (right side): *KB1; rep from * to end.
2nd row: *PB1; rep from * to end.
3rd row: P2, *C2F, p2; rep from * to end.
4th row: K2, *p2, k2; rep from * to end.
5th row: As 1st row.
6th row: As 2nd row.
7th row: K2, *p2, C2F; rep from * to last 4 sts, p2, k2.
8th row: P2, *k2, p2; rep from * to end.
Rep these 8 rows.

Ric Rac Pattern

Multiple of 3+1
Special Abbreviation
M1K = pick up horizontal strand of yarn lying between stitch just worked and next stitch and knit into the back of it.
1st row (right side): KB1, *M1K (see Special Abbreviation), k2tog tbl, KB1; rep from * to end.
2nd row: PB1, *p2, PB1; rep from * to end.
3rd row: KB1, *k2tog, M1K, KB1; rep from * to end.
4th row: As 2nd row.
Rep these 4 rows.

Patterns for Texture and Colour

Loaf Pattern

Multiple of 8 + 7

Note: Stitches should only be counted after the 6th and 12th rows of this pattern.
1st row (right side): P7, *(k1, p1, k1) into next st, p7; rep from * to end.
2nd row: K7, *p3, k7; rep from * to end.
3rd row: P7, *k3, p7; rep from * to end.
Rep the last 2 rows once more.
6th row: K7, *p3tog, k7; rep from * to end.
7th row: P3, *(k1, p1, k1) into next st, p7; rep from * to last 4 sts, (k1, p1, k1) into next st, p3.
8th row: K3, *p3, k7; rep from * to last 6 sts, p3, k3.
9th row: P3, *k3, p7; rep from * to last 6 sts, k3, p3.
Rep the last 2 rows once more.
12th row: K3, *p3tog, k7; rep from * to last 6 sts, p3tog, k3.
Rep these 12 rows.

Embossed Lozenge Stitch

Multiple of 8 + 1

1st row (right side): P3, *KB1, p1, KB1, p5; rep from * to last 6 sts, KB1, p1, KB1, p3.
2nd row: K3, *PB1, k1, PB1, k5; rep from * to last 6 sts, PB1, k1, PB1, k3.
Rep the last 2 rows once more.
5th row: P2, *KB1, p3; rep from * to last 3 sts, KB1, p2.
6th row: K2, *PB1, k3; rep from * to last 3 sts, PB1, k2.
7th row: P1, *KB1, p5, KB1, p1; rep from * to end.
8th row: K1, *PB1, k5, PB1, k1; rep from * to end.
9th row: As 7th row.
10th row: As 8th row.
11th row: As 5th row.
12th row: As 6th row.
Rep these 12 rows.

Mock Ribbing

Multiple of 2 + 1

1st row (right side): K1, *p1, k1; rep from * to end.
2nd row: P1, *keeping yarn at front of work sl 1 purlwise, p1; rep from * to end.
Rep these 2 rows.

Double Mock Ribbing

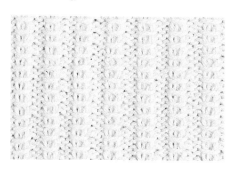

Multiple of 4 + 2

1st row (wrong side): K2, *p2, k2; rep from * to end.
2nd row: P2, *keeping yarn at front of work sl 2 purlwise, p2; rep from * to end.
Rep these 2 rows.

Dash Stitch

Multiple of 6 + 1

1st row (wrong side): K3, *PB1, k5; rep from * to last 4 sts, PB1, k3.
2nd row: P3, *KB1, p5; rep from * to last 4 sts, KB1, p3.
Rep these 2 rows twice more.

7th row: *PB1, k5; rep from * to last st, PB1.
8th row: *KB1, p5; rep from * to last st, KB1.
Rep these 2 rows twice more.
Rep these 12 rows.

Embossed Check Stitch

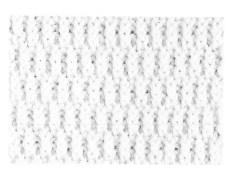

Multiple of 2 + 1

1st row (right side): *KB1; rep from * to end.
2nd row: K1, *PB1, k1; rep from * to end.
3rd row: P1, *KB1, p1; rep from * to end.
4th row: As 2nd row.
5th row: As 1st row.
6th row: PB1, *k1, PB1; rep from * to end.
7th row: KB1, *p1, KB1; rep from * to end.
8th row: As 6th row.
Rep these 8 rows.

Small Cable Check

Multiple of 12 + 7

1st row (right side): *P1, [KB1] 5 times, [p1, C2F] twice; rep from * to last 7 sts, p1, [KB1] 5 times, p1.
2nd row: *K1, [PB1] 5 times, [k1, p2] twice; rep from * to last 7 sts, k1, [PB1] 5 times, k1.
Rep the last 2 rows twice more.
7th row: *[P1, C2F] twice, p1, [KB1] 5 times; rep from * to last 7 sts, [p1, C2F] twice, p1.
8th row: *[K1, p2] twice, k1, [PB1] 5 times; rep from * to last 7 sts, [k1, p2] twice, k1.
Rep the last 2 rows twice more.
Rep these 12 rows.

Woven Horizontal Herringbone

Multiple of 4

1st row (right side): K3, *yf, sl 2, yb, k2; rep from * to last st, k1.
2nd row: P2, *yb, sl 2, yf, p2; rep from * to last 2 sts, p2.
3rd row: K1, yf, sl 2, yb, *k2, yf, sl 2, yb; rep from * to last st, k1.
4th row: P4, *yb, sl 2, yf, p2; rep from * to end.
Rep the last 4 rows twice more.
13th row: As 3rd row.
14th row: As 2nd row.
15th row: As 1st row.
16th row: As 4th row.
Rep the last 4 rows twice more.
Rep these 24 rows.

Pyramids

Multiple of 15 + 7

1st row (right side): *P1, [KB1] 5 times, p1, k8; rep from * to last 7 sts, p1, [KB1] 5 times, p1.
2nd row: *K1, [PB1] 5 times, k1, p8; rep from * to last 7 sts, k1, [PB1] 5 times, k1.
3rd row: P1, *[KB1] 5 times, p10; rep from * to last 6 sts, [KB1] 5 times, p1.
4th row: K1, *[PB1] 5 times, k10; rep from * to last 6 sts, [PB1] 5 times, k1.
5th row: P2, *[KB1] 3 times, p3, k6, p3; rep from * to last 5 sts, [KB1] 3 times, p2.
6th row: K2, *[PB1] 3 times, k3, p6, k3; rep from * to last 5 sts, [PB1] 3 times, k2.
7th row: P2, *[KB1] 3 times, p12; rep from * to last 5 sts, [KB1] 3 times, p2.
8th row: K2, *[PB1] 3 times, k12; rep from * to last 5 sts, [PB1] 3 times, k2.
9th row: P3, *KB1, p5, k4, p5; rep from * to last 4 sts, KB1, p3.

10th row: K3, *PB1, k5, p4, k5; rep from * to last 4 sts, PB1, k3.
11th row: P3, *KB1, p14; rep from * to last 4 sts, KB1, p3.
12th row: K3, *PB1, k14; rep from * to last 4 sts, PB1, k3.
Rep these 12 rows.

Twisted Knit Tweed

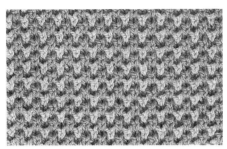

Multiple of 2 + 1

1st and 2nd foundation rows: Using A, knit.
1st row (right side): Using B, k1, *K1B, k1; rep from * to end.
2nd row: Using B, knit.
3rd row: Using A, K1B, *k1, K1B; rep from * to end.
4th row: Using A, knit.
Rep these 4 rows.

Little Birds

Multiple of 14 + 8

1st row (right side): Knit.
2nd row: Purl.
3rd row: K10, *sl 2 purlwise, k12; rep from * to last 12 sts, sl 2 purlwise, k10.
4th row: P10, *sl 2 purlwise, p12; rep from * to last 12 sts, sl 2 purlwise, p10.
5th row: K8, *C3R, C3L, k8; rep from * to end.
6th row: Purl.
Rep 1st and 2nd rows once.
9th row: K3, *sl 2, k12; rep from * to last 5 sts, sl 2, k3.
10th row: P3, *sl 2, p12; rep from * to last 5 sts, sl 2, p3.
11th row: K1, *C3R, C3L, k8; rep from * to last 7 sts, C3R, C3L, k1.
12th row: Purl.
Rep these 12 rows.

Houndstooth Tweed

Multiple of 3
Cast on in A.

1st row (right side): Using A, *k2 sl 1 purlwise; rep from * to end.
2nd row: Using A, knit.
3rd row: Using B, *sl 1 purlwise, k2; rep from * to end.
4th row: Using B, knit.
Rep these 4 rows.

Double Rice Stitch I

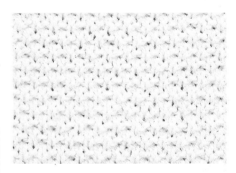

Multiple of 2 + 1

1st row (wrong side): P1, *KB1, p1; rep from * to end.
2nd row: Knit.
3rd row: *KB1, p1; rep from * to last st, KB1.
4th row: Knit.
Rep these 4 rows.

Double Rice Stitch II

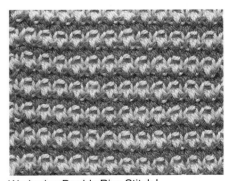

Worked as Double Rice Stitch I.

1st and 2nd rows worked in A, 3rd and 4th rows in B throughout.

Patterns for Texture and Colour

Little Cable Stitch

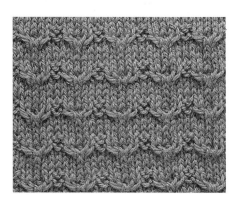

Multiple of 6 + 2
1st row (right side): Knit.
2nd row: Purl.
3rd row: P2, *C2F, C2B, p2; rep from * to end.
4th row: K2, *p4, k2; rep from * to end.
5th row: Knit.
6th row: Purl.
Rep these 6 rows.

Slipped Rib I

Multiple of 4 + 3
1st row (right side): K1, sl 1 purlwise, *k3, sl 1 purlwise; rep from * to last st, k1.
2nd row: P1, sl 1 purlwise, *p3, sl 1 purlwise; rep from * to last st, p1.
3rd row: *K3, sl 1 purlwise; rep from * to last 3 sts, k3.
4th row: *P3, sl 1 purlwise; rep from * to last 3 sts, p3.
Rep these 4 rows.

Slipped Rib II

Worked as Slipped Rib I.
Work 2 rows in A, 2 rows in B and 2 rows in C throughout.

Knotted Rib

Multiple of 5
(Note: stitches should only be counted after the 2nd row.)
1st row (right side): P2, *knit into front and back of next st, p4; rep from * to last 3 sts, knit into front and back of next st, p2.
2nd row: K2, *p2tog, k4; rep from * to last 4 sts, p2tog, k2.
Rep these 2 rows.

Diamond Drops I

Multiple of 4
1st row (right side): Knit.
2nd row: P1, *yrn, p2, pass made st over purl sts, p2; rep from * to last 3 sts, yrn, p2, pass made st over purl sts, p1.
3rd row: Knit.
4th row: P3, *yrn, p2, pass made st over purl sts, p2; rep from * to last st, p1.
Rep these 4 rows.

Diamond Drops II

Worked as Diamond Drops I.
1st and 2nd rows worked in A, 3rd and 4th rows in B throughout.

Smocking Stitch

Multiple of 8 + 2
1st and every alt row (wrong side): K2, *p2, k2; rep from * to end.
2nd row: P2, *k2, p2; rep from * to end.
4th row: P2, *yb, insert right-hand needle from front between 6th and 7th sts on left-hand needle and draw through a loop, slip this loop onto left-hand needle and knit it tog with the first st, k1, p2, k2, p2; rep from * to end.
6th row: As 2nd row.
8th row: P2, k2, p2, *yb, draw loop as before from between 6th and 7th sts and knit it with 1st st, k1, p2, k2, p2; rep from * to last 4 sts, k2, p2.
Rep these 8 rows.

Cable Squares

Multiple of 12 + 2
1st row (right side): [P1, k1] twice, p1, k5, *p1, [k1, p1] 3 times, k5; rep from * to last 4 sts, [p1, k1] twice.
2nd row: [K1, p1] twice, k1, p5, *[k1, p1] 3 times, k1, p5; rep from * to last 4 sts, [p1, k1] twice.
3rd row: P1, [k1, p1] twice, *C4B, [k1, p1] 4 times; rep from * to last 9 sts, C4B, k1, [p1, k1] twice.
4th row: As 2nd row.
Rep the last 4 rows twice more.
13th row: Knit.
14th row: Purl.
15th row: K1, *C4B; rep from * to last st, k1.
16th row: Purl.
Rep these 16 rows.

Woven Stitch I

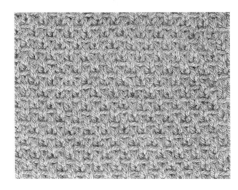

Multiple of 2 + 1
1st row (right side): K1, *yf, sl 1, yb, k1; rep from * to end.
2nd row: Purl.
3rd row: K2, *yf, sl 1, yb, k1; rep from * to last st, k1.
4th row: Purl.
Rep these 4 rows.

Woven Stitch II

Worked as Woven Stitch I.
Work 1st and 2nd rows in A, 3rd and 4th rows in B.

Alternate Bobble Stripe

Multiple of 10 + 5
1st row (right side): P2, k1, *p4, k1; rep from * to last 2 sts, p2.
2nd row: K2, p1, *k4, p1; rep from * to last 2 sts, k2.
3rd row: P2, *MB (Make bobble) as follows: work [k1, p1, k1, p1, k1] into the next st, turn and k5, turn and k5tog (bobble completed), p4, k1, p4; rep from * to last 3 sts, MB, p2.

4th row: As 2nd row.
Rep the last 4 rows 4 times more.
21st row: As 1st row.
22nd row: As 2nd row.
23rd row: P2, *k1, p4, MB, p4; rep from * to last 3 sts, k1, p2.
24th row: As 2nd row.
Rep the last 4 rows 4 times more.
Rep these 40 rows.

Double Woven Stitch I

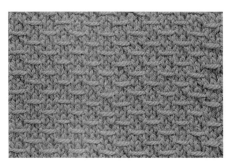

Multiple of 4
1st row (right side): K3, *yf, sl 2, yb, k2; rep from * to last st, k1.
2nd row: Purl.
3rd row: K1, *yf, sl 2, yb, k2; rep from * to last 3 sts, yf, sl 2, yb, k1.
4th row: Purl.
Rep these 4 rows.

Double Woven Stitch II

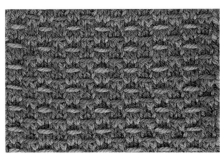

Worked as Double Woven Stitch I.
Work 1st and 2nd rows in A, 3rd and 4th rows in B.

Little Cable Fabric

Multiple of 4 + 1
1st row (right side): K1, *sl 1 purlwise, k3; rep from * to end.
2nd row: *P3, sl 1 purlwise; rep from * to last st, p1.
3rd row: K1, *C3L, k1; rep from * to end.
4th row: Purl.
5th row: K5, *sl 1, k3; rep from * to end.
6th row: *P3, sl 1; rep from * to last 5 sts, p5.
7th row: K3, *C3R, k1; rep from * to last 2 sts, k2.
8th row: Purl.
Rep these 8 rows.

Open Check Stitch

Multiple of 2.
1st row (right side): Purl.
2nd row: Knit.
3rd row: K2, *sl 1, k1; rep from * to end.
4th row: *K1, yf, sl 1, yb; rep from * to last 2 sts, k2.
5th row: K1, *yf, k2tog; rep from * to last st, k1.
6th row: Purl.
Rep these 6 rows.

Horizontal Herringbone

Multiple of 2
1st row (right side): K1, *sl 1, k1, psso but instead of dropping slipped st from left-hand needle, knit into the back of it; rep from * to last st, k1.
2nd row: *P2tog, then purl first st again slipping both sts off needle tog; rep from * to end.
Rep these 2 rows.

Patterns for Texture and Colour

Crosses

Multiple of 12 + 1
1st row (right side): Purl.
2nd row: Knit.
3rd row: P5, *[KB1] 3 times, p9; rep from * to last 8 sts, [KB1] 3 times, p5.
4th row: K5, *p3, k9; rep from * to last 8 sts, p3, k5.
Rep the last 2 rows once more.
7th row: P2, *[KB1] 9 times, p3; rep from * to last 11 sts, [KB1] 9 times, p2.
8th row: K2, *p9, k3; rep from * to last 11 sts, p9, k2.
Rep the last 2 rows once more.
11th row: As 3rd row.
12th row: As 4th row.
Rep the last 2 rows once more.
15th row: Purl.
16th row: Knit.
Rep these 16 rows.

Bordered Diamonds

Multiple of 16 + 2
Note: Slip sts purlwise throughout.
1st row (right side): K6, *p6, k10; rep from * to last 12 sts, p6, k6.
2nd row: P5, sl 1, k6, yf, sl 1, *p8, sl 1, k6, yf, sl 1; rep from * to last 5 sts, p5.
3rd row: K5, *C2L, p4, C2R, k8; rep from * to last 13 sts, C2L, p4, C2R, k5.
4th row: P1, sl 1, p4, sl 1, k4, yf, sl 1, p4, *sl 2, p4, sl 1, k4, yf, sl 1, p4; rep from * to last 2 sts, sl 1, p1.
5th row: K1, *T2F, k3, C2L, p2, C2R, k3, T2B; rep from * to last st, k1.
6th row: P1, k1, yf, sl 1, p4, sl 1, *k2, yf, sl 1, p4, sl 1; rep from * to last 2 sts, k1, p1.
7th row: K1, p1, *T2F, k3, C2L, C2R, k3, T2B, p2; rep from * to last 16 sts, T2F, k3, C2L, C2R, k3, T2B, p1, k1.
8th row: P1, k2, yf, sl 1, *p4, sl 2, p4, sl 1, k4, yf, sl 1; rep from * to last 14 sts, p4, sl 2, p4, sl 1, k2, p1.
9th row: K1, p2, *T2F, k8, T2B, p4; rep

from * to last 15 sts, T2F, k8, T2B, p2, k1.
10th row: P1, k3, yf, sl 1, *p8, sl 1, k6, yf, sl 1; rep from * to last 13 sts, p8, sl 1, k3, p1.
11th row: K1, p3, *k10, p6; rep from * to last 14 sts, k10, p3, k1.
12th row: As 10th row.
13th row: K1, p2, *C2R, k8, C2L, p4; rep from * to last 15 sts, C2R, k8, C2L, p2, k1.
14th row: As 8th row.
15th row: K1, p1, *C2R, k3, T2B, T2F, k3, C2L, p2; rep from * to last 16 sts, C2R, k3, T2B, T2F, k3, C2L, p1, k1.
16th row: As 6th row.
17th row: K1, *C2R, k3, T2B, p2, T2F, k3, C2L; rep from * to last st, k1.
18th row: As 4th row.
19th row: K5, *T2B, p4, T2F, k8; rep from * to last 13 sts, T2B, p4, T2F, k5.
20th row: As 2nd row.
Rep these 20 rows.

Herringbone

Multiple of 7 + 1
Special Abbreviation
K1B Back = From the top, insert point of right-hand needle into back of st below next st on left-hand needle and knit it.
1st row (wrong side): Purl.
2nd row: *K2tog, k2, K1B Back then knit st above, k2; rep from * to last st, k1.
3rd row: Purl.
4th row: K3, K1B Back then knit st above, k2, k2tog, *k2, K1B Back then knit st above, k2, k2tog; rep from * to end.
Rep these 4 rows.

Twisted Check

Multiple of 4 + 2
1st row (right side): Knit all sts through back loops.
2nd row: Purl.

3rd row: [KB1] twice, *p2, [KB1] twice; rep from * to end.
4th row: P2, *k2, p2; rep from * to end.
Rep 1st and 2nd rows once more.
7th row: P2, *[KB1] twice, p2; rep from * to end.
8th row: K2, *p2, k2; rep from * to end.
Rep these 8 rows.

Bobbles

Bobbles may be used to decorate any plain fabric or simple stitch pattern in any arrangement. The example shown is worked over a multiple of 10 + 5 on a background of stocking stitch.
Commence Pattern:
Work 4 rows in st st, starting knit.
5th row: K7, *MB, k9; rep from * to last 8 sts, MB, k7.
Work 5 rows in st st.
11th row: K2, *MB, k9; rep from * to last 3 sts, MB, k2.
Purl 1 row.
Rep these 12 rows.

Bud Stitch

Multiple of 6 + 5
Note: Stitches should only be counted after the 6th or 12th rows.
1st row (right side): P5, *k1, yfrn, p5; rep from * to end.
2nd row: K5, *p2, k5; rep from * to end.
3rd row: P5, *k2, p5; rep from * to end.
Rep the last 2 rows once more.
6th row: K5, *p2tog, k5; rep from * to end.
7th row: P2, *k1, yfrn, p5; rep from * to last 3 sts, k1, yfrn, p2.
8th row: K2, *p2, k5; rep from * to last 4 sts, p2, k2.
9th row: P2, *k2, p5; rep from * to last 4

sts, k2, p2.
Rep the last 2 rows once more.

12th row: K2, *p2tog, k5; rep from * to last 4 sts, p2tog, k2.
Rep these 12 rows.

Mock Cable on Moss Stitch

Multiple of 9+5

1st row (right side): [K1, p1] twice, k1, *KB1, p2, KB1, [k1, p1] twice, k1; rep from * to end.
2nd row: *[K1, p1] 3 times, k2, p1; rep from * to last 5 sts, [k1, p1] twice, k1.
Rep these 2 rows once more.
5th row: [K1, p1] twice, k1, *yf, k1, p2, k1, lift yf over last 4 sts and off needle, [k1, p1] twice, k1; rep from * to end.
6th row: As 2nd row.
Rep these 6 rows.

Diagonal Bobble Stitch

Multiple of 6

1st row (right side): *K2, Make Bobble (MB) as follows: [knit into front and back] 3 times into next st, take 1st, 2nd, 3rd, 4th and 5th sts over 6th made st, (bobble completed), p3; rep from * to end.
2nd row: *K3, p3; rep from * to end.
3rd row: P1, *k2, MB, p3; rep from * to last 5 sts, k2, MB, p2.
4th row: K2, *p3, k3; rep from * to last 4 sts, p3, k1.
5th row: P2, *k2, MB, p3; rep from * to last 4 sts, k2, MB, p1.
6th row: K1, *p3, k3; rep from * to last 5 sts, p3, k2.
7th row: *P3, k2, MB; rep from * to end.
8th row: *P3, k3; rep from * to end.
9th row: *MB, p3, k2; rep from * to end.
10th row: P2, *k3, p3; rep from * to last 4 sts, k3, p1.

11th row: K1, *MB, p3, k2; rep from * to last 5 sts, MB, p3, k1.
12th row: P1, *k3, p3; rep from * to last 5 sts, k3, p2.
Rep these 12 rows.

Spaced Knots

Multiple of 6+5
Note: Stitches should not be counted after the 5th or 11th rows.
Commence Pattern:
Work 4 rows in st st, starting knit.
5th row: K5, *[k1, p1] twice into next st, k5; rep from * to end.
6th row: P5, *sl 3, k1, pass 3 sl sts separately over last st (knot completed), p5; rep from * to end.
Work 4 rows in st st.
11th row: K2, *[k1, p1] twice into next st, k5; rep from * to last 3 sts, [k1, p1] twice into next st, k2.
12th row: P2, *sl 3, k1, pass sl sts over as before, p5; rep from * to last 6 sts, sl 3, k1, pass sl sts over as before, p2.
Rep these 12 rows.

Bells and Bell Ropes

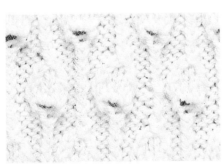

Multiple of 8+7
Note: Stitches should only be counted after the 1st, 7th, 8th, 9th, 15th and 16th rows.
1st row (right side): P3, *KB1, p3; rep from * to end.
2nd row: K3, PB1, k3, *[k1, p1, k1, p1, k1] into next st, k3, PB1, k3; rep from * to end.
3rd row: P3, KB1, p3, *k5, p3, KB1, p3; rep from * to end.
4th row: K3, PB1, k3, *p5, k3, PB1, k3; rep from * to end.
5th row: P3, KB1, p3, *sl 1, k1, psso, k1, k2tog, p3, KB1, p3; rep from * to end.
6th row: K3, PB1, k3, *p3, k3, PB1, k3; rep from * to end.
7th row: P3, KB1, p3, *sl 1, k2tog, psso, p3, KB1, p3; rep from * to end.

8th row: K3, *PB1, k3; rep from * to end.
9th row: As 1st row.
10th row: K3, [k1, p1, k1, p1, k1] into next st, k3, *PB1, k3, [k1, p1, k1, p1, k1] into next st, k3; rep from * to end.
11th row: P3, k5, p3, *KB1, p3, k5, p3; rep from * to end.
12th row: K3, p5, k3, *PB1, k3, p5, k3; rep from * to end.
13th row: P3, sl 1, k1, psso, k1, k2tog, p3, *KB1, p3, sl 1, k1, psso, k1, k2tog, p3; rep from * to end.
14th row: K3, p3, k3, *PB1, k3, p3, k3; rep from * to end.
15th row: P3, sl 1, k2tog, psso, p3, *KB1, p3, sl 1, k2tog, psso, p3; rep from * to end.
16th row: As 8th row.
Rep these 16 rows.

Half Brioche Stitch (Purl Version)

Multiple of 2+1
1st row (wrong side): Purl.
2nd row: K1, *K1B, k1; rep from * to end.
3rd row: Purl.
4th row: K1B, *k1, K1B; rep from * to end.
Rep these 4 rows.

Garter Stitch Twisted Rib

Multiple of 4
1st row (right side): K1, *C2B, k2; rep from * to last 3 sts, C2B, k1.
2nd row: K1, *yf, C2P, yb, k2; rep from * to last 3 sts, yf, C2P, yb, k1.
Rep these 2 rows.

Patterns for Texture and Colour

Rose Stitch

Multiple of 2 + 1

1st row (wrong side): K2, *p1, k1; rep from * to last st, k1.
2nd row: K1, *K1B, k1; rep from * to end.
3rd row: K1, *p1, k1; rep from *to end.
4th row: K2, *K1B, k1; rep from * to last st, k1.
Rep these 4 rows.

Twisted Stocking Stitch

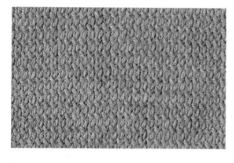

Any number of stitches
1st row (right side): Knit into the back of every st.
2nd row: Purl.
Rep these 2 rows.

Houndstooth Pattern

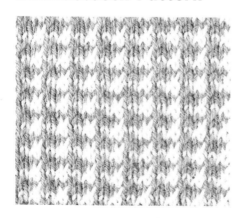

Multiple of 3
Cast on in A.

1st row (right side): Using A, k1, *sl 1 purlwise, k2; rep from * to last 2 sts, sl 1 purlwise, k1.
2nd row: Using A, purl.
3rd row: Using B, *sl 1 purlwise, k2; rep from * to end.
4th row: Using B, purl.
Rep these 4 rows.

Eyelet Knot Stitch

Multiple of 2
Note: Stitches should not be counted after the 1st row.
1st row (right side): K1, *k2tog; rep from * to last st, k1.
2nd row: K2, *M1, k1; rep from * to end.
3rd row: Knit.
4th row: Purl.
Rep these 4 rows.

Whelk Pattern

Multiple of 4 + 3
1st row (right side): K3, *sl 1 purlwise, k3; rep from * to end.
2nd row: K3, *yf, sl 1 purlwise, yb, k3; rep from * to end.
3rd row: K1, *sl 1 purlwise, k3; rep from * to last 2 sts, sl 1 purlwise, k1.
4th row: P1, sl 1 purlwise, *p3, sl 1 purlwise; rep from * to last st, p1.
Rep these 4 rows.

Knotted Cords

Multiple of 6 + 5
Knotted cords can be used singly in Aran patterns. (**Note**: stitches should not be counted after the 3rd row.)
1st row (right side): P5, *k1, p5; rep from * to end.
2nd row: K5, *p1, k5; rep from * to end.
3rd row: P5, *knit into front, back and front of next st, p5; rep from * to end.
4th row: K5, *p3tog, k5; rep from * to end.
Rep these 4 rows.

Little Leaves

Multiple of 6 + 5
Note: Stitches should not be counted after the 3rd – 12th or 19th – 28th rows inclusive.
1st row (right side): P5, *k1, p5; rep from * to end.
2nd row: K5, *p1, k5; rep from * to end.
3rd row: P5, *M1, k1, M1, p5; rep from * to end.
4th row: K5, *p3, k5; rep from * to end.
5th row: P5, *k1, [yf, k1] twice, p5; rep from * to end.
6th row: K5, *p5, k5; rep from * to end.
7th row: P5, *k2, yf, k1, yf, k2, p5; rep from * to end.
8th row: K5, *p7, k5; rep from * to end.
9th row: P5, *k2, sl 2 tog knitwise, k1, p2sso, k2, p5; rep from * to end.
10th row: As 6th row.
11th row: P5, *k1, sl 2tog knitwise, k1, p2sso, k1, p5; rep from * to end.
12th row: As 4th row.

13th row: P5, *yb, sl 2tog knitwise, k1, p2sso, p5; rep from * to end.
14th row: As 2nd row.
15th row: Purl.
16th row: Knit.
17th row: P2, *k1, p5; rep from * to last 3 sts, k1, p2.
18th row: K2, *p1, k5; rep from * to last 3 sts, p1, k2.
19th row: P2, *M1, k1, M1, p5; rep from * to last 3 sts, M1, k1, M1, p2.
20th row: K2, *p3, k5; rep from * to last 5 sts, p3, k2.
21st row: P2, *k1, [yf, k1] twice, p5; rep from * to last 5 sts, k1, [yf, k1] twice, p2.
22nd row: K2, *p5, k5; rep from * to last 7 sts, p5, k2.
23rd row: P2, *k2, yf, k1, yf, k2, p5; rep from * to last 7 sts, k2, yf, k1, yf, k2, p2.
24th row: K2, *p7, k5; rep from * to last 9 sts, p7, k2.
25th row: P2, *k2, sl 2tog knitwise, k1, p2sso, k2, p5; rep from * to last 9 sts, k2, sl 2tog knitwise, k1, p2sso, k2, p2.
26th row: As 22nd row.
27th row: P2, *k1, sl 2tog knitwise, k1, p2sso, k1, p5; rep from * to last 7 sts, k1, sl 2tog knitwise, k1, p2sso, k1, p2.
28th row: As 20th row.
29th row: P2, *yb, sl 2tog knitwise, k1, p2sso, p5; rep from * to last 5 sts, yb, sl 2tog knitwise, k1, p2sso, p2.
30th row: As 18th row.
31st row: Purl.
32nd row: Knit.
Rep these 32 rows.

Chain Stitch

Multiple of of 5 + 4
Cast on in A.
Foundation row (right side): Using B, k1, *yfrn, yrn (2 loops made), sl 2 purlwise, yb, k3; rep from * to last 3 sts, yfrn, yrn, sl 2 purlwise, yb, k1.

1st row: Using B, p1, *yb, [take yarn over top of needle and round to back (called yonb) twice, (2 loops made), sl 2 purlwise, yf, drop the 2 loops made in previous row, p3; rep from * to last 5 sts (including 2 loops made in previous row), yb, [yonb] twice, sl 2, yf, drop 2 loops made in previous row, p1.
2nd row: Using A, k3, drop the 2 loops made in previous row, *k5, drop the 2 loops made in previous row; rep from * to last st, k1.
3rd row: Using A, purl.
4th row: Using A, knit.
5th row: Using A, purl.
6th row: Using B, k1, *yfrn, yrn, place right-hand needle below the 2 B loops at front of work and pick them up, sl next 2 A sts purlwise, lift B loops over the 2 slipped sts and off the needle, yb, k3; rep from * to last 3 sts, yfrn, yrn, pick up the 2 B loops as before, sl next 2 A sts purlwise, lift B loops over the 2 slipped sts and off the needle, yb, k1.
Rep these 6 rows.
For single colour version omit colour changes.

Texture Tweed

Multiple of 4 + 3
1st row: Using A, k1, *sl 1, k3; rep from * to last 2 sts, sl 1, k1.
2nd row: Using A, k1, *yf, sl 1, yb, k3; rep from * to last 2 sts, yf, sl 1, yb, k1.
3rd row: Using B, k3, *sl 1, k3; rep from * to end.
4th row: Using B, k3, *yf, sl 1, yb, k3; rep from * to end.
5th row: As 1st row *but* using C instead of A.
6th row: As 2nd row *but* using C instead of A.
7th row: As 3rd row *but* using A instead of B.
8th row: As 4th row *but* using A instead of B.
9th row: As 1st row *but* using B instead of A.
10th row: As 2nd row *but* using B instead of A.
11th row: As 3rd row *but* using C instead of B.
12th row: As 4th row *but* using C instead of B.
Rep these 12 rows.

Rosehip Stitch

Multiple of 4 + 3
1st row (right side): K3, *sl 1 purlwise, k3; rep from * to end.
2nd row: K3, *yf, sl 1 purlwise, yb, k3; rep from * to end.
3rd row: K1, *sl 1 purlwise, k3; rep from * to last 2 sts, sl 1 purlwise, k1.
4th row: K1, *yf, sl 1 purlwise, yb, k3; rep from * to last 2 sts, yf, sl 1 purlwise, yb, k1.
Rep these 4 rows.

Brick Rib

Multiple of 3 + 1
1st row (right side): *P2, KB1; rep from * to last st, p1.
2nd row: K1, *PB1, k2; rep from * to end.
Rep the last 2 rows once more.
5th row: P1, *[KB1] twice, p1; rep from * to end.
6th row: K1, *[PB1] twice, k1; rep from * to end.
Rep the last 2 rows once more.
9th row: P1, *KB1, p2; rep from * to end.
10th row: *K2, PB1; rep from * to last st, k1.
Rep the last 2 rows once more.
Rep these 12 rows.

Patterns for Texture and Colour

Garter Slip Stitch

Multiple of 2 + 1

Cast on in M.

1st row (right side): Using Main colour, knit.

2nd row: As 1st row.

3rd row: Using Contrast, k1, * sl 1 purlwise, k1; rep from * to end.

4th row: Using Contrast, knit.

Rep these 4 rows.

For single colour version omit colour changes.

Little Sheaf Stitch

Multiple of 2 + 1

Cast on in M.

1st row (right side): Using M, knit.

2nd row: Using M, purl.

3rd row: P1M, yb, *k1A, using M yf, p1, yb; rep from * to end.

4th row: P1M, *using A yb, k1, yf, p1M; rep from * to end.

5th row: Using M only p1, *k1, p1; rep from * to end.

Using M work 3 rows in st st, starting purl.

9th row: Using B k1, *using M yf, p1, yb, using B k1; rep from * to end.

10th row: Using B k1, yf, *p1M, using B yb, k1, yf; rep from * to end.

11th row: Using M only k1, *p1, k1; rep from * to end.

12th row: Using M, purl.

Rep these 12 rows.

Ribbon Stitch

Multiple of 4 + 3

1st row (right side): Using A, knit.

2nd row: Using A, purl.

3rd row: Using B, k1, *sl 1, k3; rep from * to last 2 sts, sl 1, k1.

4th row: Using B, p1, *sl 1, p3; rep from * to last 2 sts, sl 1, p1.

5th row: As 1st row.

6th row: As 2nd row.

7th row: Using C, k3, *sl 1, k3; rep from * to end.

8th row: Using C, p3, *sl 1, p3; rep from * to end.

Rep the last 2 rows once more.

Rep the first 6 rows once.

17th row: As 7th row *but* using D instead of C.

18th row: As 8th row *but* using D instead of C.

Rep the last 2 rows once more.

Rep these 20 rows.

Diamond Slip Stitch

Multiple of of 10 + 3

Note: Slipped sts should be slipped purlwise throughout. Cast on in A.

Foundation row: Using A, knit.

1st row (right side): Using B, k1, *sl 1, k9; rep from * to last 2 sts, sl 1, k1.

2nd row: Using B, k1, *yf, sl 1, yb, k9; rep from * to last 2 sts, yf, sl 1, yb, k1.

3rd row: Using A, k3, *[sl 1, k1] 3 times, sl 1, k3; rep from * to end.

4th row: Using A, p3, *[sl 1, yb, k1, yf] 3 times, sl 1, p3; rep from * to end.

5th row: Using B, k2, *sl 1, k7, sl 1, k1; rep from * to last st, k1.

6th row: Using B, k2, *yf, sl 1, yb, k7, yf, sl 1, yb, k1; rep from * to last st, k1.

7th row: Using A, *k4, [sl 1, k1] 3 times; rep from * to last 3 sts, k3.

8th row: Using A, p4, [sl 1, yb, k1, yf] twice, sl 1, *p5, [sl 1, yb, k1, yf] twice, sl 1; rep from * to last 4 sts, p4.

9th row: Using B, [k1, sl 1] twice, *k5, [sl 1, k1] twice, sl 1; rep from * to last 9 sts, k5, [sl 1, k1] twice.

10th row: Using B, [k1, yf, sl 1, yb] twice, *k5, [yf, sl 1, yb, k1] twice, yf, sl 1, yb; rep from * to last 9 sts, k5, [yf, sl 1, yb, k1] twice.

11th row: Using A, k5, sl 1, k1, sl 1, *k7, sl 1, k1, sl 1; rep from * to last 5 sts, k5.

12th row: Using A, p5, sl 1, yb, k1, yf, sl 1, *p7, sl 1, yb, k1, yf, sl 1; rep from * to last 5 sts, p5.

13th row: Using B, k2, sl 1, k1, sl 1, k3, *[sl 1, k1] 3 times, sl 1, k3; rep from * to last 5 sts, sl 1, k1, sl 1, k2.

14th row: Using B, k2, yf, sl 1, yb, k1, yf, sl 1, yb, k3, *[yf, sl 1, yb, k1] 3 times, yf, sl 1, yb, k3; rep from * to last 5 sts, yf, sl 1, yb, k1, yf, sl 1, yb, k2.

15th row: Using A, k6, *sl 1, k9; rep from * to last 7 sts, sl 1, k6.

16th row: Using A, p6, *sl 1, p9; rep from * to last 7 sts, sl 1, p6.

17th and 18th rows: As 9th and 10th rows.

19th and 20th rows: As 11th and 12th rows.

21st and 22nd rows: As 5th and 6th rows.

23rd and 24th rows: As 7th and 8th rows.

Rep these 24 rows.

Eyelets

Multiple of 3 + 2
Work 2 rows in st st, starting knit.
3rd row (right side): K2, *yf, k2tog, k1;
rep from * to end.
4th row: Purl.
Rep these 4 rows.

Braided Openwork

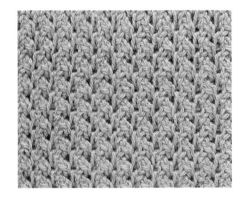

Multiple of 2
1st row (wrong side): Purl.
2nd row (right side): K1, *sl 1, k1, psso,
M1; rep from * to last st, k1.
3rd row: Purl.
4th row: K1, *M1, k2tog; rep from * to
last st, k1.
Rep these 4 rows.

Butterfly Lace

Multiple of 8 + 7
1st row (right side): K1, *k2tog, yf, k1,
yf, sl 1, k1, psso, k3; rep from * to last 6

sts, k2tog, yf, k1, yf, sl 1, k1, psso, k1.
2nd row: P3, *sl 1 purlwise, p7; rep from
* to last 4 sts, sl 1 purlwise, p3.
Rep the last 2 rows once more.
5th row: K5, *k2tog, yf, k1, yf, sl 1, k1,
psso, k3; rep from * to last 2 sts, k2.
6th row: P7, *sl 1 purlwise, p7; rep from
* to end.
Rep the last 2 rows once more.
Rep these 8 rows.

Knotted Openwork

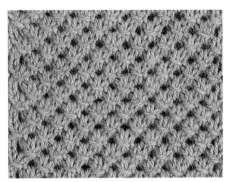

Multiple of 3
1st row (wrong side): Purl.
2nd row: K2, *yf, k3, with left-hand
needle lift first of the 3 sts just knitted
over the last 2; rep from * to last st, k1.
3rd row: Purl.
4th row: K1, *k3, with left-hand needle
lift first of the 3 sts just knitted over the
last 2, yf; rep from * to last 2 sts, k2.
Rep these 4 rows.

Eyelet Panes

Multiple of 6 + 3
Note: Stitches should *not* be counted
after the 3rd, 4th, 9th or 10th rows of this
pattern.
1st row (right side): K2, *yf, sl 1, k1,
psso, k1, k2tog, yf, k1; rep from * to last
st, k1.
2nd and every alt row: Purl.
3rd row: K3, *yf, k3; rep from * to end.
5th row: K1, k2tog, *yf, sl 1, k1, psso,
k1, k2tog, yf, sl 1, k1, psso, psso; rep from *
to last 8 sts, yf, sl 1, k1, psso, k1, k2tog,
yf, sl 1, k1, psso, k1.
7th row: K2, *k2tog, yf, k1, yf, sl 1, k1,
psso, k1; rep from * to last st, k1.
9th row: As 3rd row.

11th row: K2, *k2tog, yf, sl 1, k2tog,
psso, yf, sl 1, k1, psso, k1; rep from * to
last st, k1.
12th row: Purl.
Rep these 12 rows.

Tunnel Lace

Multiple of 3 + 2
Note: Stitches should only be counted
after the 4th row of this pattern.
1st row (right side): P2, *yon, k1, yfrn,
p2; rep from * to end.
2nd row: K2, *p3, k2; rep from * to end.
3rd row: P2, *k3, p2; rep from * to end.
4th row: K2, *p3tog, k2; rep from * to
end.
Rep these 4 rows.

Diamond Lace

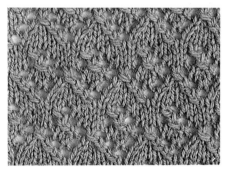

Multiple of 6 + 3
1st row (right side): *K4, yf, sl 1, k1,
psso; rep from * to last 3 sts, k3.
2nd and every alt row: Purl.
3rd row: K2, *k2tog, yf, k1, yf, sl 1, k1,
psso, k1; rep from * to last st, k1.
5th row: K1, k2tog, yf, *k3, yf, sl 1,
k2tog, psso, yf; rep from * to last 6 sts,
k3, yf, sl 1, k1, psso, k1.
7th row: K3, *yf, sl 1, k2tog, psso, yf, k3;
rep from * to end.
9th row: As 1st row.
11th row: K1, *yf, sl 1, k1, psso, k4; rep
from * to last 2 sts, yf, sl 1, k1, psso.
13th row: K2, *yf, sl 1, k1, psso, k1,
k2tog, yf, k1; rep from * to last st, k1.
15th row: As 7th row.
17th row: As 5th row.
19th row: As 11th row.
20th row: Purl.
Rep these 20 rows.

All-over Lace Patterns

Falling Leaves

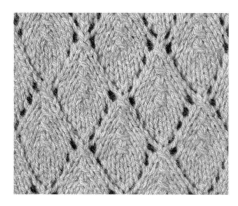

Multiple of 10 + 3

1st row (right side): K1, k2tog, k3, *yf, k1, yf, k3, sl 1, k2tog, psso, k3; rep from * to last 7 sts, yf, k1, yf, k3, sl 1, k1, psso, k1.

2nd and every alt row: Purl.

3rd row: K1, k2tog, k2, *yf, k3, yf, k2, sl 1, k2tog, psso, k2; rep from * to last 8 sts, yf, k3, yf, k2, sl 1, k1, psso, k1.

5th row: K1, k2tog, k1, *yf, k5, yf, k1, sl 1, k2tog, psso, k1; rep from * to last 9 sts, yf, k5, yf, k1, sl 1, k1, psso, k1.

7th row: K1, k2tog, yf, k7, *yf, sl 1, k2tog, psso, yf, k7; rep from * to last 3 sts, yf, sl 1, k1, psso, k1.

9th row: K2, yf, k3, *sl 1, k2tog, psso, k3, yf, k1, yf, k3; rep from * to last 8 sts, sl 1, k2tog, psso, k3, yf, k2.

11th row: K3, yf, k2, *sl 1, k2tog, psso, k2, yf, k3, yf, k2; rep from * to last 8 sts, sl 1, k2tog, psso, k2, yf, k3.

13th row: K4, yf, k1, *sl 1, k2tog, psso, k1, yf, k5, yf, k1; rep from * to last 8 sts, sl 1, k2tog, psso, k1, yf, k4.

15th row: K5, *yf, sl 1, k2tog, psso, yf, k7; rep from * to last 8 sts, yf, sl 1, k2tog, psso, yf, k5.

16th row: Purl.

Rep these 16 rows.

Herringbone Lace Rib

Multiple of 7 + 1

1st row (right side): K1, *p1, k1, yfrn, p2tog, k1, p1, k1; rep from * to end.

2nd row: P1, *k2, yfrn, p2tog, k2, p1; rep from * to end.

Rep these 2 rows.

Garter Stitch Lacy Diamonds

Multiple of 10 + 1

1st and every alt row (right side): Knit.

2nd row: K3, *k2tog, yf, k1, yf, k2tog, k5; rep from * to last 8 sts, k2tog, yf, k1, yf, k2tog, k3.

4th row: K2, *k2tog, yf, k3, yf, k2tog, k3; rep from * to last 9 sts, k2tog, yf, k3, yf, k2tog, k2.

6th row: K1, *k2tog, yf, k5, yf, k2tog, k1; rep from * to end.

8th row: K1, *yf, k2tog, k5, k2tog, yf, k1; rep from * to end.

10th row: K2, *yf, k2tog, k3, k2tog, yf, k3; rep from * to last 9 sts, yf, k2tog, k3, k2tog, yf, k2.

12th row: K3, *yf, k2tog, k1, k2tog, yf, k5; rep from * to last 8 sts, yf, k2tog, k1, k2tog, yf, k3.

Rep these 12 rows.

Diamond Lace

Multiple of 8 + 7

1st row (right side): Knit.

2nd row: and every alt row: Purl.

3rd row: K3, *yf, sl 1, k1, psso, k6; rep from * to last 4 sts, yf, sl 1, k1, psso, k2.

5th row: K2, *yf, sl 1, k2tog, psso, yf, k5; rep from * to last 5 sts, yf, sl 1, k2tog, psso, yf, k2.

7th row: As 3rd row.

9th row: Knit.

11th row: K7, *yf, sl 1, k1, psso, k6; rep from * to end.

13th row: K6, *yf, sl 1, k2tog, psso, yf, k5; rep from * to last st, k1.

15th row: As 11th row.

16th row: Purl.

Rep these 16 rows.

Open Diamonds with Bobbles

Multiple of 10 + 1

1st row (right side): P1, *yon, sl 1, k1, psso, p5, k2tog, yfrn, p1; rep from * to end.

2nd row: K2, *p1, k5, p1, k3; rep from * to last 9 sts, p1, k5, p1, k2.

3rd row: P2, *yon, sl 1, k1, psso, p3, k2tog, yfrn, p3; rep from * to last 9 sts, yon, sl 1, k1, psso, p3, k2tog, yfrn, p2.

4th row: K3, *p1, k3, p1, k5; rep from * to last 8 sts, p1, k3, p1, k3.

5th row: P3, *yon, sl 1, k1, psso, p1, k2tog, yfrn, p5; rep from * to last 8 sts, yon, sl 1, k1, psso, p1, k2tog, yfrn, p3.

6th row: K4, *p1, k1, p1, k7; rep from * to last 7 sts, p1, k1, p1, k4.

7th row: P4, *yon, sl 1, k2tog, psso, yfrn, p3, make bobble (MB) as follows: [k1, p1, k1, p1, k1] into next st, turn and k5, turn and p5, turn and sl 1, k1, psso, k1, k2tog, turn and p3tog, (bobble completed), p3; rep from * to last 7 sts, yon, sl 1, k2tog, psso, yfrn, p4.

8th row: K4, *p3, k3, PB1, k3; rep from * to last 7 sts, p3, k4.

9th row: P3, *k2tog, yfrn, p1, yon, sl 1, k1, psso, p5; rep from * to last 8 sts, k2tog, yfrn, p1, yon, sl 1, k1, psso, p3.

10th row: K3, *p1, k3, p1, k5; rep from * to last 8 sts, p1, k3, p1, k3.

11th row: P2, *k2tog, yfrn, p3, yon, sl 1, k1, psso, p3; rep from * to last 9 sts, k2tog, yfrn, p3, yon, sl 1, k1, psso, p2.

12th row: K2, *p1, k5, p1, k3; rep from * to last 9 sts, p1, k5, p1, k2.

13th row: P1, *k2tog, yfrn, p5, yon, sl 1, k1, psso, p1; rep from * to end.

14th row: K1, *p1, k7, p1, k1; rep from * to end.

15th row: K2tog, *yfrn, p3, MB, p3, yon, sl 1, k2tog, psso; rep from * to last 9 sts, yfrn, p3, MB, p3, yon, sl 1, k1, psso.

16th row: P2, *k3, PB1, k3, p3; rep from * to last 9 sts, k3, PB1, k3, p2.

Rep these 16 rows.

Fishtail Lace

Multiple of 8 + 1
1st row (right side): K1, *yf, k2, sl 1, k2tog, psso, k2, yf, k1; rep from * to end.
2nd row: Purl.
3rd row: K2, *yf, k1, sl 1, k2tog, psso, k1, yf, k3; rep from * to last 7 sts, yf, k1, sl 1, k2tog, psso, k1, yf, k2.
4th row: Purl.
5th row: K3, *yf, sl 1, k2tog, psso, yf, k5; rep from * to last 6 sts, yf, sl 1, k2tog, psso, yf, k3.
6th row: Purl.
Rep these 6 rows.

Ridged Lace Pattern

Multiple of 2 + 1
Purl 3 rows.
4th row (right side): K1, *yf, sl 1, k1, psso; rep from * to end.
Purl 3 rows.
8th row: K1, *yf, k2tog; rep from * to end.
Rep these 8 rows.

Feather Lace

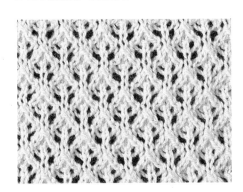

Multiple of 6 + 1
1st row (right side): K1, *yf, k2tog tbl, k1, k2tog, yf, k1; rep from *. to end.
2nd and every alt row: Purl.
3rd row: K1, *yf, k1, sl 1, k2tog, psso, k1, yf, k1; rep from * to end.
5th row: K1, *k2tog, yf, k1, yf, k2tog tbl, k1; rep from * to end.
7th row: K2tog, *[k1, yf] twice, k1, sl 1, k2tog, psso; rep from * to last 5 sts, [k1, yf] twice, k1, k2tog tbl.
8th row: Purl.
Rep these 8 rows.

Trellis Lace

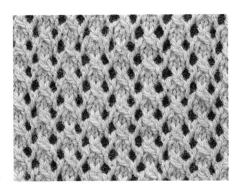

Multiple of 6 + 5
1st row (right side): K4, *yf, sl 1, k2tog, psso, yf, k3; rep from * to last st, k1.
2nd row: Purl.
3rd row: K1, *yf, sl 1, k2tog, psso, yf, k3; rep from * to last 4 sts, yf, sl 1, k2tog, psso, yf, k1.
4th row: Purl.
Rep these 4 rows.

Diamond and Eyelet Pattern

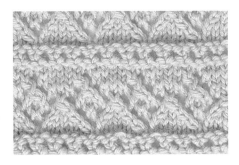

Multiple of 6 + 3
1st row (wrong side): Knit.
2nd row: P1, *yrn, p2tog; rep from * to end.
3rd and 4th rows: Knit.
5th row and every wrong side row to 15th row: Purl.
6th row: *K4, yf, sl 1, k1, psso; rep from * to last 3 sts, k3.
8th row: K2, *k2tog, yf, k1, yf, sl 1, k1, psso, k1; rep from * to last st, k1.
10th row: K1, k2tog, yf, *k3, yf, sl 1, k2tog, psso, yf; rep from * to last 6 sts, k3, yf, sl 1, k1, psso, k1.

12th row: K3, *yf, sl 1, k2tog, psso, yf, k3; rep from * to end.
14th row: As 6th row.
16th row: Knit.
Rep these 16 rows.

Lattice Lace

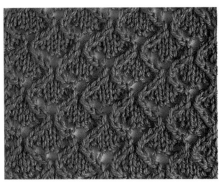

Multiple of 7 + 2
1st row (right side): K3, *k2tog, yf, k5; rep from * to last 6 sts, k2tog, yf, k4.
2nd row: P2, *p2tog tbl, yrn, p1, yrn, p2tog, p2; rep from * to end.
3rd row: K1, *k2tog, yf, k3, yf, sl 1, k1, psso; rep from * to last st, k1.
4th row: Purl.
5th row: K1, *yf, sl 1, k1, psso, k5; rep from * to last st, k1.
6th row: *P1, yrn, p2tog, p2, p2tog tbl, yrn; rep from * to last 2 sts, p2.
7th row: *K3, yf, sl 1, k1, psso, k2tog, yf; rep from * to last 2 sts, k2.
8th row: Purl.
Rep these 8 rows.

Lacy Checks

Multiple of 6 + 5
1st row (right side): K1, *yf, sl 1, k2tog, psso, yf, k3; rep from * to last 4 sts, yf, sl 1, k2tog, psso, yf, k1.
2nd and every alt row: Purl.
3rd row: As 1st row.
5th row: Knit.
7th row: K4, *yf, sl 1, k2tog, psso, yf, k3; rep from * to last st, k1.
9th row: As 7th row.
11th row: Knit.
12th row: Purl.
Rep these 12 rows.

All-over Lace Patterns

Ridged Lace

Multiple of 2

1st row (right side): K1, *yf, k2tog tbl; rep from * to last st, k1.

2nd row: P1, *yrn, p2tog; rep from * to last st, p1.

Rep these 2 rows.

Double Lace Rib

Multiple of.6 + 2

1st row (right side): K2, *p1, yon, k2tog tb1,p1, k2; rep from * to end.

2nd row: P2, *k1, p2; rep from * to end.

3rd row: K2, *p1, k2tog, yfrn, p1, k2; rep from * to end.

4th row: As 2nd row.

Rep these 4 rows.

Trellis Pattern

Multiple of 4 + 2

1st row (right side): K1, yf, *sl 1, k1, psso, k2tog, [yfon] twice (2 sts made); rep from * to last 5 sts, sl 1, k1, psso, k2tog, yf, k1.

2nd row: K2, p2, *k into front of first loop

---

of double yfon, then k into back of 2nd loop, p2; rep from * to last 2 sts, k2.

3rd row: K1, p1, *C2B, p2; rep from * to last 4 sts, C2B, p1, k1.

4th row: K2, *p2, k2; rep from * to end.

5th row: K1, k2tog, *[yfon] twice, sl 1, k1, psso, k2tog; rep from * to last 3 sts, [yfon] twice, sl 1, k1, psso, k1.

6th row: K1, p1, k into front of first loop of double yfon, then k into back of 2nd loop, *p2, work into double yfon as before; rep from * to last 2 sts, p1, k1.

7th row: K2, *p2, C2B; rep from * to last 4 sts, p2, k2.

8th row: K1, p1, k2, *p2, k2; rep from * to last 2 sts, p1, k1.

Rep these 8 rows.

Chequerboard Lace

Multiple of 12 + 8

1st row (right side): K7, *[yf, k2tog] 3 times, k6; rep from * to last st, k1.

2nd and every alt row: Purl.

3rd row: K7, *[k2tog, yf] 3 times, k6; rep from * to last st, k1.

5th row: As 1st row.

7th row: As 3rd row.

9th row: K1, *[yf, k2tog] 3 times, k6; rep from * to last 7 sts, [yf, k2tog] 3 times, k1.

11th row: K1, *[k2tog, yf] 3 times, k6; rep from * to last 7 sts, [k2tog, yf] 3 times, k1.

13th row: As 9th row.

15th row: As 11th row.

16th row: Purl.

Rep these 16 rows.

Fancy Openwork

Multiple of 4

Note: Stitches should only be counted after the 2nd and 4th rows.

1st row (right side): K2, *yf, k4; rep from * to last 2 sts, yf, k2.

2nd row: P2tog, *(k1, p1) into the yf of previous row, [p2tog] twice; rep from * to last 3 sts, (k1, p1) into the yf, p2tog.

3rd row: K4, *yf, k4; rep from * to end.

4th row: P2, p2tog, *(k1, p1) into the yf of previous row, [p2tog] twice; rep from * to last 5 sts, (k1, p1) into the yf, p2tog, p2.

Rep these 4 rows.

Bell Lace

Multiple of 8 + 3

1st row (right side): K1, p1, k1, *p1, yon, sl 1, k2tog, psso, yfrn, [p1, k1] twice; rep from * to end.

2nd row: P1, k1, p1, *k1, p3, [k1, p1] twice; rep from * to end.

Rep last 2 rows twice more.

7th row: K1, k2tog, *yfrn, [p1, k1] twice, p1, yon, sl 1, k2tog, psso; rep from * to last 8 sts, yfrn, [p1, k1] twice, p1, yon, sl 1, k1, psso, k1.

8th row: P3, *[k1, p1] twice, k1, p3; rep from * to end.

Rep the last 2 rows twice more.

Rep these 12 rows.

Diamond Rib

Multiple of 9 + 2

1st row (right side): P2, *k2tog, [k1, yf] twice, k1, sl 1, k1, psso, p2; rep from * to end.

2nd and every alt row: K2, *p7, k2; rep from * to end.

3rd row: P2, *k2tog, yf, k3, yf, sl 1, k1, psso, p2; rep from * to end.

5th row: P2, *k1, yf, sl 1, k1, psso, k1, k2tog, yf, k1, p2; rep from * to end.

7th row: P2, *k2, yf, sl 1, k2tog, psso, yf, k2, p2; rep from * to end.

8th row: As 2nd row.

Rep these 8 rows.

Eyelet Rib

Multiple of 11 + 4

1st row (right side): K1, yfrn, p2tog, k1, *p1, k2, yf, sl 1, k1, psso, k1, p1, k1, yfrn, p2tog, k1; rep from * to end.

2nd and every alt row: K1, yfrn, p2tog, *k2, p5, k2, yfrn, p2tog; rep from * to last st, k1.

3rd row: K1, yfrn, p2tog, k1, *p1, k1, yf, sl 1, k2tog, psso, yf, k1, p1, k1, yfrn, p2tog, k1; rep from * to end.

5th row: As 1st row.

7th row: K1, yfrn, p2tog, k1, *p1, k5, p1, k1, yfrn, p2tog, k1; rep from * to end.

8th row: As 2nd row.

Rep these 8 rows.

Moss Lace Diamonds

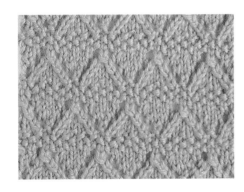

Multiple of 8 + 1

1st row (right side): K1, *p1, k1; rep from * to end.

2nd row: K1, *p1, k1; rep from * to end.

Rep the last 2 rows once more.

5th row: K1, *yf, sl 1, k1, psso, k3, k2tog, yf, k1; rep from * to end.

6th row: Purl.

7th row: K2, *yf, sl 1, k1, psso, k1, k2tog, yf, k3; rep from * to last 7 sts, yf, sl 1, k1, psso, k1, k2tog, yf, k2.

8th row: Purl.

9th row: K3, *yf, sl 1, k2tog, psso, yf, k5; rep from * to last 6 sts, yf, sl 1, k2tog, psso, yf, k3.

10th row: Purl.

11th row: K1, *p1, k1; rep from * to end.

Rep the last row 3 times more.

15th row: K2, *k2tog, yf, k1, yf, sl 1, k1, psso, k3; rep from * to last 7 sts, k2tog, yf, k1, yf, sl 1, k1, psso, k2.

16th row: Purl.

17th row: K1, *k2tog, yf, k3, yf, sl 1, k1, psso, k1; rep from * to end.

18th row: Purl.

19th row: K2tog, *yf, k5, yf, sl 1, k2tog, psso; rep from * to last 7 sts, yf, k5, yf, sl 1, k1, psso.

20th row: Purl.

Rep these 20 rows.

Scallop Pattern

Multiple of 13 + 2

Note: Stitches should only be counted after the 5th or 6th row of pattern.

1st row (right side): K1, *sl 1, k1, psso, k9, k2tog; rep from * to last st, k1.

2nd row: Purl.

3rd row: K1, *sl 1, k1, psso, k7, k2tog; rep from * to last st, k1.

4th row: Purl.

5th row: K1, *sl 1, k1, psso, yf, [k1, yf] 5 times, k2tog; rep from * to last st, k1.

6th row: Knit.

Rep these 6 rows.

Astrakhan Bobbles

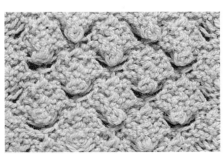

Multiple of 12 + 3

Either side of this stitch may be used.

1st row: K2, *yf, k4, p3tog, k4, yf, k1; rep from * to last st, k1.

Rep this row 5 times more.

7th row: K1, p2tog, *k4, yf, k1, yf, k4, p3tog; rep from * to last 12 sts, k4, yf, k1, yf, k4, p2tog, k1.

Rep this row 5 times more.

Rep these 12 rows.

Chevron Rib

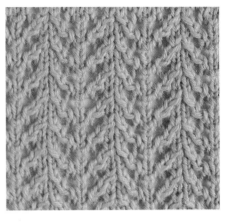

Multiple of 7 + 2

1st row (right side): K2, *k2tog, yf, k1, yf, sl 1, k1, psso, k2; rep from * to end.

2nd row: Purl.

3rd row: K1, *k2tog, yf, k3, yf, sl 1, k1, psso; rep from * to last st, k1.

4th row: Purl.

Rep these 4 rows.

Slanting Eyelets

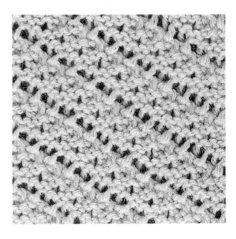

Multiple of 8 + 2

1st row (right side): K1, *yfrn, p2tog, k1, p2tog, yon, k3; rep from * to last st, k1.

2nd row: K6, *p2tog, yon, k6; rep from * to last 4 sts, p2tog, yon, k2.

3rd row: K3, *yfrn, p2tog, k1, p2tog, yon, k3; rep from * to last 7 sts, yfrn, p2tog, k1, p2tog, yon, k2.

4th row: K4, *p2tog, yon, k6; rep from * to last 6 sts, p2tog, yon, k4.

5th row: *P2tog, yon, k3, yfrn, p2tog, k1; rep from * to last 2 sts, k2.

6th row: K2, *p2tog, yon, k6; rep from * to end.

7th row: K2, *p2tog, yon, k3, yfrn, p2tog, k1; rep from * to end.

8th row: *P2tog, yon, k6; rep from * to last 2 sts, k2.

Rep these 8 rows.

All-over Lace Patterns

All-over Eyelets

Multiple of 10 + 1
1st row (right side): Knit.
2nd and every alt row: Purl.
3rd row: K3, *k2tog, yf, k1, yf, sl 1, k1, psso, k5; rep from * to last 8 sts, k2tog, yf, k1, yf, sl 1, k1, psso, k3.
5th row: Knit.
7th row: K1, *yf, sl 1, k1, psso, k5, k2tog, yf, k1; rep from * to end.
8th row: Purl.
Rep these 8 rows.

Snakes and Ladders

Multiple of 8 + 2
1st row (right side): K7, *k2tog, yf, k6; rep from * to last 3 sts, k2tog, yf, k1.
2nd row: K2, *yfrn, p2tog, k6; rep from * to end.
3rd row: K5, *k2tog, yf, k6; rep from * to last 5 sts, k2tog, yf, k3.
4th row: K4, *yfrn, p2tog, k6; rep from * to last 6 sts, yfrn, p2tog, k4.
5th row: K3, *k2tog, yf, k6; rep from * to last 7 sts, k2tog, yf, k5.
6th row: *K6, yfrn, p2tog; rep from * to last 2 sts, k2.
7th row: K1, *k2tog, yf, k6; rep from * to last st, k1.
8th row: K7, *p2tog tbl, yon, k6; rep from * to last 3 sts, p2tog tbl, yon, k1.
9th row: K2, *yf, k2tog tbl, k6; rep from * to end.
10th row: K5, *p2tog tbl, yon, k6; rep from * to last 5 sts, p2tog tbl, yon, k3.
11th row: K4, *yf, k2tog tbl, k6; rep from * to last 6 sts, yf, k2tog tbl, k4.
12th row: K3, *p2tog tbl, yon, k6; rep from * to last 7 sts, p2tog tbl, yon, k5.
13th row: *K6, yf, k2tog tbl; rep from * to last 2 sts, k2.
14th row: K1, *p2tog tbl, yon, k6; rep

from * to last st, k1.
Rep these 14 rows.

Eyelet Lace

Multiple of 6 + 2
Note: Stitches should only be counted after the 2nd and 4th row.

1st row (right side): K1, yf, *k2tog tbl, k2, k2tog, yf; rep from * to last st, k1.
2nd row: K1, p5, *p into front and back of next st, p4; rep from * to last 2 sts, p1,k1.
3rd row: K2, *k2tog, yf, k2tog tbl, k2; rep from * to end.
4th row: K1, p2, *p into front and back of next st, p4; rep from * to last 4 sts, p into front and back of next st, p2, k1.
Rep these 4 rows.

Travelling Vine

Multiple of 8 + 2
Note: Stitches should only be counted after wrong side rows.

1st row (right side): K1, *yf, KB1, yf, k2tog tbl, k5; rep from * to last st, k1.
2nd row: P5, *p2tog tbl, p7; rep from * to last 6 sts, p2tog tbl, p4.
3rd row: K1, *yf, KB1, yf, k2, k2tog tbl, k3; rep from * to last st, k1.
4th row: P3, *p2tog tbl, p7; rep from * to last 8 sts, p2tog tbl, p6.
5th row: K1, *KB1, yf, k4, k2tog tbl, k1, yf; rep from * to last st, k1.
6th row: P2, *p2tog tbl, p7; rep from * to end.
7th row: K6, *k2tog, yf, KB1, yf, k5; rep from * to last 4 sts, k2tog, yf, KB1, yf, k1.
8th row: P4, *p2tog, p7; rep from * to last 7 sts, p2tog, p5.
9th row: K4, *k2tog, k2, yf, KB1, yf, k3; rep from * to last 6 sts, k2tog, k2, yf, KB1, yf, k1.
10th row: P6, *p2tog, p7; rep from * to last 5 sts, p2tog, p3.

11th row: K1, *yf, k1, k2tog, k4, yf, KB1; rep from * to last st, k1.
12th row: *P7, p2tog; rep from * to last 2 sts, p2.
Rep these 12 rows.

Imitation Crochet

Multiple of 6 + 3
Note: Stitches should *not* be counted after the 1st and 5th row.
1st row (wrong side): K1, *yf, k1; rep from * to end.
2nd row: Knit, dropping yfs of previous row.
3rd row: K1, k3tog, *[yfon] twice (2 sts made), k1, [yfon] twice, sl 2, k3tog, pass both sl sts over; rep from * to last 5 sts, [yfon] twice, k1, [yfon] twice, k3tog, k1.
4th row: K2, *k into front of first loop and back of 2nd loop of double yfon of previous row, k1; rep from * to last st, k1.
5th row: As 1st row.
6th row: As 2nd row.
7th row: K2, *[yfon] twice, sl 2, k3tog, pass both sl sts over, [yfon] twice, k1; rep from * to last st, k1.
8th row: As 4th row.
Rep these 8 rows.

Climbing Leaf Pattern

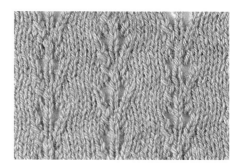

Multiple of 16 + 1
1st row (right side): K1, *yf, k5, k2tog, k1, k2tog tbl, k5, yf, k1; rep from * to end.
2nd and every alt row: Purl.
3rd row: As 1st row.
5th row: K1, *k2tog tbl, k5, yf, k1, yf, k5, k2tog, k1; rep from * to end.
7th row: As 5th row.
8th row: Purl.
Rep these 8 rows.

Florette Pattern

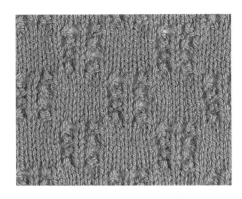

Multiple of 12 + 7
1st row (right side): K1, *p2tog, yon, k1, yfrn, p2tog, k7; rep from * to last 6 sts, p2tog, yon, k1, yfrn, p2tog, k1.
2nd and every alt row: Purl.
3rd row: K1, *yfrn, p2tog, k1, p2tog, yon, k7; rep from * to last 6 sts, yfrn, p2tog, k1, p2tog, yon, k1.
5th row: As 3rd row.
7th row: As 1st row.
9th row: K7, *p2tog, yon, k1, yfrn, p2tog, k7; rep from * to end.
11th row: K7, *yfrn, p2tog, k1, p2tog, yon, k7; rep from * to end.
13th row: As 11th row.
15th row: As 9th row.
16th row: Purl.
Rep these 16 rows.

Gothic Windows

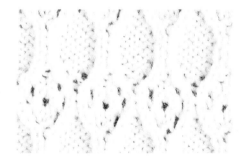

Multiple of 8 + 2
Note: Stitches should *not* be counted after the 3rd, 7th, 9th and 11th rows.
1st row (right side): P4, *k2, p6; rep from * to last 6 sts, k2, p4.
2nd row: K4, *p2, k6; rep from * to last 6 sts, p2, k4.
3rd row: P3, *k2tog, yf, sl 1, k1, psso, p4; rep from * to last 7 sts, k2tog, yf, sl 1, k1, psso, p3.
4th row: K3, *p1, k into back then front of next st, p1, k4; rep from * to last 6 sts, p1, k into back then front of next st, p1, k3.
5th row: P2, *k2tog, yf, k2, yf, sl 1, k1, psso, p2; rep from * to end.
6th row: K2, *p6, k2; rep from * to end.
7th row: K1, *k2tog, yf, k2tog, [yf, sl 1, k1, psso] twice; rep from * to last st, k1.
8th row: P4, *k into front then back of next st, p6; rep from * to last 5 sts, k into front then back of next st, p4.

9th row: K1, *[yf, sl 1, k1, psso] twice, k2tog, yf, k2tog; rep from * to last st, yf, k1.
10th row: K1, KB1, *p6, k into back then front of next st; rep from * to last 8 sts, p6, KB1, k1.
11th row: P2, *yon, k3tog tbl, yf, k3tog, yfrn, p2; rep from * to end.
12th row: K2, *KB1, p1, k into back then front of next st, p1, KB1, k2; rep from * to end.
13th row: P3, *yon, sl 1, k1, psso, k2tog, yfrn, p4; rep from * to last 7 sts, yon, sl 1, k1, psso, k2tog, yfrn, p3.
14th row: K3, *KB1, p2, KB1, k4; rep from * to last 7 sts, KB1, p2, KB1, k3.
Rep these 14 rows.

Simple Lace Rib

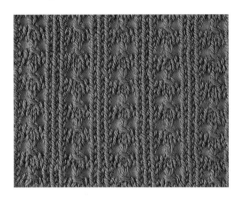

Multiple of 6 + 1
1st row (right side): [KB1] twice, *k3, [KB1] 3 times; rep from * to last 5 sts, k3, [KB1] twice.
2nd row: [PB1] twice, *p3, [PB1] 3 times; rep from * to last 5 sts, p3, [PB1] twice.
3rd row: [KB1] twice, *yf, sl 1, k2tog, psso, yf, [KB1] 3 times; rep from * to last 5 sts, yf, sl 1, k2tog, psso, yf, [KB1] twice.
4th row: As 2nd row.
Rep these 4 rows.

Diamond Diagonal

Multiple of 8 + 2
1st row (right side): K1, *yf, k2tog tbl, k6; rep from * to last st, k1.
2nd row: K1, *yfrn, p2tog, k3, p2tog tbl, yon, k1; rep from * to last st, k1.
3rd row: *K3, yf, k2tog tbl, k1, k2tog, yf; rep from * to last 2 sts, k2.

4th row: K3, *yfrn, p3tog tbl, yon, k5; rep from * to last 7 sts, yfrn, p3tog tbl, yon, k4.
5th row: K5, *yf, k2tog tbl, k6; rep from * to last 5 sts, yf, k2tog tbl, k3.
6th row: K2, *p2tog tbl, yon, k1, yfrn, p2tog, k3; rep from * to end.
7th row: K2, *k2tog, yf, k3, yf, k2tog tbl, k1; rep from * to end.
8th row: P2tog tbl, *yon, k5, yfrn, p3tog tbl; rep from * to last 8 sts, yon, k5, yfrn, p2tog, k1.
Rep these 8 rows.

Wheatear Stitch

Multiple of 8 + 6
1st row (right side): P5, *k2, yf, sl 1, k1, psso, p4; rep from * to last st, p1.
2nd row: K5, *p2, yrn, p2tog, k4; rep from * to last st, k1.
Rep the last 2 rows 3 times more.
9th row: P1, *k2, yf, sl 1, k1, psso, p4; rep from * to last 5 sts, k2, yf, sl 1, k1, psso, p1.
10th row: K1, *p2, yrn, p2tog, k4; rep from * to last 5 sts, p2, yrn, p2tog, k1.
Rep the last 2 rows 3 times more.
Rep these 16 rows.

Flower Buds

Multiple of 8 + 5
1st row (right side): K3, *yf, k2, p3tog, k2, yf, k1; rep from * to last 2 sts, k2.
2nd row: Purl.
Rep the last 2 rows twice more.
7th row: K2, P2tog, *k2, yf, k1, yf, k2, p3tog; rep from * to last 9 sts, k2, yf, k1, yf, k2, p2tog, k2.
8th row: Purl.
Rep the last 2 rows twice more.
Rep these 12 rows.

All-over Lace Patterns

Zigzag Lace

Multiple of 4 + 3

1st row (right side): K4, *k2tog, yf, k2; rep from * to last 3 sts, k2tog, yf, k1.
2nd row: *P2, yrn, p2tog; rep from * to last 3 sts, p3.
3rd row: *K2, k2tog, yf; rep from * to last 3 sts, k3.
4th row: P4, *yrn, p2tog, p2; rep from * to last 3 sts, yrn, p2tog, p1.
5th row: K1, *yf, sl 1, k1, psso, k2; rep from * to last 2 sts, k2.
6th row: P3, *p2tog tbl, yrn, p2; rep from * to end.
7th row: K3, *yf, sl 1, k1, psso, k2; rep from * to end
8th row: P1, *p2tog tbl, yrn, p2; rep from * to last 2 sts, p2.
Rep these 8 rows.

Horizontal Leaf Pattern

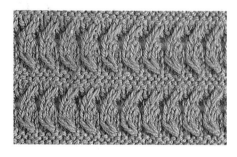

Multiple of 3

1st row (right side): K2, *sl 1 purlwise, k2; rep from * to last st, k1.
2nd row: P3, *sl 1 purlwise, p2; rep from * to end.
3rd row: K2, *C3L; rep from * to last st, k1.
4th row: Purl.
5th row: K2, *yf, k2tog, k1; rep from * to last st, k1.
6th row: Purl.
7th row: K4, *sl 1 purlwise, k2; rep from * to last 2 sts, sl 1 purlwise, k1.
8th row: P1, *sl 1 purlwise, p2; rep from * to last 2 sts, p2.
9th row: K2, *C3R; rep from * to last st, k1.
10th row: Knit.
11th row: Purl.
12th row: Purl.
Rep these 12 rows.

Lace And Cables

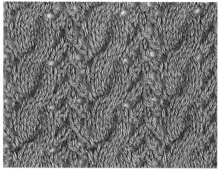

Multiple of 11 + 7

1st row (right side): K1, *yf, sl 1, k1, psso, k1, k2tog, yf, k6; rep from * to last 6 sts, yf, sl 1, k1, psso, k1, k2tog, yf, k1.
2nd and every alt row: Purl.
3rd row: K2, *yf, sl 1, k2tog, psso, yf, k8; rep from * to last 5 sts, yf, sl 1, k2tog, psso, yf, k2.
5th row: As 1st row.
7th row: K2, *yf, sl 1, k2tog, psso, yf, k1, C6B, k1; rep from * to last 5 sts, yf, sl 1, k2tog, psso, yf, k2.
8th row: Purl.
Rep these 8 rows.

Wavy Cable Lace

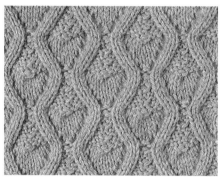

Multiple of 14 + 1

1st row (right side): K1, *yf, k2, p3, p3tog, p3, k2, yf, k1; rep from * to end.
2nd row: P4, *k7, p7; rep from * to last 11 sts, k7, p4.
3rd row: K2, *yf, k2, p2, p3tog, p2, k2, yf, k3; rep from * to last 13 sts, yf, k2, p2, p3tog, p2, k2, yf, k2.
4th row: P5, *k5, p9; rep from * to last 10 sts, k5, p5.
5th row: K3, *yf, k2, p1, p3tog, p1, k2, yf, k5; rep from * to last 12 sts, yf, k2, p1, p3tog, p1, k2, yf, k3.
6th row: P6, *k3, p11; rep from * to last 9 sts, k3, p6.
7th row: K4, *yf, k2, p3tog, k2, yf, k7; rep from * to last 11 sts, yf, k2, p3tog, k2, yf, k4.
8th row: P7, *k1, p13; rep from * to last 8 sts, k1, p7.
9th row: P2tog, *p3, k2, yf, k1, yf, k2, p3, p3tog; rep from * to last 13 sts, p3, k2, yf, k1, yf, k2, p3, p2tog.
10th row: K4, *p7, k7; rep from * to last 11 sts, p7, k4.

11th row: P2tog, *P2, k2, yf, k3, yf, k2, p2, p3tog; rep from * to last 13 sts, p2, k2, yf, k3, yf, k2, p2, p2tog.
12th row: K3, *p9, k5; rep from * to last 12 sts, p9, k3.
13th row: P2tog, *p1, k2, yf, k5, yf, k2, p1, p3tog; rep from * to last 13 sts, p1, k2, yf, k5, yf, k2, p1, p2tog.
14th row: K2, *p11, k3; rep from * to last 13 sts, p11, k2.
15th row: P2tog, *k2, yf, k7, yf, k2, p3tog; rep from * to last 13 sts, k2, yf, k7, yf, k2, p2tog.
16th row: K1, *p13, k1; rep from * to end.
Rep these 16 rows.

Waterfall Pattern

Multiple of 6 + 3

Note: Sts should only be counted after the 4th, 5th and 6th rows.

1st row (right side): P3, *k3, yfrn, p3; rep from * to end.
2nd row: K3, *p4, k3; rep from * to end.
3rd row: P3, *k1, k2tog, yf, k1, p3; rep from * to end.
4th row: K3, *p2, p2tog, k3; rep from * to end.
5th row: P3, *k1, yf, k2tog, p3; rep from * to end.
6th row: K3, *p3, k3; rep from * to end.
Rep these 6 rows.

Lacy Bubbles

Multiple of 6 + 3

1st row (right side): Purl.
2nd row: Knit.
3rd row: Purl.
4th row: K1, p3tog, [k1, p1, k1, p1, k1] into next st, *p5tog, [k1, p1, k1, p1, k1] into next st; rep from * to last 4 sts,

p3tog, k1.
5th row: Purl.
6th row: K1, [k1, p1, k1] into next st, p5tog, *[k1, p1, k1, p1, k1] into next st, p5tog; rep from * to last 2 sts, [k1, p1, k1] into next st, k1.
7th row: Purl.
8th row: Knit.
Rep these 8 rows.

Lacy Diamonds

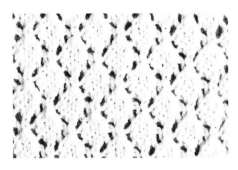

Multiple of 6 + 1
1st row (right side): *K1, k2tog, yf, k1, yf, k2tog tbl; rep from * to last st, k1.
2nd and every alt row: Purl.
3rd row: K2tog, *yf, k3, yf, [sl 1] twice, k1, p2sso; rep from * to last 5 sts, yf, k3, yf, k2tog tbl.
5th row: *K1, yf, k2tog tbl, k1, k2tog, yf; rep from * to last st, k1.
7th row: K2, *yf, [sl 1] twice, k1, p2sso, yf, k3; rep from * to last 5 sts, yf, [sl 1] twice, k1, p2sso, yf, k2.
8th row: Purl.
Rep these 8 rows.

Twist Cable and Ladder Lace

Multiple of 7 + 6
1st row (right side): K1, *k2tog, [yf] twice, sl 1, k1, psso, k3; rep from * to last 5 sts, k2tog, [yf] twice, sl 1, k1, psso, k1.
2nd row: K2, *[KB1, k1] into double yf of previous row, k1, p3, k1; rep from * to last 4 sts, [KB1, k1] into double yf of previous row, k2.
3rd row: K1, *k2tog, [yf] twice, sl 1, k1, psso, knit into 3rd st on left-hand needle, then knit into 2nd st, then knit into 1st st, slipping all 3 sts onto right-hand needle tog; rep from * to last 5 sts, k2tog, [yf] twice, sl 1, k1, psso, k1.
4th row: As 2nd row.
Rep these 4 rows.

Large Lattice Lace

Multiple of 6 + 2
1st row (right side): K1, p1, *yon, k2tog tbl, k2tog, yfrn, p2; rep from * to last 6 sts, yon, k2tog tbl, k2tog, yfrn, p1, k1.
2nd row: K2, *p4, k2; rep from * to end.
3rd row: K1, p1, *k2tog, [yf] twice, k2tog tbl, p2; rep from * to last 6 sts, k2tog, [yf] twice, k2tog tbl, p1, k1.
4th row: K2, *p1, [k1, p1] into double yf of previous row, p1, k2; rep from * to end.
5th row: K1, *k2tog, yfrn, p2, yon, k2tog tbl; rep from * to last st, k1.
6th row: K1, p2, *k2, p4; rep from * to last 5 sts, k2, p2, k1.
7th row: K1, yf, *k2tog tbl, p2, k2tog, [yf] twice; rep from * to last 7 sts, k2tog tbl, p2, k2tog, yf, k1.
8th row: K1, p2, k2, p1, *[k1, p1] into double yf of previous row, p1, k2, p1; rep from * to last 2 sts, p1, k1.
Rep these 8 rows.

Fuchsia Stitch

Multiple of 6
Note: Stitches should only be counted after the 11th and 12th rows.
1st row (right side): P2, *k2, yfrn, p4; rep from * to last 4 sts, k2, yfrn, p2.
2nd row: K2, *p3, k4; rep from * to last 5 sts, p3, k2.
3rd row: P2, *k3, yfrn, p4; rep from * to last 5 sts, k3, yfrn, p2.
4th row: K2, *p4, k4; rep from * to last 6 sts, p4, k2.
5th row: P2, *k4, yfrn, p4; rep from * to last 6 sts, k4, yfrn, p2.
6th row: K2, *p5, k4; rep from * to last 7 sts, p5, k2.
7th row: P2, *k3, k2tog, p4; rep from * to last 7 sts, k3, k2tog, p2.
8th row: As 4th row.
9th row: P2, *k2, k2tog, p4; rep from * to last 6 sts, k2, k2tog, p2.
10th row: As 2nd row.
11th row: P2, *k1, k2tog, p4; rep from * to last 5 sts, k1, k2tog, p2.

12th row: K2, *p2, k4; rep from * to last 4 sts, p2, k2.
Rep these 12 rows.

Dewdrop Pattern

Multiple 6 + 1
1st row (wrong side): K2, *p3, k3; rep from * to last 5 sts, p3, k2.
2nd row: P2, *k3, p3; rep from * to last 5 sts, k3, p2.
3rd row: As 1st row.
4th row: K2, *yf, sl 1, k2tog, psso, yf, k3; rep from * to last 5 sts, yf, sl 1, k2tog, psso, yf, k2.
5th row: As 2nd row.
6th row: K2, *p3, k3; rep from * to last 5 sts, p3, k2.
7th row: As 2nd row.
8th row: K2tog, *yf, k3, yf, sl 1, k2tog, psso; rep from * to last 5 sts, yf, k3, yf, sl 1, k1, psso.
Rep these 8 rows.

Eyelet Check

Multiple of 8 + 7
1st row (right side): K2, *p3, k5; rep from * to last 5 sts, p3, k2.
2nd row: P2, *k3, p5; rep from * to last 5 sts, k3, p2.
3rd row: K2, *p1, yrn, p2tog, k5; rep from * to last 5 sts, p1, yrn, p2tog, k2.
4th row: As 2nd row.
5th row: As 1st row.
6th row: Purl.
7th row: K6, *p3, k5; rep from * to last 9 sts, p3, k6.
8th row: P6, *k3, p5; rep from * to last 9 sts, k3, p6.
9th row: K6, *p1, yrn, p2tog, k5; rep from * to last 9 sts, p1, yrn, p2tog, k6.
10th row: As 8th row.
11th row: K6, *p3, k5; rep from * to last 9 sts, p3, k6.
12th row: Purl.
Rep these 12 rows.

All-over Lace Patterns

Alternating Lace

Multiple of 6 + 5
1st row (right side): K1, *yf, sl 1, k2tog, psso, yf, k3; rep from * to last 4 sts, yf, sl 1, k2tog, psso, yf, k1.
2nd row: Purl.
Rep the last 2 rows 3 times more.
9th row: K4, *yf, sl 1, k2tog, psso, yf, k3; rep from * to last st, k1.
10th row: Purl.
Rep the last 2 rows 3 times more.
Rep these 16 rows.

Faggotting

Multiple of 3
Note: Stitches should only be counted after the 2nd and 4th rows.
1st row (right side): *K1, [yf] twice, k2tog; rep from * to end.
2nd row: P1, *purl into first yf of previous row, drop second yf off needle, p2; rep from * to last 3 sts, purl into first yf, drop second yf off needle, p1.
3rd row: *K2tog, [yf] twice, k1; rep from * to end.
4th row: As 2nd row.
Rep these 4 rows.

Lace Check

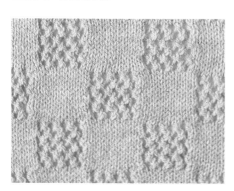

Multiple of 18 + 9
1st row (wrong side): Purl.
2nd row: K1, *[yf, k2tog] 4 times, k10; rep from * to last 8 sts, [yf, k2tog] 4 times.
3rd row: Purl.
4th row: *[Sl 1, k1, psso, yf] 4 times, k10; rep from * to last 9 sts, [sl 1, k1, psso, yf] 4 times, k1.
Rep the last 4 rows twice more.
13th row: Purl.
14th row: *K10, [yf, k2tog] 4 times; rep from * to last 9 sts, k9.
15th row: Purl.
16th row: K9, *[sl 1, k1, psso, yf] 4 times, k10; rep from * to end.
Rep the last 4 rows twice more.
Rep these 24 rows.

Single Lace Rib

Multiple of 4 + 1
1st row (right side): K1, *yf, k2tog, p1, k1; rep from * to end.
2nd row: P1, *yrn, p2tog, k1, p1; rep from * to end.
Rep these 2 rows.

Ridged Openwork

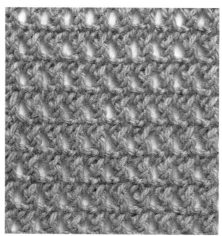

Multiple of 2 + 1
Note: Stitches should only be counted after the 1st, 3rd or 4th rows of this pattern.
1st row (right side): Purl.
2nd row: *P2tog; rep from * to last st, p1.
3rd row: P1, *purl through horizontal strand of yarn lying between stitch just worked and next st, p1; rep from * to end.
4th row: P1, *yrn, p2tog; rep from * to end.
Rep these 4 rows.

Wavy Eyelet Rib

Multiple of 7 + 2
1st row (right side): *P2, yon, sl 1, k1, psso, k1, k2tog, yfrn; rep from * to last 2 sts, p2.
2nd row: K2, *p5, k2; rep from * to end.
Rep the last 2 rows twice more.
7th row: *P2, k5; rep from * to last 2 sts, p2.
8th row: As 2nd row.
9th row: *P2, k2tog, yf, k1, yf, sl 1, k1, psso; rep from * to last 2 sts, p2.
10th row: As 2nd row.
Rep the last 2 rows twice more.
15th row: As 7th row.
16th row: As 2nd row.
Rep these 16 rows.

Loose Lattice Lace

Multiple of 8 + 3

Note: Sts should only be counted after the 5th, 6th, 11th and 12th rows.

1st row (right side): K1, *k2tog, k1, yf, k1, sl 1, k1, psso, k2; rep from * to last 2 sts, k2.

2nd and every alt row: Purl.

3rd row: *K2tog, k1, [yf, k1] twice, sl 1, k1, psso; rep from * to last 3 sts, k3.

5th row: K2, *yf, k3, yf, k1, sl 1, k1, psso, k1; rep from * to last st, k1.

7th row: K4, *k2tog, k1, yf, k1, sl 1, k1, psso, k2; rep from * to last 7 sts, k2tog, k1, yf, k1, sl 1, k1, psso, k1.

9th row: K3, *k2tog, k1, [yf, k1] twice, sl 1, k1, psso; rep from * to end.

11th row: K2, *k2tog, k1, yf, k3, yf, k1; rep from * to last st, k1.

12th row: Purl.

Rep these 12 rows.

Fir Cone

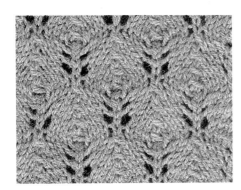

Multiple of 10 + 1

1st row (wrong side): Purl.

2nd row: K1, *yf, k3, sl 1, k2tog, psso, k3, yf, k1; rep from * to end.

Rep the last 2 rows 3 times more.

9th row: Purl.

10th row: K2tog, *k3, yf, k1, yf, k3, sl 1, k2tog, psso; rep from * to last 9 sts, k3, yf, k1, yf, k3, sl 1, k1, psso.

Rep the last 2 rows 3 times more.

Rep these 16 rows.

Staggered Eyelets

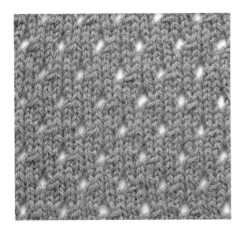

Multiple of 4 + 3

Work 2 rows in st st, starting knit.

3rd row (right side): *K2, k2tog, yf; rep from * to last 3 sts, k3.

Work 3 rows in st st, starting purl.

7th row: *K2tog, yf, k2; rep from * to last 3 sts, k2tog, yf, k1.

8th row: Purl.

Rep these 8 rows.

Layette Stitch

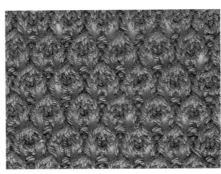

Multiple of 4 + 1

1st row (right side): K2, *p1, k3; rep from * to last 3 sts, p1, k2.

2nd row: P2, *k1, p3; rep from * to last 3 sts, k1, p2.

3rd row: K2tog, yfrn, *p1, yon, k3tog, yfrn; rep from * to last 3 sts, p1, yon, k2tog.

4th row: K1, *p3, k1; rep from * to end.

5th row: P1, *k3, p1; rep from * to end.

6th row: As 4th row.

7th row: P1, *yon, k3tog, yfrn, p1; rep from * to end.

8th row: As 2nd row.

Rep these 8 rows.

Eyelet Chevron

Mutliple of 12 + 1

1st row (right side): K4, *k2tog, yf, k1, yf, sl 1, k1, psso, k7; rep from * to last 9 sts, k2tog, yf, k1, yf, sl 1, k1, psso, k4.

2nd and every alt row: Purl.

3rd row: K3, *k2tog, yf, k3, yf, sl 1, k1, psso, k5; rep from * to last 10 sts, k2tog, yf, k3, yf, sl 1, k1, psso, k3.

5th row: K2, *k2tog, yf, k5, yf, sl 1, k1, psso, k3; rep from * to last 11 sts, k2tog, yf, k5, yf, sl 1, k1, psso, k2.

7th row: K1, *k2tog, yf, k7, yf, sl 1, k1,

psso, k1; rep from * to end.

9th row: K2tog, yf, k9, *yf, sl 1, k2tog, psso, yf, k9; rep from * to last 2 sts, yf, sl 1, k1, psso.

10th row: Purl.

Rep these 10 rows.

Tulip Lace

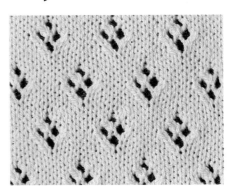

Multiple of 8 + 7

1st row (right side): Knit.

2nd and every alt row: Purl.

3rd row: K3, *yf, sl 1, k1, psso, k6; rep from * to last 4 sts, yf, sl 1, k1, psso, k2.

5th row: K1, *k2tog, yf, k1, yf, sl 1, k1, psso, k3; rep from * to last 6 sts, k2tog, yf, k1, yf, sl 1, k1, psso, k1.

7th row: As 3rd row.

9th row: Knit.

11th row: K7, *yf, sl 1, k1, psso, k6; rep from * to end.

13th row: K5, *k2tog, yf, k1, yf, sl 1, k1, psso, k3; rep from * to last 2 sts, k2.

15th row: As 11th row.

16th row: Purl.

Rep these 16 rows.

Snowdrop Lace

Multiple of 8 + 5

1st row (right side): K1, *yf, sl 1 purlwise, k2tog, psso, yf, k5; rep from * to last 4 sts, yf, sl 1 purlwise, k2tog, psso, yf, k1.

2nd and every alt row: Purl.

3rd row: As 1st row.

5th row: K4, *yf, sl 1 purlwise, k1, psso, k1, k2tog, yf, k3; rep from * to last st, k1.

7th row: K1, *yf, sl 1 purlwise, k2tog, psso, yf, k1; rep from * to end.

8th row: Purl.

Rep these 8 rows.

All-over Lace Patterns

Diagonal Lace

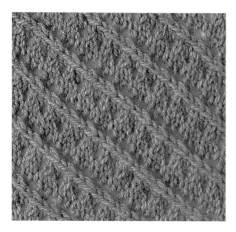

Multiple of 8 + 4

1st row (right side): K2, *yf, sl 1, k1, psso, k1, k2tog, yf, k3; rep from * to last 2 sts, k2.

2nd row: P7, *p2tog tbl, yrn, p6; rep from * to last 5 sts, p2tog tbl, yrn, p3.

3rd row: K4, *yf, sl 1, k1, psso, k1, k2tog, yf, k3; rep from * to end.

4th row: P5, *p2tog tbl, yrn, p6; rep from * to last 7 sts, p2tog tbl, yrn, p5.

5th row: K1, *k2tog, yf, k3, yf, sl 1, k1, psso, k1; rep from * to last 3 sts, k2tog, yf, k1.

6th row: P3, *p2tog tbl, yrn, p6; rep from * to last st, p1.

7th row: K3, *k2tog, yf, k3, yf, sl 1, k1, psso, k1; rep from * to last st, k1.

8th row: P1, *p2tog tbl, yrn, p6; rep from * to last 3 sts, p2tog tbl, yrn, p1.

Rep these 8 rows.

Lacy Rib

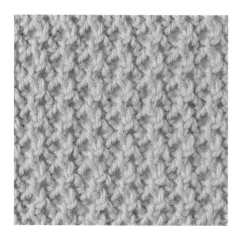

Multiple of 3 + 1

1st row (right side): K1, *k2tog, yfrn, p1; rep from * to last 3 sts, k2tog, yf, k1.

2nd row: P3, *k1, p2; rep from * to last 4 sts, k1, p3.

3rd row: K1, yf, sl 1, k1, psso, *p1, sl 1, yon, k1, psso; rep from * to last st, k1.

4th row: As 2nd row.

Rep these 4 rows.

Zigzag Openwork

Multiple of 2 + 1

Note: Stitches should only be counted after the 2nd or 4th rows of this pattern.

1st row (right side): K1, *k2tog; rep from * to end.

2nd row: K1, *M1, k1; rep from * to end.

3rd row: *K2tog; rep from * to last st, k1.

4th row: As 2nd row.

Rep these 4 rows.

Fern Diamonds

Multiple of 10 + 1

1st row (right side): K3, *k2tog, yf, k1, yf, sl 1, k1, psso, k5; rep from * to last 8 sts, k2tog, yf, k1, yf, sl 1, k1, psso, k3.

2nd and every alt row: Purl.

3rd row: K2, *k2tog, [k1, yf] twice, k1, sl 1, k1, psso, k3; rep from * to last 9 sts, k2tog, [k1, yf] twice, k1, sl 1, k1, psso, k2.

5th row: K1, *k2tog, k2, yf, k1, yf, k2, sl 1, k1, psso, k1; rep from * to end.

7th row: K2tog, *k3, yf, k1, yf, k3, sl 1, k2tog, psso; rep from * to last 9 sts, k3, yf, k1, yf, k3, sl 1, k1, psso.

9th row: K1, *yf, sl 1, k1, psso, k5, k2tog, yf, k1; rep from * to end.

11th row: K1, *yf, k1, sl 1, k1, psso, k3, k2tog, k1, yf, k1; rep from * to end.

Hourglass Eyelets

13th row: K1, *yf, k2, sl 1, k1, psso, k1, k2tog, k2, yf, k1; rep from * to end.

15th row: K1, *yf, k3, sl 1, k2tog, psso, k3, yf, k1; rep from * to end.

16th row: Purl.

Rep these 16 rows.

Multiple of 6 + 1

1st row (right side): K6, *p1, k5; rep from * to last st, k1.

2nd row: K1, *p5, k1; rep from * to end.

3rd row: K1, *yf, sl 1, k1, psso, p1, k2tog, yf, k1; rep from * to end.

4th row: K1, p2, *k1, p5; rep from * to last 4 sts, k1, p2, k1.

5th row: K3, *p1, k5; rep from * to last 4 sts, p1, k3.

6th row: As 4th row.

7th row: K1, *k2tog, yf, k1, yf, sl 1, k1, psso, p1; rep from * to last 6 sts, k2tog, yf, k1, yf, sl 1, k1, psso, k1.

8th row: As 2nd row.

Rep these 8 rows.

Garter Stitch Eyelet Chevron

Multiple of 9 + 1

1st row (right side): K1, *yf, sl 1, k1, psso, k4, k2tog, yf, k1; rep from * to end.

2nd row: P2, *k6, p3; rep from * to last 8 sts, k6, p2.

3rd row: K2, *yf, sl 1, k1, psso, k2, k2tog, yf, k3; rep from * to last 8 sts, yf, sl 1, k1, psso, k2, k2tog, yf, k2.

4th row: P3, *k4, p5; rep from * to last 7 sts, k4, p3.

5th row: K3, *yf, sl 1, k1, psso, k2tog, yf, k5; rep from * to last 7 sts, yf, sl 1, k1, psso, k2tog, yf, k3.

6th row: P4, *k2, p7; rep from * to last 6 sts, k2, p4.

Rep these 6 rows.

Fern Lace

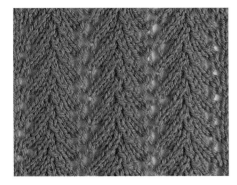

Multiple of 9 + 4
1st row (wrong side): Purl.
2nd row: K3, *yf, k2, sl 1, k1, psso, k2tog, k2, yf, k1; rep from * to last st, k1.
3rd row: Purl.
4th row: K2, *yf, k2, sl 1, k1, psso, k2tog, k2, yf, k1; rep from * to last 2 sts, k2.
Rep these 4 rows.

Lacy Zigzag

Multiple of 6 + 1
1st row (right side): *Sl 1, k1, psso, k2, yf, k2; rep from * to last st, k1.
2nd row: Purl.
Rep the last 2 rows twice more.
7th row: K3, *yf, k2, k2tog, k2; rep from * to last 4 sts, yf, k2, k2tog.
8th row: Purl.
Rep the last 2 rows twice more.
Rep these 12 rows.

Foaming Waves

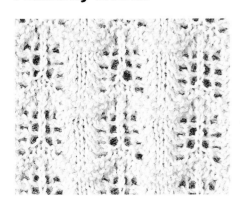

Multiple of 12 + 1
Knit 4 rows.
5th row (right side): K1, *[k2tog] twice, [yf, k1] 3 times, yf, [sl 1, k1, psso] twice, k1; rep from * to end.
6th row: Purl.
Rep the last 2 rows 3 times more.
Rep these 12 rows.

Arrowhead Lace

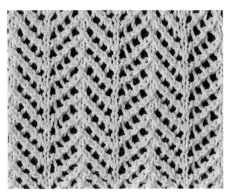

Multiple of 10 + 1
1st row (right side): K1, *[yf, sl 1, k1, psso] twice, k1, [k2tog, yf] twice, k1; rep from * to end.
2nd row: Purl.
3rd row: K2, *yf, sl 1, k1, psso, yf, sl 1, k2tog, psso, yf, k2tog, yf, k3; rep from * to last 9 sts, yf, sl 1, k1, psso, yf, sl 1, k2tog, psso, yf, k2tog, yf, k2.
4th row: Purl.
Rep these 4 rows.

Leafy Lace

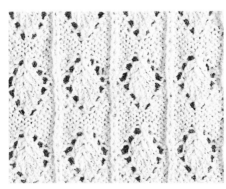

Multiple of 10 + 1
1st row (right side): KB1, *p9, KB1; rep from * to end.
2nd row: P1, *k9, p1; rep from * to end.
Rep the last 2 rows once more.
5th row: KB1, *p2, p2tog, yon, KB1, yfrn, p2tog, p2, KB1; rep from * to end.
6th row: P1, *k4, PB1, k4, p1; rep from * to end.
7th row: KB1, *p1, p2tog, yon, [KB1] 3 times, yfrn, p2tog, p1, KB1; rep from * to end.
8th row: P1, *k3, [PB1] 3 times, k3, p1; rep from * to end.
9th row: KB1, *p2tog, yon, [KB1] 5 times, yfrn, p2tog, KB1; rep from * to end.
10th row: P1, *k2, [PB1] 5 times, k2, p1; rep from * to end.
11th row: KB1, *p1, yon, [KB1] twice, sl 1, k2tog, psso, [KB1] twice, yfrn, p1, KB1; rep from * to end.
12th row: As 10th row.
13th row: KB1, *p2, yon, KB1, sl 1, k2tog, psso, KB1, yfrn, p2, KB1; rep from * to end.
14th row: As 8th row.
15th row: KB1, *p3, yon, sl 1, k2tog, psso, yfrn, p3, KB1; rep from * to end.
16th row: As 6th row.
Rep these 16 rows.

Little Arrowhead

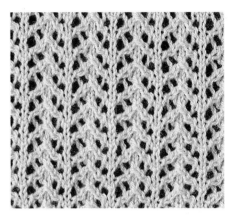

Multiple of 6 + 1
1st row (right side): K1, *yf, sl 1, k1, psso, k1, k2tog, yf, k1; rep from * to end.
2nd row: Purl.
3rd row: K2, *yf, sl 1, k2tog, psso, yf, k3; rep from * to last 5 sts, yf, sl 1, k2tog, psso, yf, k2.
4th row: Purl.
Rep these 4 rows.

Bluebell Ribs

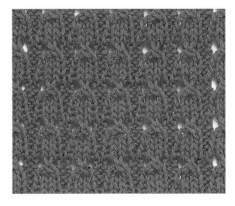

Multiple of 5 + 2
1st row (right side): P2, *k3, p2; rep from * to end.
2nd row: K2, *p3, k2; rep from * to end.
Rep the last 2 rows once more.
5th row: P2, *yon, sl 1, k2tog, psso, yfrn, p2; rep from * to end.
6th row: As 2nd row.
Rep these 6 rows.

Lace Panel Stitches

Lace Diamond Border

Multiple of 8.
Worked on a background of st st.
1st row (right side): *K1, yf, k3, pass 3rd st on right-hand needle over first 2 sts; rep from * to end.
2nd and every alt row: Purl.
3rd row: Knit.
5th row: K3, *yf, sl 1, k1, psso, k6; rep from * to last 5 sts, yf, sl 1, k1, psso, k3.
7th row: K2, *[yf, sl 1, k1, psso] twice, k4; rep from * to last 6 sts, [yf, sl 1, k1, psso] twice, k2.
9th row: K1, *[yf, sl 1, k1, psso] 3 times, k2; rep from * to last 7 sts, [yf, sl 1, k1, psso] 3 times, k1.
11th row: As 7th row.
13th row: As 5th row.
15th row: Knit.
17th row: As 1st row.

Candelabra Panel

Worked over 13 sts on a background of st st.
1st row (right side): Knit.
2nd and every alt row: Purl.
3rd row: Knit.
5th row: K4, k2tog, yf, k1, yf, sl 1, k1, psso, k4.
7th row: K3, k2tog, yf, k3, yf, sl 1, k1, psso, k3.
9th row: K2, [k2tog, yf] twice, k1, [yf, sl 1, k1, psso] twice, k2.
11th row: K1, [k2tog, yf] twice, k3, [yf, sl 1, k1, psso] twice, k1.
13th row: [K2tog, yf] 3 times, k1, [yf, sl 1, k1, psso] 3 times.
14th row: Purl.
Rep these 14 rows.

Ridged Eyelet Border

Multiple of 2 + 1
Worked on a background of st st.
1st, 2nd and 3rd rows: Knit.
4th row (wrong side): *P2tog, yrn; rep from * to last st, p1.
5th, 6th and 7th rows: Knit.
8th row: Purl.
Rep the first 6 rows once more.

Faggoted Panel

Worked over 9 sts on a st st background.
1st row (right side): P1, k1, k2tog, yf, k1, yf, k2tog tbl, k1, p1.
2nd row: K1, p7, k1.
3rd row: P1, k2tog, yf, k3, yf, k2tog tbl, p1.
4th row: As 2nd row.
Rep these 4 rows.

Diamond Panel

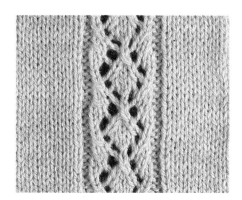

Worked over 11 sts on a background of st st.

Parasol Stitch

1st row (right side): P2, k2tog, [k1, yf] twice, k1, sl 1, k1, psso, p2.
2nd and every alt row: K2, p7, k2.
3rd row: P2, k2tog, yf, k3, yf, sl 1, k1, psso, p2.
5th row: P2, k1, yf, sl 1, k1, psso, k1, k2tog, yf, k1, p2.
7th row: P2, k2, yf, sl 1, k2tog, psso, yf, k2, p2.
8th row: As 2nd row.
Rep these 8 rows.

Worked over 17 sts on a background of st st. (**Note**: Sts should only be counted after the 11th and 12th rows of this pattern.)
1st row (right side): Yf, k1, [p3, k1] 4 times, yf.
2nd and every alt row: Purl.
3rd row: K1, yf, k1, [p3, k1] 4 times, yf, k1.
5th row: K2, yf, k1, [p3, k1] 4 times, yf, k2.
7th row: K3, yf, k1, [p2tog, p1, k1] 4 times, yf, k3.
9th row: K4, yf, k1, [p2tog, k1] 4 times, yf, k4.
11th row: K5, yf, k1, [k3tog, k1] twice, yf, k5.
12th row: Purl.
Rep these 12 rows.

Leaf Panel

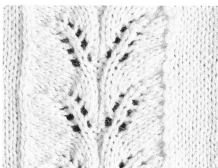

Worked over 24 sts on a background of st st.
1st row (right side): Sl 1, k2tog, psso, k7, yf, k1, yfrn, p2, yon, k1, yf, k7, k3tog.
2nd and every alt row: P11, k2, p11.
3rd row: Sl 1, k2tog, psso, k6 [yf, k1] twice, p2, [k1, yf] twice, k6, k3tog.

5th row: Sl 1, k2tog, psso, k5, yf, k1, yf, k2, p2, k2, yf, k1, yf, k5, k3tog.

7th row: Sl 1, k2tog, psso, k4, yf, k1, yf, k3, p2, k3, yf, k1, yf, k4, k3tog.

9th row: Sl 1, k2tog, psso, k3, yf, k1, yf, k4, p2, k4, yf, k1, yf, k3, k3tog.

10th row: As 2nd row.

Rep these 10 rows.

Fishtail Lace Panel

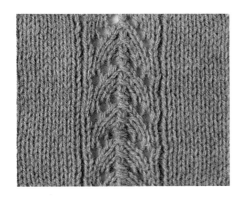

Worked over 11 sts on a background of st st.

1st row (right side): P1, k1, yf, k2, sl 1, k2tog, psso, k2, yf, k1, p1.

2nd row: K1, p9, k1.

3rd row: P1, k2, yf, k1, sl 1, k2tog, psso, k1, yf, k2, p1.

4th row: As 2nd row.

5th row: P1, k3, yf, sl 1, k2tog, psso, yf, k3, p1.

6th row: As 2nd row.

Rep these 6 rows.

Vandyke Lace Panel I

Worked over 17 sts on a background of st st.

1st row (right side): *K2tog, yf, k1, yf, sl 1, k1, psso*, k3, yf, sl 1, k1, psso, k2, rep from * to * once more.

2nd row: Purl.

3rd row: [K2tog, yf, k1, yf, sl 1, k1, psso, k1] twice, k2tog, yf, k1, yf, sl 1, k1, psso.

4th row: Purl.

5th row: *K2tog, yf, k1, yf, sl 1, k1, psso*, k2tog, yf, k3, yf, sl 1, k1, psso, rep from * to * once more.

6th row: Purl.

Rep these 6 rows.

Vandyke Lace Panel II

Worked over 9 sts on a background of st st.

1st row (right side): K4, yf, sl 1, k1, psso, k3.

2nd and every alt row: Purl.

3rd row: K2, k2tog, yf, k1, yf, sl 1, k1, psso, k2.

5th row: K1, k2tog, yf, k3, yf, sl 1, k1, psso, k1.

7th row: K2tog, yf, k5, yf, sl 1, k1, psso.

8th row: Purl.

Rep these 8 rows.

Bear Paw Panel

Worked over 23 sts on a background of st st.

1st row (right side): K2, [p4, k1] 3 times, p4, k2.

2nd row: P2, [k4, p1] 3 times, k4, p2.

3rd row: K1, yf, k1, p2, p2tog, [k1, p4] twice, k1, p2tog, p2, k1, yf, k1.

4th row: P3, k2, p2, k4, p1, k4, p2, k2, p3.

5th row: K2, yf, k1, p3, k1, p2, p2tog, k1, p2tog, p2, k1, p3, k1, yf, k2.

6th row: P4, k3, p1, k2, p3, k2, p1, k3, p4.

7th row: K3, yf, k1, p1, p2tog, [k1, p3] twice, k1, p2tog, p1, k1, yf, k3.

8th row: P5, k1, p2, k3, p1, k3, p2, k1, p5.

9th row: K4, yf, k1, p2, k1, p1, p2tog, k1, p2tog, p1, k1, p2, k1, yf, k4.

10th row: P6, k2, p1, k1, p3, k1, p1, k2, p6.

11th row: K5, yf, k1, p2tog, [k1, p2] twice, k1, p2tog, k1, yf, k5.

12th row: P9, k2, p1, k2, p9.

13th row: K6, yf, k1, p1, k1, [p2tog, k1] twice, p1, k1, yf, k6.

14th row: P8, k1, p5, k1, p8.

Rep these 14 rows.

Lace and Cable Pattern

Worked over 21 sts on a st st background.

Special Abbreviation

CB4F or CB4B (Cable-Back 4 Front or Back) = slip next 2 sts onto a cable needle and hold at front (or back) of work, knit into the back of next 2 sts on left-hand needle, then knit into the back of sts on cable needle.

1st row (right side): P2, [KB1] 4 times, k1, yf, k2tog tbl, k3, k2tog, yf, k1, [KB1] 4 times, p2.

2nd and every alt row: K2, [PB1] 4 times, k1, p7, k1, [PB1] 4 times, k2.

3rd row: P2, [KB1] 4 times, k2, yf, k2tog tbl, k1, k2tog, yf, k2, [KB1] 4 times, p2.

5th row: P2, CB4F (see Special Abbreviation), k3, yf, sl 1, k2tog, psso, yf, k3, CB4B, p2.

7th row: P2, [KB1] 4 times, k9, [KB1] 4 times, p2.

8th row: As 2nd row.

Rep these 8 rows.

Fan Lace Panel

Worked over 11 sts on a background of st st.

1st row (right side): Sl 1, k1, psso, [KB1] 3 times, yf, k1, yf, [KB1] 3 times, k2tog.

2nd and every alt row: Purl.

3rd row: Sl 1, k1, psso, [KB1] twice, yf, k1, yf, sl 1, k1, psso, yf, [KB1] twice, k2tog.

5th row: Sl 1, k1, psso, KB1, yf, k1, [yf, sl 1, k1, psso] twice, yf, KB1, k2tog.

7th row: Sl 1, k1, psso, yf, k1, [yf, sl 1, k1, psso] 3 times, yf, k2tog.

8th row: Purl.

Rep these 8 rows.

Lace Panel Stitches

Lozenge Lace Panel

Worked over 11 sts on a background of st st.

1st row (right side): K1, yf, sl 1, k1, psso, k5, k2tog, yf, k1.
2nd and every alt row: Purl.
3rd row: K2, yf, sl 1, k1, psso, k3, k2tog, yf, k2.
5th row: K3, yf, sl 1, k1, psso, k1, k2tog, yf, k3.
7th row: K4, yf, sl 1, k2tog, psso, yf, k4.
9th row: K3, k2tog, yf, k1, yf, sl 1, k1, psso, k3.
11th row: K2, k2tog, yf, k3, yf, sl 1, k1, psso, k2.
13th row: K1, k2tog, yf, k5, yf, sl 1, k1, psso, k1.
15th row: K2tog, yf, k7, yf, sl 1, k1, psso.
16th row: Purl.
Rep these 16 rows.

Lace Chain Panel

Worked over 10 sts on a background of st st.

1st row (right side): K2, k2tog, yf, k2tog but do not slip from needle, knit the first of these 2 sts again, then slip both sts from needle together, yf, sl 1, k1, psso, k2.
2nd row: Purl.
3rd row: K1, k2tog, yf, k4, yf, sl 1, k1, psso, k1.
4th row: Purl.
5th row: K2tog, yf, k1, k2tog, [yf] twice, sl 1, k1, psso, k1, yf, sl 1, k1, psso.
6th row: P4, k1 into first yf, p1 into 2nd yf, p4.
7th row: K2, yf, sl 1, k1, psso, k2, k2tog, yf, k2.
8th row: Purl.
9th row: K3, yf, sl 1, k1, psso, k2tog, yf, k3.
10th row: Purl.
Rep these 10 rows.

Lace Rib Panel

Worked over 7 sts on a background of reversed st st.

1st row (right side): P1, yon, sl 1, k1, psso, k1, k2tog, yfrn, p1.
2nd row: K1, p5, k1.
3rd row: P1, k1, yf, sl 1, k2tog, psso, yf, k1, p1.
4th row: K1, p5, k1.
Rep these 4 rows.

Openweave Panel

Worked over 11 sts on a background of st st.

1st row (right side): P2, yb, sl 1, k1, psso, yf, k3, yf, k2tog, p2.
2nd row: K2, p7, k2.
3rd row: P2, k2, yf, sl 1, k2tog, psso, yf, k2, p2.
4th row: K2, p7, k2.
Rep these 4 rows.

Arch Lace Panel

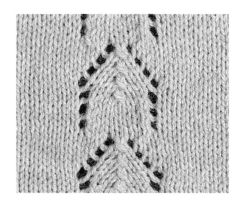

Worked over 11 sts on a background of st st.

1st row (right side): K1, yf, k2tog, k5, sl 1, k1, psso, yf, k1.
2nd and every alt row: Purl.
3rd row: As 1st row.
5th row: As 1st row.
7th row: K1, yf, k3, sl 1, k2tog, psso, k3, yf, k1.
9th row: K2, yf, k2, sl 1, k2tog, psso, k2, yf, k2.
11th row: K3, yf, k1, sl 1, k2tog, psso, k1, yf, k3.
13th row: K4, yf, sl 1, k2tog, psso, yf, k4.
14th row: Purl.
Rep these 14 rows.

Little Lace Panel

Worked on 5 sts on a background of st st.
Note: Sts should not be counted after the 1st or 2nd rows of this pattern.
1st row (right side): K1, yf, k3, yf, k1.
2nd row: Purl.
3rd row: K2, sl 1, k2tog, psso, k2.
4th row: Purl.
Rep these 4 rows.

Quatrefoil Panel

Worked over 15 sts on a background of st st.

Note: Stitches should not be counted after the 6th, 7th, 8th or 9th rows.
1st row (right side): K5, k2tog, yf, k1, yf, sl 1, k1, psso, k5.
2nd row: P4, p2tog tbl, yrn, p3, yrn, p2tog, p4.
3rd row: K3, k2tog, yf, k5, yf, sl 1, k1, psso, k3.

4th row: P2, p2tog tbl, yrn, p1, yrn, p2tog, p1, p2tog tbl, yrn, p1, yrn, p2tog, p2.

5th row: K1, k2tog, yf, k3, yf, k3tog, yf, k3, yf, sl 1, k1, psso, k1.

6th row: P2, yrn, p5, yrn, p1, yrn, p5, yrn, p2.

7th row: [K3, yf, sl 1, k1, psso, k1, k2tog, yf] twice, k3.

8th row: P4, p3tog, yrn, p5, yrn, p3tog, p4.

9th row: K6, yf, sl 1, k1, psso, k1, k2tog, yf, k6.

10th row: P3, p2tog tbl, p2, yrn, p3tog, yrn, p2, p2tog, p3.

Rep these 10 rows.

Eyelet Twigs

Worked over 14 sts on a background of st st.

1st row (right side): K1, yf, k3tog, yf, k3, yf, sl 1, k2tog, psso, yf, k4.

2nd and every alt row: Purl.

3rd row: Yf, k3tog, yf, k5, yf, sl 1, k2tog, psso, yf, k3.

5th row: K5, yf, k3tog, yf, k1, yf, sl 1, k2tog, psso, yf, k2.

7th row: K4, yf, k3tog, yf, k3, yf, sl 1, k2tog, psso, yf, k1.

9th row: K3, yf, k3tog, yf, k5, yf, sl 1, k2tog, psso, yf.

11th row: K2, yf, k3tog, yf, k1, yf, sl 1, k2tog, psso, yf, k5.

12th row: Purl.
Rep these 12 rows.

Diamond Medallion Panel

Worked over 17 sts on a background of st st.

1st row (right side): K6, k2tog, yf, k1, yf, sl 1, k1, psso, k6.

2nd and every alt row: Purl.

3rd row: K5, k2tog, yf, k3, yf, sl 1, k1, psso, k5.

5th row: K4, [k2tog, yf] twice, k1, [yf, sl 1, k1, psso] twice, k4.

7th row: K3, [k2tog, yf] twice, k3, [yf, sl 1, k1, psso] twice, k3.

9th row: K2, [k2tog, yf] 3 times, k1, [yf, sl 1, k1, psso] 3 times, k2.

11th row: K1, [k2tog, yf] 3 times, k3, [yf, sl 1, k1, psso] 3 times, k1.

13th row: [K2tog, yf] 3 times, k5, [yf, sl 1, k1, psso] 3 times.

15th row: K1, [yf, sl 1, k1, psso] 3 times, k3, [k2tog, yf] 3 times, k1.

17th row: K2, [yf, sl 1, k1, psso] 3 times, k1, [k2tog, yf] 3 times, k2.

19th row: K3, [yf, sl 1, k1, psso] twice, yf, sl 1, k2tog, psso, yf, [k2tog, yf] twice, k3.

21st row: K4, [yf, sl 1, k1, psso] twice, k1, [k2tog, yf] twice, k4.

23rd row: K5, yf, sl 1, k1, psso, yf, sl 1, k2tog, psso, yf, k2tog, yf, k5.

25th row: K6, yf, sl 1, k1, psso, k1, k2tog, yf, k6.

27th row: K7, yf, sl 1, k2tog, psso, yf, k7.

28th row: Purl.

Tulip Bud Panel

Worked over 33 sts on a background of garter st.

1st row (wrong side): K16, p1, k16.

2nd row: K14, k2tog, yf, k1, yf, sl 1, k1, psso, k14.

3rd row: K14, p5, k14.

4th row: K13, k2tog, yf, k3, yf, sl 1, k1, psso, k13.

5th row: K13, p7, k13.

6th row: K12, [k2tog, yf] twice, k1, [yf, sl 1, k1, psso] twice, k12.

7th row: K12, p9, k12.

8th row: K11, [k2tog, yf] twice, k3, [yf, sl 1, k1, psso] twice, k11.

9th row: K11, p4, k1, p1, k1, p4, k11.

10th row: K10, [k2tog, yf] twice, k5, [yf, sl 1, k1, psso] twice, k10.

11th row: K10, p4, k2, p1, k2, p4, k10.

12th row: K9, [k2tog, yf] twice, k3, yf, k1, yf, k3, [yf, sl 1, k1, psso] twice, k9. (35 sts)

13th row: K9, p4, k3, p3, k3, p4, k9.

14th row: K1, yf, sl 1, k1, psso, k5, [k2tog, yf] twice, k5, yf, k1, yf, k5, [yf, sl 1, k1, psso] twice, k5, k2tog, yf, k1. (37 sts)

15th row: K1, p2, k5, p4, k4, p5, k4, p4, k5, p2, k1.

16th row: K2, yf, sl 1, k1, psso, k3, [k2tog, yf] twice, k7, yf, k1, yf, k7, [yf, sl 1, k1, psso] twice, k3, k2tog, yf, k2. (39 sts)

17th row: K2, p2, k3, p4, k5, p7, k5, p4, k3, p2, k2.

18th row: K3, yf, sl 1, k1, psso, k1, [k2tog, yf] twice, k9, yf, k1, yf, k9, [yf, sl 1, k1, psso] twice, k1, k2tog, yf, k3. (41 sts)

19th row: K3, p2, k1, p4, k6, p9, k6, p4, k1, p2, k3.

20th row: K4, yf, sl 1, k2tog, psso, yf, k2tog, yf, k7, sl 1, k1, psso, k5, k2tog, k7, yf, sl 1, k1, psso, yf, k3tog, yf, k4. (39 sts)

21st row: K4, p5, k7, p7, k7, p5, k4.

22nd row: K16, sl 1, k1, psso, k3, k2tog, k16. (37 sts)

23rd row: K16, p5, k16.

24th row: K16, sl 1, k1, psso, k1, k2tog, k16. (35 sts)

25th row: K16, p3, k16.

26th row: K16, sl 1, k2tog, psso, k16. (33 sts)

27th row: As 1st row.

Twin Leaf Lace Panel

Worked over 23 sts on a background of st st.

1st row (right side): K8, k2tog, yf, k1, p1, k1, yf, sl 1, k1, psso, k8.

2nd row: P7, p2tog tbl, p2, yon, k1, yfrn, p2, p2tog, p7.

3rd row: K6, k2tog, k1, yf, k2, p1, k2, yf, k1, sl 1, k1, psso, k6.

4th row: P5, p2tog tbl, p3, yrn, p1, k1, p1, yrn, p3, p2tog, p5.

5th row: K4, k2tog, k2, yf, k3, p1, k3, yf, k2, sl 1, k1, psso, k4.

6th row: P3, p2tog tbl, p4, yrn, p2, k1, p2, yrn, p4, p2tog, p3.

7th row: K2, k2tog, k3, yf, k4, p1, k4, yf, k3, sl 1, k1, psso, k2.

8th row: P1, p2tog tbl, p5, yrn, p3, k1, p3, yrn, p5, p2tog, p1.

9th row: K2tog, k4, yf, k5, p1, k5, yf, k4, sl 1, k1, psso.

10th row: P11, k1, p11.

11th row: K11, p1, k11.

12th row: P11, k1, p11.
Rep these 12 rows.

Lace Panel Stitches

Shetland Fern Panel

Worked over 13 sts on a background of st st.

1st row (right side): K6, yf, sl 1, k1, psso, k5.
2nd row: Purl.
3rd row: K4, k2tog, yf, k1, yf, sl 1, k1, psso, k4.
4th row: Purl.
5th row: K3, k2tog, yf, k3, yf, sl 1, k1, psso, k3.
6th row: Purl.
7th row: K3, yf, sl 1, k1, psso, yf, sl 1, k2tog, psso, yf, k2tog, yf, k3.
8th row: Purl.
9th row: K1, k2tog, yf, k1, yf, sl 1, k1, psso, k1, k2tog, yf, k1, yf, sl 1, k1, psso, k1.
10th row: Purl.
11th row: K1, [yf, sl 1, k1, psso] twice, k3, [k2tog, yf] twice, k1.
12th row: P2, [yrn, p2tog] twice, p1, [p2tog tbl, yrn] twice, p2.
13th row: K3, yf, sl 1, k1, psso, yf, sl 1, k2tog, psso, yf, k2tog, yf, k3.
14th row: P4, yrn, p2tog, p1, p2tog tbl, yrn, p4.
15th row: K5, yf, sl 1, k2tog, psso, yf, k5.
16th row: Purl.
Rep these 16 rows.

Staggered Fern Lace Panel

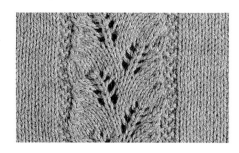

Worked over 20 sts on a background of st st.

1st row (right side): P2, k9, yf, k1, yf, k3, sl 1, k2tog, psso, p2.
2nd and every alt row: Purl.
3rd row: P2, k10, yf, k1, yf, k2, sl 1, k2tog, psso, p2.
5th row: P2, k3tog, k4, yf, k1, yf, k3, [yf, k1] twice, sl 1, k2tog, psso, p2.
7th row: P2, k3tog, k3, yf, k1, yf, k9, p2.

9th row: P2, k3tog, k2, yf, k1, yf, k10, p2.
11th row: P2, k3tog, [k1, yf] twice, k3, yf, k1, yf, k4, sl 1, k2tog, psso, p2.
12th row: Purl.
Rep these 12 rows.

Shetland Eyelet Panel

Worked over 9 sts on a background of st st.

1st row (right side): K2, k2tog, yf, k1, yf, sl 1, k1, psso, k2.
2nd and every alt row: Purl.
3rd row: K1, k2tog, yf, k3, yf, sl 1, k1, psso, k1.
5th row: K1, yf, sl 1, k1, psso, yf, sl 2 knitwise, k1, p2sso, yf, k2tog, yf, k1.
7th row: K3, yf, sl 2 knitwise, k1, p2sso, yf, k3.
8th row: Purl.
Rep these 8 rows.

Travelling Ribbed Eyelet Panel

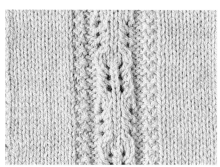

Worked over 13 sts on a background of st st.

1st row (right side): K2, p2, yon, sl 1, k1, psso, k1, k2tog, yfrn, p2, k2.
2nd row: K4, p5, k4.
Rep 1st and 2nd rows twice more.
7th row: K2, p2, k5, p2, k2.
8th row: As 2nd row.
9th row: K2, p2, k2tog, yf, k1, yf, sl 1, k1, psso, p2, k2.
10th row: As 2nd row.
Rep 9th and 10th rows twice more.
15th row: As 7th row.
16th row: As 2nd row.
Rep these 16 rows.

Zigzag Eyelet Panel

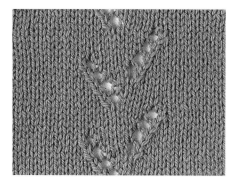

Worked over 11 sts on a background of st st.

1st row (right side): K6, yf, sl 1, k1, psso, k3.
2nd and every alt row: Purl.
3rd row: K7, yf, sl 1, k1, psso, k2.
5th row: K3, k2tog, yf, k3, yf, sl 1, k1, psso, k1.
7th row: K2, k2tog, yf, k5, yf, sl 1, k1, psso.
9th row: K1, k2tog, yf, k8.
11th row: K2tog, yf, k9.
12th row: Purl.
Rep these 12 rows.

Pyramid Lace Panel

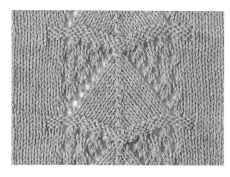

Worked over 25 sts on a background of st st.

1st row (right side): Purl.
2nd row: Knit.
3rd row: K3, yf, k8, sl 1, k2tog, psso, k8, yf, k3.
4th and every following alt row to 18th row: Purl.
5th row: K4, yf, k7, sl 1, k2tog, psso, k7, yf, k4.
7th row: K2, k2tog, yf, k1, yf, k6, sl 1, k2tog, psso, k6, yf, k1, yf, sl 1, k1, psso, k2.
9th row: K6, yf, k5, sl 1, k2tog, psso, k5, yf, k6.
11th row: K3, yf, sl 1, k2tog, psso, yf, k1, yf, k4, sl 1, k2tog, psso, k4, yf, k1, yf, sl 1, k2tog, psso, yf, k3.
13th row: K8, yf, k3, sl 1, k2tog, psso, k3, yf, k8.
15th row: K2, k2tog, yf, k1, yf, sl 1, k2tog, psso, yf, k1, yf, k2, sl 1, k2tog, psso, k2, yf, k1, yf, sl 1, k2tog, psso, yf, k1, yf, sl 1, k1, psso, k2.
17th row: K10, yf, k1, sl 1, k2tog, psso, k1, yf, k10.

19th row: K3, [yf, sl 1, k2tog, psso, yf, k1] 4 times, yf, sl 1, k2tog, psso, yf, k3.
20th row: Knit.
Rep these 20 rows.

Fish Scale Lace Panel

Worked over 17 sts on a background of st st.
1st row (right side): K1, yf, k3, sl 1, k1, psso, p5, k2tog, k3, yf, k1.
2nd row: P6, k5, p6.
3rd row: K2, yf, k3, sl 1, k1, psso, p3, k2tog, k3, yf, k2.
4th row: P7, k3, p7.
5th row: K3, yf, k3, sl 1, k1, psso, p1, k2tog, k3, yf, k3.
6th row: P8, k1, p8.
7th row: K4, yf, k3, sl 1, k2tog, psso, k3, yf, k4.
8th row: Purl.
Rep these 8 rows.

Diamond and Bobble Panel

Worked over 11 sts on a background of reversed st st.
1st row (right side): P1, yon, sl 1, k1, psso, p5, k2tog, yfrn, p1.
2nd row: K2, p1, k5, p1, k2.
3rd row: P2, yon, sl 1, k1, psso, p3, k2tog, yfrn, p2.
4th row: K3, [p1, k3] twice.
5th row: P3, yon, sl 1, k1, psso, p1, k2tog, yfrn, p3.
6th row: K4, p1, k1, p1, k4.
7th row: P4, yon, sl 1, k2tog, psso, yfrn, p4.
8th row: K5, p1, k5.
9th row: P3, k2tog, yfrn, p1, yon, sl 1, k1, psso, p3.

10th row: As 4th row.
11th row: P2, k2tog, yfrn, p3, yon, sl 1, k1, psso, p2.
12th row: As 2nd row.
13th row: P1, k2tog, yfrn, p5, yon, sl 1, k1, psso, p1.
14th row: K1, p1, k7, p1, k1.
15th row: K2tog, yfrn, p3, make bobble as follows: into next st work [k1, yf, k1, yf, k1] turn, p5, turn, k5, turn p2tog, p1, p2tog tbl, turn, sl 1, k2tog, psso, p3, yon, sl 1, k1, psso.
16th row: K1, p1, k3, KB1, k3, p1, k1.
Rep these 16 rows.

Eyelet Twigs and Bobbles

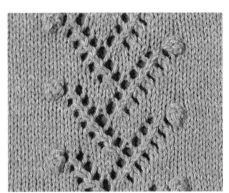

Worked over 16 sts on a background of st st.
1st row (right side): K2, yf, k3tog, yf, k3, yf, sl 1, k2tog, psso, yf, k5.
2nd and every alt row: Purl.
3rd row: K1, yf, k3tog, yf, k5, yf, sl 1, k2tog, psso, yf, k4.
5th row: MB, k5, yf, k3tog, yf, k1, yf, sl 1, k2tog, psso, yf, k3.
7th row: K5, yf, k3tog, yf, k3, yf, sl 1, k2tog, psso, yf, k2.
9th row: K4, yf, k3tog, yf, k5, yf, sl 1, k2tog, psso, yf, MB.
11th row: K3, yf, k3tog, yf, k1, yf, sl 1, k2tog, psso, yf, k6.
12th row: Purl.
Rep these 12 rows.

Challice Cup Panel

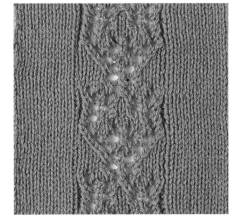

Worked over 13 sts on a background of st st.
Note: Sts should not be counted after the 7th, 8th, 15th or 16th rows of this pattern.
1st row (right side): P1, k3, k2tog, yf, k1, yf, sl 1, k1, psso, k3, p1.
2nd row: K1, p11, k1.
3rd row: P1, k2, k2tog, yf, k3, yf, sl 1, k1, psso, k2, p1.
4th row: As 2nd row.
5th row: P1, k1, k2tog, yf, k1, yf, sl 1, k2tog, psso, yf, k1, yf, sl 1, k1, psso, k1, p1.
6th row: As 2nd row.
7th row: P1, k2tog, yf, k3, yf, k1, yf, k3, yf, sl 1, k1, psso, p1.
8th row: K1, p13, k1.
9th row: P1, k2tog, yf, sl 1, k1, psso, k5, k2tog, yf, sl 1, k1, psso, p1.
10th row: As 2nd row.
11th row: P1, k2tog, yf, k1, yf, sl 1, k1, psso, k1, k2tog, yf, k1, yf, sl 1, k1, psso, p1.
12th row: As 2nd row.
Rep the last 2 rows once more.
15th row: P1, k1, yf, k3, yf, sl 1, k2tog, psso, yf, k3, yf, k1, p1.
16th row: As 8th row.
17th row: P1, k3, k2tog, yf, sl 1, k2tog, psso, yf, sl 1, k1, psso, k3, p1.
18th row: As 2nd row.
Rep these 18 rows.

Lacy Chain

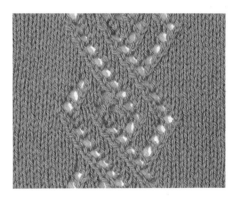

Worked over 16 sts on a background of st st.
1st row (right side): K5, yf, sl 1, k1, psso, k2, yf, sl 1, k1, psso, k5.
2nd and every alt row: Purl.
3rd row: K3, k2tog, yf, k1, yf, sl 1, k1, psso, k2, yf, sl 1, k1, psso, k4.
5th row: K2, k2tog, yf, k3, yf, sl 1, k1, psso, k2, yf, sl 1, k1, psso, k3.
7th row: K1, k2tog, yf, k2, k2tog, yf, k1, yf, sl 1, k1, psso, k2, yf, sl 1, k1, psso, k2.
9th row: K2tog, yf, k2, k2tog, yf, k3, yf, sl 1, k1, psso, k2, yf, sl 1, k1, psso, k1.
11th row: K2, yf, sl 1, k1, psso, k2, sl 1, k1, psso, yf, k2, k2tog, yf, k2tog.
13th row: K3, yf, sl 1, k1, psso, k2, yf, sl 1, k2tog, psso, yf, k2, k2tog, yf, k2.
15th row: K4, yf, sl 1, k1, psso, k2, yf, sl 1, k1, psso, k1, k2tog, yf, k3.
16th row: Purl.
Rep these 16 rows.

Rib Patterns

3-Stitch Twisted Rib

Multiple of 5 + 2
1st row (wrong side): K2, *p3, k2; rep from * to end.
2nd row: P2, *C3, p2; rep from * to end.
Rep these 2 rows.

Broken Rib

Multiple of of 2 + 1
1st row (right side): Knit.
2nd row: P1, *k1, p1; rep from * to end.
Rep these 2 rows.

Embossed Rib

Multiple of 6 + 2
1st row (right side): P2, *KB1, k1, p1, KB1, p2; rep from * to end.
2nd row: K2, *PB1, k1, p1, PB1, k2; rep from * to end.
3rd row: P2, *KB1, p1, k1, KB1, p2; rep from * to end.
4th row: K2, *PB1, p1, k1, PB1, k2; rep from * to end.
Rep these 4 rows.

Corded Rib

Multiple of 4 + 2
1st row: K1, *k2tog tbl, pick up horizontal strand of yarn lying between stitch just worked and next st and knit into back of it, p2; rep from * to last st, k1.
Rep this row.

Moss Rib

Multiple of 4 + 1
1st row: K2, *p1, k3; rep from * to last 3 sts, p1, k2.
2nd row: P1, *k3, p1; rep from * to end.
Rep these 2 rows.

Diagonal Rib

Multiple of 4
1st row (right side): *K2, p2; rep from * to end.
2nd row: As 1st row.
3rd row: K1, *p2, k2; rep from * to last 3 sts, p2, k1.
4th row: P1, *k2, p2; rep from * to last 3 sts, k2, p1.
5th row: *P2, k2; rep from * to end.
6th row: As 5th row.

7th row: As 4th row.
8th row: As 3rd row.
Rep these 8 rows.

Open Twisted Rib

Multiple of 5 + 3
Note: Sts should not be counted after the 2nd or 3rd rows of this pattern.
1st row (wrong side): K1, PB1, k1, *p2, k1, PB1, k1; rep from * to end.
2nd row: P1, KB1, p1, *k1, yf, k1, p1, KB1, p1; rep from * to end.
3rd row: K1, PB1, k1, *p3, k1, PB1, k1; rep from * to end.
4th row: P1, KB1, p1, *k3, pass 3rd st on right-hand needle over first 2 sts, p1, KB1, p1; rep from * to end.
Rep these 4 rows.

Broken Rib Diagonal

Multiple of 6
1st row (right side): *K4, p2; rep from * to end.
2nd row: *K2, p4; rep from * to end.
3rd row: As 1st row.
4th row: As 2nd row.
5th row: K2, *p2, k4; rep from * to last 4 sts, p2, k2.
6th row: P2, *k2, p4; rep from * to last 4 sts, k2, p2.
7th row: As 5th row.
8th row: As 6th row.
9th row: *P2, k4; rep from * to end.
10th row: *P4, k2; rep from * to end.
11th row: As 9th row.
12th row: As 10th row.
Rep these 12 rows.

Piqué Rib

Multiple of 10 + 3

1st row (right side): K3, *p3, k1, p3, k3; rep from * to end.
2nd row: P3, *k3, p1, k3, p3; rep from * to end.
3rd row: As 1st row.
4th row: Knit.
Rep these 4 rows.

Bobble Rib

Multiple of 8 + 3

1st row (right side): K3, *p2, [p1, k1] twice into next st, pass the first 3 of these sts, one at a time, over the 4th st (bobble made), p2, k3; rep from * to end.
2nd row: P3, *k2, p1, k2, p3; rep from * to end.
3rd row: K3, *p2, k1, p2, k3; rep from * to end.
4th row: As 2nd row.
Rep these 4 rows.

Granite Rib

Multiple of 8 + 2

1st row (right side): K2, *[C2F]3 times, k2; rep from * to end.
2nd row: Purl.
3rd row: K2, *[knit 3rd st from left-hand needle, then 2nd st, then 1st stitch, slipping all 3 sts off needle together] twice, k2; rep from * to end.
4th row: Purl.
Rep these 4 rows.

Basket Weave Rib

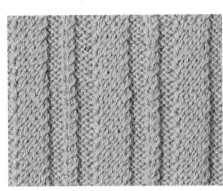

Multiple of 15 + 8

1st row (right side): *P3, k2, p3, k1, [C2F] 3 times; rep from * to last 8 sts, p3, k2, p3.
2nd row: *K3, purl into 2nd st on needle, then purl first st slipping both sts off needle together (called C2P), k3, p1, [C2P] 3 times; rep from * to last 8 sts, k3, C2P, k3.
Rep these 2 rows.

Spiral Rib

Multiple of 6 + 3

1st row (right side): K3, *p3, k3; rep from * to end.
2nd row: P3, *k3, p3; rep from * to end.
3rd row: As 1st row.
4th row: K1, *p3, k3; rep from * to last 2 sts, p2.
5th row: K2, *p3, k3; rep from * to last st, p1.
6th row: As 4th row.
7th row: As 4th row.
8th row: As 5th row.
9th row: As 4th row.
10th row: K3, *p3, k3; rep from * to end.
11th row: As 2nd row.

12th row: As 10th row.
13th row: P2, *k3, p3; rep from * to last st, k1.
14th row: P1, *k3, p3; rep from * to last 2 sts, k2.
15th row: As 13th row.
16th row: As 13th row.
17th row: As 14th row.
18th row: As 13th row.
Rep these 18 rows.

Chain Stitch Rib

Multiple of 3 + 2

1st row (wrong side): K2, *p1, k2; rep from * to end.
2nd row: P2, *k1, p2; rep from * to end.
3rd row: As 1st row.
4th row: P2, *yb, insert needle through centre of st 3 rows below next st on needle and knit this in the usual way, slipping st above off needle at the same time, p2; rep from * to end.
Rep these 4 rows.

Mock Cable Rib

Multiple of 7 + 2

1st row (right side): P2, *C2B, k3, p2; rep from * to end.
2nd and every alt row: K2, *p5, k2; rep from * to end.
3rd row: P2, *k1, C2B, k2, p2; rep from * to end.
5th row: P2, *k2, C2B, k1, p2; rep from * to end.
7th row: P2, *k3, C2B, p2; rep from * to end.
8th row: K2, *p5, k2; rep from * to end.
Rep these 8 rows.

Rib Patterns

Wavy Rib

Multiple of 3 + 1
1st row (wrong side): K1, *p2, k1; rep from * to end.
2nd row: P1, *C2F, p1; rep from * to end.
3rd row: As 1st row.
4th row: P1, *C2B, p1; rep from * to end.
Rep these 4 rows.

Square Rib

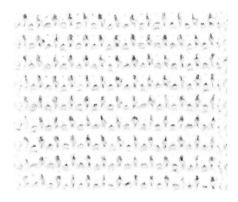

Multiple of 2 + 1
1st row (right side): K2, p1, *k1, p1; rep from * to last 2 sts, k2.
2nd row: K1, *p1, k1; rep from * to end.
3rd row: As 1st row.
4th row: K1, p1, *yb, insert needle through centre of st 2 rows below next st on needle and knit this in the usual way slipping st above off needle at the same time, p1; rep from * to last st, k1.
Rep these 4 rows.

Single Eyelet Rib

Multiple of 5 + 2
1st row (right side): P2, *k3, p2; rep from * to end.
2nd and every alt row: K2, *p3, k2; rep from * to end.
3rd row: P2, *k2tog, yf, k1, p2; rep from * to end.
5th row: As 1st row.
7th row: P2, *k1, yf, sl 1, k1, psso, p2; rep from * to end.
8th row: As 2nd row.
Rep these 8 rows.

Double Eyelet Rib

Multiple of 7 + 2
1st row (right side): P2, *k5, p2; rep from * to end.
2nd row: K2, *p5, k2; rep from * to end.
3rd row: P2, *k2tog, yf, k1, yf, sl 1, k1, psso, p2; rep from * to end.
4th row: As 2nd row.
Rep these 4 rows.

Little Hour Glass Ribbing

Multiple of 4 + 2
Note: Sts should not be counted after 3rd row.
1st row (wrong side): K2, *p2, k2; rep from * to end.
2nd row: P2, *k2tog tbl, then knit same 2 sts tog through front loops, p2; rep from * to end.
3rd row: K2, *p1, yrn, p1, k2; rep from * to end.
4th row: P2, *yb, sl 1, k1, psso, k1, p2; rep from * to end.
Rep these 4 rows.

Fisherman's Rib

Note: Each set of instructions gives the same appearance but a different 'feel'. For example (C) is a firmer fabric than (A).

(A) Multiple of 2 + 1
Foundation row: Knit.
1st row (right side): Sl 1, *K1B, p1; rep from * to end.
2nd row: Sl 1, *p1, K1B; rep from * to last 2 sts, p1, k1.
Rep the last 2 rows only.

(B) Multiple of 2 + 1
Foundation row: Knit.
1st row (right side): Sl 1, *K1B, k1; rep from * to end.
2nd row: Sl 1, *k1, K1B; rep from * to last 2 sts, k2.
Rep the last 2 rows only.

(C) Multiple of 3 + 1
1st row (right side): Sl 1, *k2tog, yfon, sl1 purlwise; rep from * to last 3 sts, k2tog, k1.
2nd row: Sl 1, *yfon, sl 1 purlwise, k2tog (the yfon and sl 1 of previous row); rep from * to last 2 sts, yfon, sl 1 purlwise, k1.
Rep the last 2 rows.

Half Fisherman's Rib

Note: Both sets of instructions give the same appearance but a different 'feel'. (B) is a firmer fabric than (A).
(A) Multiple of 2 + 1
1st row (right side): Sl 1, knit to end.
2nd row: Sl 1, *K1B, p1; rep from * to end.
Rep these 2 rows.

(B) Multiple of 2 + 1
1st row (right side): Sl 1, *p1, k1; rep from * to end.
2nd row: Sl 1, *K1B, p1; rep from * to end.
Rep these 2 rows.

'Faggotted' Rib

Multiple of 4 + 2
1st row: K3, *yf, sl 1, k1, psso, k2; rep from * to last 3 sts, yf, sl 1, k1, psso, k1.
2nd row: P3, *yrn, p2tog, p2; rep from * to last 3 sts, yrn, p2tog, p1.
Rep these 2 rows.

Slipped Rib

Multiple of 2 + 1
1st row (right side): K1, *yf, sl 1 purlwise, yb, k1; rep from * to end.
2nd row: Purl.
Rep these 2 rows.

Contrary Fisherman's Rib

Multiple of 2 + 1
Foundation row: Knit.
1st row (right side): Sl 1, *K1B, k1; rep from * to end.
2nd row: Sl 1, *k1, K1B; rep from * to last 2 sts, k2.

3rd row: As 1st row.
4th row: As 2nd row.
5th row: As 1st row.
6th row: Sl 1,*K1B, k1; rep from * to end.
7th row: As 2nd row.
8th row: As 6th row.
9th row: As 2nd row.
10th row: As 6th row.
Rep the last 10 rows only.

Mock Wavy Cable Rib

Multiple of 4 + 2
1st row (right side): P2, *k2, p2; rep from * to end.
2nd and every alt row: K2, *p2, k2; rep from * to end.
3rd row: P2, *C2B, p2; rep from * to end.
5th row: As 1st row.
7th row: P2, *k2tog but do not slip off needle, then insert right-hand needle between these 2 sts and knit the 1st st again, slipping both sts off needle tog, p2; rep from * to end.
8th row: As 2nd row.
Rep these 8 rows.

Mock Cable - Right

Multiple of 4 + 2
1st row (right side): P2, *k2, p2; rep from * to end.
2nd row: K2, *p2, k2; rep from * to end.
3rd row: P2, *C2F, p2; rep from * to end.
4th row: As 2nd row.
Rep these 4 rows.

Mock Cable - Left

Multiple of 4 + 2
1st row (right side): P2, *k2, p2; rep from * to end.
2nd row: K2, *p2, k2; rep from * to end.
3rd row: P2, *C2B, p2; rep from * to end.
4th row: As 2nd row.
Rep these 4 rows.

Fancy Slip Stitch Rib

Multiple of 5 + 2
1st row (right side): P2, *k1, sl 1 purlwise, k1, p2; rep from * to end.
2nd row: K2, *p3, k2; rep from * to end.
Rep these 2 rows.

Supple Rib

Multiple of 3 + 1
1st row (right side): K1, *knit the next st but do not slip it off the left-hand needle, then purl the same st and the next st tog, k1; rep from * to end.
2nd row: Purl.
Rep these 2 rows.

Rib Patterns

Farrow Rib

Multiple of 3 + 1
1st row (right side): *K2, p1; rep from * to last st, k1.
2nd row: P1, *k2, p1; rep from * to end.
Rep these 2 rows.

Oblique Rib

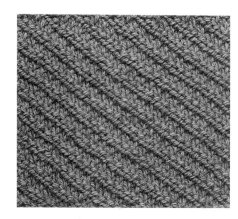

Multiple of 4
1st row (right side): *K2, p2; rep from * to end.
2nd row: K1, *p2, k2; rep from * to last 3 sts, p2, k1.
3rd row: *P2, k2; rep from * to end.
4th row: P1, *k2, p2; rep from * to last 3 sts, k2, p1.
Rep these 4 rows.

Open Chain Ribbing

Multiple of 6 + 2
1st row (wrong side): K2, *p4, k2; rep from * to end.
2nd row: P2, *k2tog, [yf] twice, sl 1, k1, psso, p2; rep from * to end.
3rd row: K2, *p1, purl into front of first yf, purl into back of 2nd yf, p1, k2; rep from * to end.
4th row: P2, *yon, sl 1, k1, psso, k2tog, yfrn, p2; rep from * to end.
Rep these 4 rows.

Beaded Rib

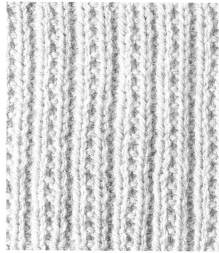

Multiple of 5 + 2
1st row (right side): P2, *k1, p1, k1, p2; rep from * to end.
2nd row: K2, *p3, k2; rep from * to end.
Rep these 2 rows.

Eyelet Mock Cable Ribbing

Multiple of 5 + 2
1st row (right side): P2, *sl 1, k2, psso, p2; rep from * to end.
2nd row: K2, *p1, yrn, p1, k2; rep from * to end.
3rd row: P2, *k3, p2; rep from * to end.
4th row: K2, *p3, k2; rep from * to end.
Rep these 4 rows.

Rib Checks

Multiple of 10 + 5
1st row (right side): P5, *[KB1, p1] twice, KB1, p5; rep from * to end.
2nd row: K5, *[PB1, k1] twice, PB1, k5; rep from * to end.
Rep the last 2 rows once more then the 1st row again.
6th row: [PB1, k1] twice, PB1, *k5, [PB1, k1] twice, PB1; rep from * to end.
7th row: [KB1, p1] twice, KB1, *p5, [KB1, p1] twice, KB1; rep from * to end.
Rep the last 2 rows once more then the 6th row again.
Rep these 10 rows.

Large Eyelet Rib

Multiple of 6 + 2
1st row (right side): *P2, k2tog, [yf] twice, sl 1, k1, psso; rep from * to last 2 sts, p2.
2nd row: K2, *p1, knit into first yf, purl into 2nd yf, p1, k2; rep from * to end.
3rd row: *P2, k4; rep from * to last 2 sts, p2.
4th row: K2, *p4, k2; rep from * to end.
Rep these 4 rows.

Woven Rib

Multiple of 6 + 3

1st row (right side): P3, *sl 1 purlwise, yb, k1, yf, sl 1 purlwise, p3; rep from * to end.
2nd row: K3, *p3, k3; rep from * to end.
3rd row: *P3, k1, yf, sl 1 purlwise, yb, k1; rep from * to last 3 sts, p3.
4th row: As 2nd row.
Rep these 4 rows.

Medallion Rib

Multiple of 8 + 4

1st row (right side): P4, *yb, sl 2 purlwise, C2B, p4; rep from * to end.
2nd row: K4, *yf, sl 2 purlwise, purl the 2nd st on left-hand needle, then the 1st st, slipping both sts from needle tog, k4; rep from * to end.
3rd row: Knit.
4th row: Purl.
Rep these 4 rows.

Twisted Cable Rib

Multiple of 4 + 2

1st row (right side): P2, *k2, p2; rep from * to end.
2nd row: K2, *p2, k2; rep from * to end.
3rd row: P2, *k2tog but do not slip off needle, then insert right-hand needle between these 2 sts and knit the 1st st again, slipping both sts off needle tog, p2; rep from * to end.
4th row: As 2nd row.
Rep these 4 rows.

Uneven Rib

Multiple of 4 + 3

1st row: *K2, p2; rep from * to last 3 sts, k2, p1.
Rep this row.

Puffed Rib

Multiple of 3 + 2

Note: Stitches should only be counted after the 4th row.
1st row (right side): P2, *yon, k1, yfrn, p2; rep from * to end.
2nd row: K2, *p3, k2; rep from * to end.
3rd row: P2, *k3, p2; rep from * to end.
4th row: K2, *p3tog, k2; rep from * to end.
Rep these 4 rows.

Linked Ribs

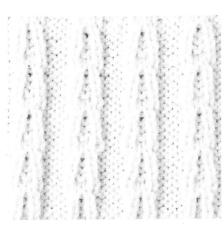

Multiple of 8 + 4

1st row (right side): P4, *k1, p2, k1, p4; rep from * to end.
2nd row: K4, *p1, k2, p1, k4; rep from * to end.
Rep the last 2 rows once more.
5th row: P4, *C2L, C2R, p4; rep from * to end.
6th row: K4, *p4, k4; rep from * to end.
Rep these 6 rows.

Chevron Rib

Multiple of 18 + 1

1st row (right side): P1, *k1, p2, k2, p2, k1, p1; rep from * to end.
2nd row: *K3, p2, k2, p2, k1, [p2, k2] twice; rep from * to last st, k1.
3rd row: *[P2, k2] twice, p3, k2, p2, k2, p1; rep from * to last st, p1.
4th row: *K1, p2, k2, p2, k5, p2, k2, p2; rep from * to last st, k1.
Rep these 4 rows.

Little Chevron Rib

Multiple of 10 + 1

1st row (right side): P1, *k1, p1, [k2, p1] twice, k1, p1; rep from * to end.
2nd row: K1, *p2, [k1, p1] twice, k1, p2, k1; rep from * to end.
3rd row: P1, *k3, p3, k3, p1; rep from * to end.
4th row: K2, *p3, k1, p3, k3; rep from * to last 9 sts, p3, k1, p3, k2.
Rep these 4 rows.

73

Cables

9-Stitch Plait

Down   Up

Downwards Plait
1st row (right side): Knit.
2nd and every alt row: Purl.
3rd row: C6F, k3.
5th row: Knit.
7th row: K3, C6B.
8th row: Purl.
Rep these 8 rows.

Upwards Plait
1st row (right side): Knit.
2nd and every alt row: Purl.
3rd row: C6B, k3.
5th row: Knit.
7th row: K3, C6F.
8th row: Purl.
Rep these 8 rows.

6-Stitch Plait

Down   Up

Downwards Plait
1st row (right side): C4F, k2.
2nd row: Purl.
3rd row: K2, C4B.
4th row: Purl.
Rep these 4 rows.

Upwards Plait
1st row (right side): C4B, k2.
2nd row: Purl.
3rd row: K2, C4F.
4th row: Purl.
Rep these 4 rows.

4-Stitch Cable I

1st row (right side): Knit.
2nd row: Purl.
3rd row: C4B.
4th row: Purl.
Rep these 4 rows.
The cable as given above twists to the right. To work the 4 st cable twisted to the left work C4F instead of C4B in the 3rd row.

4-Stitch Cable II

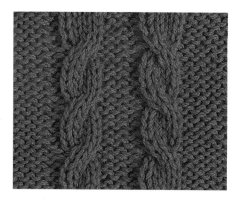

1st row (right side): Knit.
2nd row: Purl.
Rep the last 2 rows once more.
5th row: C4B.
6th row: Purl.
Rep these 6 rows.
The cable as given above twists to the right. To work the 4 st cable twisted to the left, work C4F instead of C4B in the 5th row.

6-Stitch Cable

1st row (right side): Knit.
2nd row: Purl.
3rd row: C6B.
4th row: Purl.
Rep these 4 rows.
The cable as given above twists to the right. To work the 6 st cable twisted to the left work C6F instead of C6B in the 3rd row.

8-Stitch Cable

1st row (right side): Knit.
2nd row: Purl.
Rep the last 2 rows once more.
5th row: C8B.
6th row: Purl.
Rep 1st and 2nd rows twice more.
Rep these 10 rows.
The cable as given above twists to the right. To work the 8 st cable twisted to the left, work C8F instead of C8B in the 5th row.

Claw Pattern I

Down   Up
Worked over 8 sts.
Downwards Claw
1st row (right side): Knit.
2nd row: Purl.
3rd row: C4F, C4B.
4th row: Purl.
Rep these 4 rows.

Upwards Claw
1st row (right side): Knit.
2nd row: Purl.
3rd row: C4B, C4F.
4th row: Purl.
Rep these 4 rows.

Claw Pattern II

Down   Up

Worked over 9 sts.

Downwards Claw
1st row (right side): Knit.
2nd row: Purl.
3rd row: C4L, k1, C4R.
4th row: Purl.
Rep these 4 rows.

Upwards Claw
1st row (right side): Knit.
2nd row: Purl.
3rd row: C4R, k1, C4L.
4th row: Purl.
Rep these 4 rows.

Double Cable

Down   Up

Worked over 12 sts.

Downwards Cable
1st row (right side): Knit.
2nd row: Purl.
3rd row: C6F, C6B.
4th row: Purl.
Rep 1st and 2nd rows twice more.
Rep these 8 rows.

Upwards Cable
1st row (right side): Knit.
2nd row: Purl.
3rd row: C6B, C6F.
4th row: Purl.
Rep 1st and 2nd rows twice more.
Rep these 8 rows.

Small Double Cable

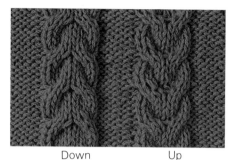

Down   Up

Worked over 8 sts

Downwards Cable
1st row (right side): Knit.
2nd row: Purl.
Rep the last 2 rows once more.
5th row: C4F, C4B.
6th row: Purl.
Rep these 6 rows.

Upwards Cable
1st row (right side): Knit.
2nd row: Purl.
Rep the last 2 rows once more.
5th row: C4B, C4F.
6th row: Purl.
Rep these 6 rows.

Braid Cable

Worked over 9 sts on a background of reversed st st.
1st row (right side): T2L, p2, T2R, T2L, p1.
2nd row: K1, [PB1, k2] twice, PB1, k1.
3rd row: P1, T2L, T2R, p2, T2L.
4th row: PB1, k4, [PB1] twice, k2.
5th row: P2, slip next st onto cable needle and hold at back of work, KB1 from left hand needle, then KB1 from cable needle, p4, KB1.
6th row: As 4th row.
7th row: P1, T2R, T2L, p2, T2R.
8th row: As 2nd row.
9th row: T2R, p2, T2L, T2R, p1.
10th row: K2, [PB1] twice, k4, PB1.
11th row: KB1, p4, slip next st onto cable needle and hold at front of work, KB1 from left-hand needle, then KB1 from cable needle, p2.
12th row: As 10th row.
Rep these 12 rows.

Round Cable

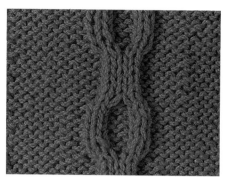

Worked over 8 sts.
1st row (right side): P2, k4, p2.
2nd row: K2, p4, k2.
Rep the last 2 rows once more.
5th row: T4B, T4F.
6th row: P2, k4, p2.
7th row: As 2nd row.
Rep the last 2 rows once more then the 6th row again.
11th row: T4F, T4B.
12th row: As 2nd row.
Rep these 12 rows.

Triple Rib Cable

Worked over 5 sts.

Cable to the Right
1st row (right side): KB1, [p1, KB1] twice.
2nd row: PB1, [k1, PB1] twice.
Rep these 2 rows twice more.

7th row: Slip first 2 sts onto a cable needle and hold at back of work, work [KB1, p1, KB1] from left-hand needle, then work [p1, KB1] from cable needle.
8th row: As 2nd row.
Rep 1st and 2nd rows 3 times more.
Rep these 14 rows.

Cable to the Left
1st row (right side): KB1, [p1, KB1] twice.
2nd row: PB1, [k1, PB1] twice.
Rep these 2 rows twice more.

7th row: Slip first 3 sts onto a cable needle and hold at front of work, work [KB1, p1] from left-hand needle, then work [KB1, p1, KB1] from cable needle.
8th row: As 2nd row.
Rep 1st and 2nd rows 3 times more.
Rep these 14 rows.

Cables

Claw Pattern with Bobbles

Worked over 9 sts.
Downwards Claw
1st row (right side): C4L, k1, C4R.
2nd row: Purl.
3rd row: K4, k into front, back and front of next st, [turn, k3] twice, slip 2nd and 3rd sts of this group over first st, k4.
4th row: Purl.
Rep these 4 rows.
Bobbles may be added to the Upwards Claw in the same way.

9-Stitch Cable

1st row (right side): Knit.
2nd row: Purl.
Rep the last 2 rows once more.
5th row: C9B.
6th row: Purl.
Rep 1st and 2nd rows 3 times more.
Rep these 12 rows.
The cable as given above twists to the right. To work the 9 st cable twisted to the left, work C9F instead of C9B in the 5th row.

13-Stitch Claw Pattern

Down   Up

Downwards Claw
1st row (right side): Knit.
2nd row: Purl.
3rd row: C6F, k1, C6B.
4th row: Purl.
Rep these 4 rows.

Upwards Claw
1st row (right side): Knit.
2nd row: Purl.
3rd row: C6B, k1, C6F.
4th row: Purl.
Rep these 4 rows.

Folded Cable

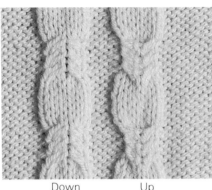

Down   Up

Worked over 6 sts.
Downwards Cable
1st row (right side): Knit.
2nd row: Purl.
Rep the last 2 rows once more.
5th row: C3L, C3R.
6th row: Purl.
Rep the last 2 rows twice more, then work 1st and 2nd rows once more.
Rep these 12 rows.

Upwards Cable
1st row (right side): Knit.
2nd row: Purl.
Rep the last 2 rows once more.
5th row: C3R, C3L.
6th row: Purl.
Rep the last 2 rows twice more, then work 1st and 2nd rows once more.
Rep these 12 rows.

Open Cable with Bobbles

Worked over 5 sts on a background of reversed st st.
Special Abbreviations
T5R (Twist 5 Right) = slip next 4 sts onto cable needle and hold at back of work, k1 from left-hand needle, then p3, k1 from cable needle.
T5L (Twist 5 Left) = slip next st onto cable needle and hold at front of work, k1, p3 from left-hand needle, then knit st from cable needle.
1st row (right side): T5R.
2nd row: P1, k3, p1.
3rd row: K1, p3, k1.
Rep 2nd and 3rd rows once more then 2nd row again.
7th row: K1, p1, MB, p1, k1.
Rep 2nd and 3rd rows twice more, then 2nd row again.
Rep these 12 rows.
The cable as given above twists to the right. To work the cable twisted to the left, work T5L instead of T5R in the 1st row.

Little Pearl Cable

Worked over 4 sts.
1st row (right side): C2F, C2B.
2nd row: Purl.
3rd row: C2B, C2F.
4th row: Purl.
Rep these 4 rows.

4-Stitch Snakey Cable

1st row (right side): Knit.
2nd row: Purl.
3rd row: C4B.
4th row: Purl.
Rep 1st and 2nd rows once more.
7th row: C4F.
8th row: Purl.
Rep these 8 rows.

Double Snakey Cable

Worked over 8 sts.
1st row (right side): Knit.
2nd row: Purl.
3rd row: C4B, C4F.
4th row: Purl.
Rep 1st and 2nd rows once more.
7th row: C4F, C4B.
8th row: Purl.
Rep these 8 rows.

Giant Cable

Worked over 12 sts.
1st row (right side): Knit.
2nd row: Purl.
Rep the last 2 rows once more.
5th row: C12B.
6th row: Purl.
Rep the 1st and 2nd rows once more.
Rep these 8 rows.
The cable as given above twists to the right. To work the 12 st cable twisted to the left, work C12F instead of C12B in the 5th row.

Wave Cable

Worked over 6 sts.
1st row (right side): Knit.
2nd row: Purl.
3rd row: C6B.
4th row: Purl.
Now work 1st and 2nd rows twice more.
9th row: C6F.
10th row: Purl.
Now work 1st and 2nd rows once more.
Rep these 12 rows.

Striped Medallion Cable

Worked over 15 sts on a background of reversed st st.
1st row (right side): Knit into the back of every st.
2nd row: Purl into the back of every st.
3rd row: C6F but working into back of sts, [KB1] 3 times, C6B working into the back of sts.
4th row: Purl into the back of every st.
Now work 1st and 2nd rows twice more.
9th row: C6B as before, [KB1] 3 times, C6F as before.
10th row: As 2nd row.
Now work 1st and 2nd rows 3 times more.
Rep these 16 rows.

Oxo Cable

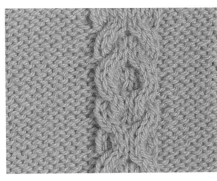

Worked over 8 sts on a background of reversed st st.
1st row (right side): Knit.
2nd row and every alt row: Purl.
3rd row: C4F, C4B.
5th row: Knit.
7th row: C4B, C4F.
9th row: Knit.
11th row: C4B, C4F.
13th row: Knit.
15th row: C4F, C4B.
16th row: Purl.
Rep these 16 rows.

Honeycomb Cable

Worked over 12 sts on a background of reversed st st.
1st row (right side): K4, C2F, C2B, k4.
2nd and every alt row: Purl.
3rd row: K2, [C2F, C2B] twice, k2.
5th row: [C2F, C2B] 3 times.
7th row: [C2B, C2F] 3 times.
9th row: K2, [C2B, C2F] twice, k2.
11th row: K4, C2B, C2F, k4.
12th row: Purl.
Rep these 12 rows.

Chain Cable

Worked over 9 sts.
1st row (right side): P2, T5R, p2.
2nd row: K2, p2, k1, p2, k2.
3rd row: P1, T3B, p1, T3F, p1.
4th row: K1, p2, k3, p2, k1.
5th row: T3B, p3, T3F.
6th row: P2, k5, p2.
7th row: K2, p5, k2.
8th row: As 6th row.
9th row: T3F, p3, T3B.
10th row: As 4th row.
11th row: P1, T3F, p1, T3B, p1.
12th row: As 2nd row.
Rep these 12 rows.
The cable as given above twists to the right. To work the cable twisted to the left, work T5L instead of T5R in the 1st row.

Cables

Rib Twist Cable

Worked over 9 sts.

Special Abbreviations

T4BR (Twist 4 Back Right) = slip next st onto cable needle and hold at back of work, KB1, p1, KB1 from left-hand needle, then purl st from cable needle.

T4FL (Twist 4 Front Left) = slip next 3 sts onto cable needle and hold at front of work, p1 from left-hand needle, then KB1, p1, KB1 from cable needle.

T7L (Twist 7 Left) = slip next 3 sts onto cable needle and hold at front of work, [KB1, p1] twice from left-hand needle, then KB1, p1, KB1 from cable needle.

T7R (Twist 7 Right) = slip next 4 sts onto cable needle and hold at back of work, KB1, p1, KB1 from left-hand needle, then [p1, KB1] twice from cable needle.

1st row (right side): T4BR, p1, T4FL.
2nd row: PB1, k1, PB1, k3, PB1, k1, PB1.
3rd row: KB1, p1, KB1, p3, KB1, p1, KB1.
4th row: As 2nd row.
5th row: T4FL, p1, T4BR.
6th row: [K1, PB1] 4 times, k1.
7th row: P1, T7L, p1.
8th row: As 6th row.
Rep these 8 rows.
The cable as given above twists to the left. To work the cable twisted to the right, work T7R instead of T7L in the 7th row.

Medallion Cable

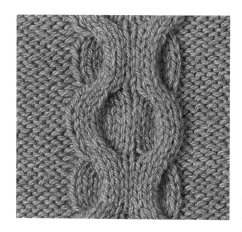

Worked over 13 sts.
1st row (right side): Knit.

2nd row: Purl.
Rep the last 2 rows once more.
5th row: C6F, k1, C6B.
6th row: As 2nd row.
7th row: As 1st row.
Rep the last 2 rows twice more.
12th row: As 2nd row.
13th row: C6B, k1, C6F.
14th row: As 2nd row.
15th row: As 1st row.
16th row: As 2nd row.
Rep these 16 rows.

Staghorn Cable I

Worked over 16 sts.
Foundation row: Purl.
1st row (right side): K4, C4B, C4F, k4.
2nd and 4th rows: Purl.
3rd row: K2, C4B, k4, C4F, k2.
5th row: C4B, k8, C4F.
6th row: Purl.
Rep these 6 rows.

Staghorn Cable II

Worked over 16 sts.
Foundation row: Purl.
1st row (right side): C4F, k8, C4B.
2nd and 4th rows: Purl.
3rd row: K2, C4F, k4, C4B, k2.
5th row: K4, C4F, C4B, k4.
6th row: Purl.
Rep these 6 rows.

Figure-of-eight Cable

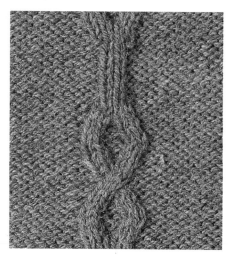

Worked over 8 sts.
1st row (right side): P3, k2, p3.
2nd row: K3, p2, k3.
3rd row: P2, k4, p2.
4th row: K2, p4, k2.
5th row: P1, T3B, T3F, p1.
6th row: K1, p2, k2, p2, k1.
7th row: T3B, p2, T3F.
8th row: As 3rd row.
9th row: T3F, p2, T3B.
10th row: As 6th row.
11th row: P1, T3F, T3B, p1.
12th row: As 4th row.
13th row: P2, C4B, p2.
14th row: As 4th row.
Rep 5th-12th rows once more.
23rd row: P3, k2, p3.
24th row: K3, p2, k3.
Rep the last 2 rows twice more.
Rep these 28 rows.
The cable as given above twists to the right. To work the figure of 8 cable twisted to the left, work C4F instead of C4B in the 13th row.

Braided Cable

Worked over 9 sts on a background of reversed st st.

1st row: T3F, T3B, T3F.
2nd row: P2, k2, p4, k1.
3rd row: P1, C4B, p2, k2.
4th row: As 2nd row.
5th row: T3B, T3F, T3B.

6th row: K1, p4, k2, p2.
7th row: K2, p2, C4F, p1.
8th row: As 6th row.
Rep these 8 rows.

Giant Oxo Cable

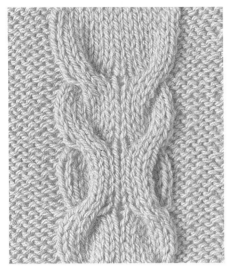

Worked over 13 sts.
1st Foundation row (right side): Knit.
2nd Foundation row: Purl.
Rep the last 2 rows once more.
1st row: C6B, k1, C6F.
2nd row: Purl.
3rd row: Knit.
Rep the last 2 rows twice more.
8th row: As 2nd row.
Rep the last 8 rows once more.
17th row: C6F, k1, C6B.
18th row: As 2nd row.
19th row: As 3rd row.
Rep the last 2 rows twice more.
24th row: As 2nd row.
Rep the last 8 rows once more.
Rep these 32 rows.

Cable With Bobbles

Worked over 9 sts.
1st row (right side): P2, T5R, p2.
2nd row: K2, p2, k1, p2, k2.
3rd row: P1, T3B, p1, T3F, p1.
4th row: K1, p2, k3, p2, k1.
5th row: T3B, p3, T3F.
6th row: P2, k5, p2.

7th row: K2, p2, MB, p2, k2.
8th row: As 6th row.
9th row: T3F, p3, T3B.
10th row: As 4th row.
11th row: P1, T3F, p1, T3B, p1.
12th row: As 2nd row.
Rep these 12 rows.
Bobbles may also be added to this cable twisted to the left.

Oxo Ripple

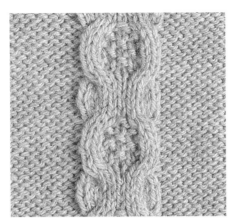

Worked over 9 sts.
1st row (right side): C4B, k1, C4F.
2nd row: P2, [k1, p1] twice, k1, p2.
3rd row: K3, p1, k1, p1, k3.
Rep the 2nd and 3rd rows once more then the 2nd row again.
7th row: C4F, k1, C4B.
8th row: Purl.
9th row: Knit.
Rep 8th and 9th rows once more.
12th row: Purl.
Rep these 12 rows.

8-Stitch Snakey Cable

1st row (right side): Knit.
2nd row: Purl.
3rd row: C8B.
4th row: Purl.
Rep 1st and 2nd rows twice more.
9th row: C8F.
10th row: Purl.
Rep 1st and 2nd rows once.
Rep these 12 rows.

Slipped 5-Stitch Cable Plait

Down   Up

Downwards Plait
1st row (right side): Sl 1 purlwise, k4.
2nd row: P4, sl 1 purlwise.
3rd row: C3L, k2.
4th row: Purl.
5th row: K4, sl 1 purlwise.
6th row: Sl 1 purlwise, p4.
7th row: K2, C3R.
8th row: Purl.
Rep these 8 rows.

Upwards Plait
1st row (right side): K2, sl 1 purlwise, k2.
2nd row: P2, sl 1 purlwise, p2.
3rd row: K2, C3L.
4th row: Purl.
Rep 1st and 2nd rows once.
7th row: C3R, k2.
8th row: Purl.
Rep these 8 rows.

Slipped Wavy Cable

Worked over 3 sts.
1st row (right side): Sl 1 purlwise, k2.
2nd row: P2, sl 1 purlwise.
3rd row: C3L.
4th row: Purl.
5th row: K2, sl 1 purlwise.
6th row: Sl 1 purlwise, p2.
7th row: C3R.
8th row: Purl.
Rep these 8 rows.

Cables

6-Stitch Slipped Double Cable

Down   Up

Downwards Cable
1st row (right side): Sl 1 purlwise, k4, sl 1 purlwise.
2nd row: Sl 1 purlwise, p4, sl 1 purlwise.
Rep the last 2 rows once more.
5th row: C3L, C3R.
6th row: Purl.
Rep these 6 rows.

Upwards Cable
1st row (right side): K2, [sl 1 purlwise] twice, k2.
2nd row: P2, [sl 1 purlwise] twice, p2.
Rep the last 2 rows once more.
5th row: C3R, C3L.
6th row: Purl.
Rep these 6 rows.

Slipped 3-Stitch Cable

Slipped to the Left
1st row (right side): Sl 1 purlwise, k2.
2nd row: P2, sl 1 purlwise.
3rd row: C3L.
4th row: Purl.
Rep these 4 rows.

Slipped to the Right
1st row (right side): K2, sl 1 purlwise.
2nd row: Sl 1 purlwise, p2.
3rd row: C3R.
4th row: Purl.
Rep these 4 rows.

Slipped Double Chain

Worked over 7 sts.
1st row (right side): Sl 1 purlwise, k5, sl 1 purlwise.
2nd row: Sl 1 purlwise, p5, sl 1 purlwise.
3rd row: C3L, k1, C3R.
4th row: Purl.
5th row: K2, sl 1 purlwise, k1, sl 1 purlwise, k2.
6th row: P2, sl 1 purlwise, p1, sl 1 purlwise, p2.
7th row: C3R, k1, C3L.
8th row: Purl.
Rep these 8 rows.

12-Stitch Plait

Down   Up

Downwards Plait
1st row (right side): Knit.
2nd and every alt row: Purl.
3rd row: C8F, k4.
5th and 7th rows: Knit.
9th row: K4, C8B.
11th row: Knit.
12th row: Purl.
Rep these 12 rows.

Upwards Plait
1st row (right side): Knit.
2nd row and every alt row: Purl.
3rd row: C8B, k4.
5th and 7th rows: Knit.
9th row: K4, C8F.
11th row: Knit.
12th row: Purl.
Rep these 12 rows.

Medallion Moss Cable

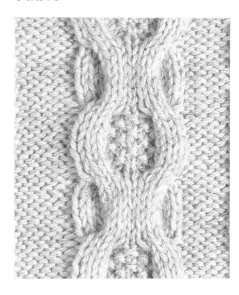

Worked over 13 sts.
1st row (right side): K4, [p1, k1] 3 times, k3.
2nd row: P3, [k1, p1] 4 times, p2.
Rep the last 2 rows once more.
5th row: C6F, k1, C6B.
6th row: Purl.
7th row: Knit.
Rep the last 2 rows twice more.
12th row: Purl.
13th row: C6B, k1, C6F.
14th row: As 2nd row.
15th row: As 1st row.
16th row: As 2nd row.
Rep these 16 rows.

6-Stitch Spiral Cable

1st row (right side): [C2F] 3 times.
2nd row: Purl.
3rd row: K1, [C2F] twice, k1.
4th row: Purl.
Rep these 4 rows.

Alternated Cable

Worked over 10 sts on a background of reversed st st.

1st row (right side): P1, k8, p1.
2nd row: K1, p8, k1.
3rd row: P1, C4B, C4F, p1.
4th row: K1, p2, k4, p2, k1.
5th row: T3B, p4, T3F.
6th row: P2, k6, p2.
7th row: K2, p6, k2.
Work the 6th and 7th rows once more, then 6th row again.
11th row: T3F, p4, T3B.
12th row: As 4th row.
13th row: P1, C4F, C4B, p1.
14th row: K1, p8, k1.
15th row: P1, C4B, C4F, p1.
16th row: K1, p8, k1.
17th row: P1, k8, p1.
Work the 14th, 15th and 16th rows once more.
Rep these 20 rows.

Trellis with Bobbles

Worked over 23 sts on a background of reversed st st.

1st row (wrong side): P2, k7, p2, k1, p2, k7, p2.
2nd row: K2, p3, make bobble as follows: — knit into front, back, front, back and front of next st, [turn and p5, turn and k5] twice, then pass 2nd, 3rd, 4th and 5th sts over the first st (bobble completed), p3, C5B, p3, make bobble as before, p3, k2.
3rd row: As 1st row.
4th row: T3F, p5, T3B, p1, T3F, p5, T3B.
5th row: K1, p2, k5, p2, k3, p2, k5, p2, k1.
6th row: P1, T3F, p3, T3B, p3, T3F, p3, T3B, p1.
7th row: K2, p2, k3, p2, k5, p2, k3, p2, k2.
8th row: P2, T3F, p1, T3B, p5, T3F, p1, T3B, p2.
9th row: K3, p2, k1, p2, k7, p2, k1, p2, k3
10th row: P3, C5F, p3, make bobble as before, p3, C5F, p3.
11th row: As 9th row.
12th row: P2, T3B, p1, T3F, p5, T3B, p1, T3F, p2.
13th row: As 7th row.
14th row: P1, T3B, p3, T3F, p3, T3B, p3, T3F, p1.
15th row: As 5th row.
16th row: T3B, p5, T3F, p1, T3B, p5, T3F.
Rep these 16 rows.

Framed Basket Weave

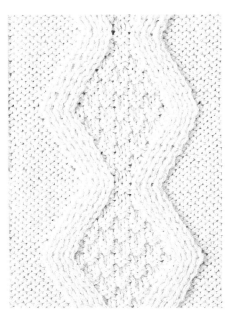

Worked over 24 sts on a background of reversed st st.

1st row (right side): P5, [T2B] 3 times, k2, [T2F] 3 times, p5.
2nd row: K5, [p1, k1] twice, p2, k2, p2, [k1, p1] twice, k5.
3rd row: P4, [T2B] 3 times, k1, p2, k1, [T2F] 3 times, p4.
4th row: K4, [p1, k1] twice, p1, k2, p2, k2, [p1, k1] twice, p1, k4.

5th row: P3, [T2B] 3 times, p2, k2, p2, [T2F] 3 times, p3.
6th row: K3, [p1, k1] 3 times, p2, k2, p2, [k1, p1] 3 times, k3.
7th row: P2, [T2B] 3 times, p1, k2, p2, k2, p1, [T2F] 3 times, p2.
8th row: K2, [p1, k1] twice, p3, k2, p2, k2, p3, [k1, p1] twice, k2.
9th row: P1, [T2B] 3 times, [k2, p2] twice, k2, [T2F] 3 times, p1.
10th row: K1, [p1, k1] twice, [p2, k2] 3 times, p2, [k1, p1] twice, k1.
11th row: [T2B] 3 times, k1, [p2, k2] twice, p2, k1, [T2F] 3 times.
12th row: [P1, k1] twice, p1, [k2, p2] 3 times, k2, [p1, k1] twice, p1.
13th row: [T2F] 3 times, p1, [k2, p2] twice, k2, p1, [T2B] 3 times.
14th row: As 10th row.
15th row: P1, [T2F] 3 times, [p2, k2] twice, p2, [T2B] 3 times, p1.
16th row: As 8th row.
17th row: P2, [T2F] 3 times, k1, p2, k2, p2, k1, [T2B] 3 times, p2.
18th row: As 6th row.
19th row: P3, [T2F] 3 times, k2, p2, k2, [T2B] 3 times, p3.
20th row: As 4th row.
21st row: P4, [T2F] 3 times, p1, k2, p1, [T2B] 3 times, p4.
22nd row: As 2nd row.
23rd row: P5, [T2F] 3 times, p2, [T2B] 3 times, p5.
24th row: K6, [p1, k1] twice, p4, [k1, p1] twice, k6.
Rep these 24 rows.

Honeycomb Pattern

Worked over a multiple of 8 sts. The example shown is worked over 24 sts.

1st row (right side): *C4B, C4F; rep from * to end of panel.
2nd row: Purl.
3rd row: Knit.
4th row: Purl.
5th row: *C4F, C4B; rep from * to end of panel.
6th row: Purl.
7th row: Knit.
8th row: Purl.
Rep these 8 rows.

Cables

Cabled Moss Stitch

Worked over 13 sts on a background of reversed st st.

1st row (right side): P3, T3B, k1, T3F, p3.
2nd row: K3, p2, k1, p1, k1, p2, k3.
3rd row: P2, T3B, k1, p1, k1, T3F, p2.
4th row: K2, p2, [k1, p1] twice, k1, p2, k2.
5th row: P1, T3B, [k1, p1] twice, k1, T3F, p1.
6th row: K1, p2, [k1, p1] 3 times, k1, p2, k1.
7th row: T3B, [k1, p1] 3 times, k1, T3F.
8th row: P2, [k1, p1] 4 times, k1, p2.
9th row: K3, [p1, k1] 3 times, p1, k3.
10th row: P3, [k1, p1] 3 times, k1, p3.
11th row: T3F, [k1, p1] 3 times, k1, T3B.
12th row: K1, p3, [k1, p1] twice, k1, p3, k1.
13th row: P1, T3F, [k1, p1] twice, k1, T3B, p1.
14th row: K2, p3, k1, p1, k1, p3, k2.
15th row: P2, T3F, k1, p1, k1, T3B, p2.
16th row: K3, p3, k1, p3, k3.
17th row: P3, T3F, k1, T3B, p3.
18th row: K4, p5, k4.
19th row: P4, T5R, p4.
20th row: K4, p2, k1, p2, k4.
21st row: P3, T3B, p1, T3F, p3.
22nd row: [K3, p2] twice, k3.
23rd row: [P3, k2] twice, p3.
24th row: As 22nd row.
25th row: P3, T3F, p1, T3B, p3.
26th row: As 20th row.
27th row: As 19th row.
28th row: As 20th row.
Rep these 28 rows.

Cable and Dot

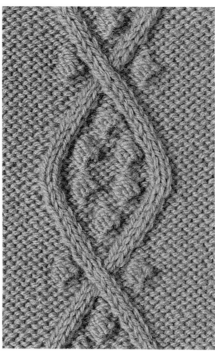

Worked over 15 sts on a background of reversed st st.

1st row (wrong side): K2, k into front, back, front, back and front of next st (bobble made), k2, p2, k1, p2, k2, make bobble in next st as before, k2.
2nd row: P2, k5tog tbl (completing bobble), p2, C5F, p2, k5tog tbl, p2.
3rd row: K5, p2, k1, p2, k5.
4th row: P4, T3B, p1, T3F, p4.
5th row: K4, p2, k3, p2, k4.
6th row: P3, T3B, p3, T3F, p3.
7th row: K3, p2, k2, make bobble in next st (as on 1st row), k2, p2, k3.
8th row: P2, T3B, p2, k5tog tbl, p2, T3F, p2.
9th row: K2, p2, k7, p2, k2.
10th row: P1, T3B, p7, T3F, p1.
11th row: K1, p2, k2, make bobble in next st, k3, make bobble in next st, k2, p2, k1.
12th row: T3B, p2, k5tog tbl, p3, k5tog tbl, p2, T3F.
13th row: P2, k11, p2.
14th row: K2, p11, k2.
15th row: P2, k3, make bobble in next st, k3, make bobble in next st, k3, p2.
16th row: T3F, p2, k5tog tbl, p3, k5tog tbl, p2, T3B.
17th row: K1, p2, k9, p2, k1.
18th row: P1, T3F, p7, T3B, p1.
19th row: K2, p2, k3, make bobble in next st, k3, p2, k2.
20th row: P2, T3F, p2, k5tog tbl, p2, T3B, p2.
21st row: K3, p2, k5, p2, k3.
22nd row: P3, T3F, p3, T3B, p3.
23rd row: K4, p2, k3, p2, k4.
24th row: P4, T3F, p1, T3B, p4.
Rep these 24 rows.
The cable as given above twists to the left. To work the cable twisted to the right, work C5B instead of C5F on the 2nd row.

Little Lattice

Worked over a multiple of 6 sts (minimum 12) on a background of reversed st st. The example shown is worked over 18 sts.

1st row (right side): P1, *T2B, T2F, p2; rep from * to 5 sts before end of panel, T2B, T2F, p1.
2nd row: K1, *p1, k2; rep from * to 2 sts before end of panel, p1, k1.
3rd row: *T2B, p2, T2F; rep from * to end of panel.
4th row: P1, *k4, C2P; rep from * to 5 sts before end of panel, k4, p1.
5th row: *T2F, p2, T2B; rep from * to end of panel.
6th row: As 2nd row.
7th row: P1, *T2F, T2B, p2; rep from * to 5 sts before end of panel, T2F, T2B, p1.
8th row: K2, *C2P, k4; rep from * to 4 sts before end of panel, C2P, k2.
Rep these 8 rows.

Wave and Dot

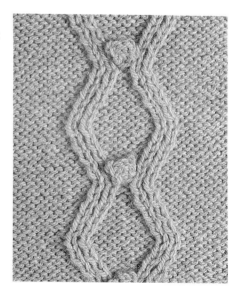

Worked over 15 sts on a background of reversed st st.

1st row (right side): P3, [T2B] twice, make bobble as follows:– k into front,

82

back and front of next st, [turn and k3, turn and p3] twice, then slip 2nd and 3rd sts of this group over first st (bobble completed), [T2F] twice, p3.

2nd row: K3, [p1, k1, p1, k3] twice.

3rd row: P2, [T2B] twice, p3, [T2F] twice, p2.

4th row: K2, p1, k1, p1, k5, p1, k1, p1, k2.

5th row: P1, [T2B] twice, p5, [T2F] twice, p1.

6th row: [K1, p1] twice, k7, [p1, k1] twice.

7th row: [T2B] twice, p7, [T2F] twice.

8th row: P1, k1, p1, k9, p1, k1, p1.

9th row: [T2F] twice, p7, [T2B] twice.

10th row: As 6th row.

11th row: P1, [T2F] twice, p5, [T2B] twice, p1.

12th row: As 4th row.

13th row: P2, [T2F] twice, p3, [T2B] twice, p2.

14th row: As 2nd row.

15th row: P3, [T2F] twice, p1, [T2B] twice, p3.

16th row: K4, [p1, k1] 3 times, p1, k4.
Rep these 16 rows.

Sloping Diamonds

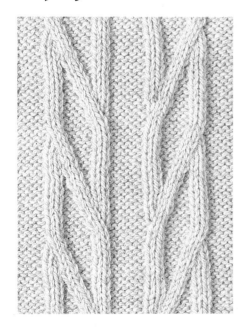

Worked over 10 sts.
Slope to the Right
1st row (right side): K2, p5, C3B.

2nd row: P3, k5, p2.

3rd row: K2, p4, C3B, k1.

4th row: P4, k4, p2.

5th row: K2, p3, T3B, k2.

6th row: P2, k1, p2, k3, p2.

7th row: K2, p2, T3B, p1, k2.

8th row: P2, [k2, p2] twice.

9th row: K2, p1, T3B, p2, k2.

10th row: P2, k3, p2, k1, p2.

11th row: K2, T3B, p3, k2.

12th row: P2, k4, p4.

13th row: K1, T3B, p4, k2.

14th row: P2, k5, p3.

15th row: T3B, p5, k2.

16th row: P2, k6, p2.
Rep these 16 rows.

Slope to the Left
1st row (right side): C3F, p5, k2.

2nd row: P2, k5, p3.

3rd row: K1, C3F, p4, k2.

4th row: P2, k4, p4.

5th row: K2, T3F, p3, k2.

6th row: P2, k3, p2, k1, p2.

7th row: K2, p1, T3F, p2, k2.

8th row: P2, [k2, p2] twice.

9th row: K2, p2, T3F, p1, k2.

10th row: P2, k1, p2, k3, p2.

11th row: K2, p3, T3F, k2.

12th row: P4, k4, p2.

13th row: K2, p4, T3F, k1.

14th row: P3, k5, p2.

15th row: K2, p5, T3F.

16th row: P2, k6, p2.
Rep these 16 rows.

Fishernet Pattern

Worked over a multiple of 8 sts (minimum 16 sts) on a background of reversed st st. The example shown is worked over 24 sts.
1st row (right side): P1, *T3F, T3B, p2; rep from * to 7 sts before end of panel, T3F, T3B, p1.

2nd row: K2, *p4, k4; rep from * to 6 sts before end of panel, p4, k2.

3rd row: P2, *C4F, p4; rep from * to 6 sts before end of panel, C4F, p2.

4th row: As 2nd row.

5th row: P1, *T3B, T3F, p2; rep from * to 7 sts before end of panel, T3B, T3F, p1.

6th row: K1, *p2, k2; rep from * to 3 sts before end of panel, p2, k1.
Rep the last 6 rows once more.

13th row: *T3B, p2, T3F; rep from * to end of panel.

14th row: P2, *k4, p4; rep from * to 6 sts before end of panel, k4, p2.

15th row: K2, *p4, C4B; rep from * to 6 sts before end of panel, p4, k2.

16th row: As 14th row.

17th row: K2, p3, *T3B, T3F, p2; rep from * to 3 sts before end of panel, p1, k2.

18th row: P2, k3, *p2, k2; rep from * to 3 sts before end of panel, k1, p2.

19th row: K2, p3, *T3F, T3B, p2; rep from * to 3 sts before end of panel, p1, k2.

20th row: As 14th row.

21st row: As 15th row.

22nd row: As 14th row.

23rd row: *T3F, p2, T3B; rep from * to end of panel.

24th row: As 6th row.
Rep these 24 rows.

In and Out

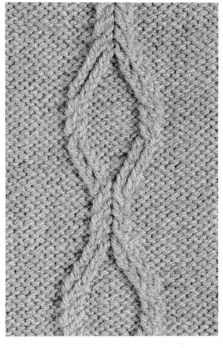

Worked over 12 sts on a background of reversed st st.
1st row (right side): P3, T3L, T3R, p3.

2nd row: K3, PB1, k1, [PB1] twice, k1, PB1, k3.

3rd row: P2, [T2R] twice, [T2L] twice, p2.

4th row: [K2, PB1, k1, PB1] twice, k2.

5th row: P1, [T2R] twice, p2, [T2L] twice, p1.

6th row: [K1, PB1] twice, k4, [PB1, k1] twice.

7th row: [T2R] twice, p4, [T2L] twice.

8th row: PB1, k1, PB1, k6, PB1, k1, PB1.

9th row: T3L, p6, T3R.
Rep the 8th and 9th rows twice more, then 8th row again.

15th row: [T2L] twice, p4, [T2R] twice.

16th row: As 6th row.

17th row: P1, [T2L] twice, p2, [T2R] twice, p1.

18th row: As 4th row.

19th row: P2, [T2L] twice, [T2R] twice, p2.

20th row: As 2nd row.

21st row: P3, T3L, T3R, p3.

22nd row: As 2nd row.
Rep the last 2 rows once more
Rep these 24 rows.

Cables

Arrow Rib

Worked over 15 sts on a background of reversed st st.
1st row (right side): KB1, p1, T2F, p3, KB1, p3, T2B, p1, KB1.
2nd row: P1, k2, p1, [k3, p1] twice, k2, p1.
3rd row: KB1, p2, T2F, p2, KB1, p2, T2B, p2, KB1.
4th row: P1, k3, p1, [k2, p1] twice, k3, p1.
5th row: KB1, p3, T2F, p1, KB1, p1, T2B, p3, KB1.
6th row: P1, k4, p1, [k1, p1] twice, k4, p1.
7th row: KB1, p4, T2F, KB1, T2B, p4, KB1.
8th row: P1, k1, p1, k4, p1, k4, p1, k1, p1.
Rep these 8 rows.

Waving Rib

Worked over 20 sts on a background of reversed st st.
1st row (right side): [P2, T3B] twice, [T3F, p2] twice.
2nd row: K2, p2, k3, p2, k2, p2, k3, p2, k2.
3rd row: P1, [T3B, p2] twice, T3F, p2, T3F, p1.

4th row: K1, p2, k3, p2, k4, p2, k3, p2, k1.
5th row: [T3B, p2] twice, [p2, T3F] twice.
6th row: P2, k3, p2, k6, p2, k3, p2.
7th row: [T3F, p2] twice, [p2, T3B] twice.
8th row: As 4th row.
9th row: P1, [T3F, p2] twice, T3B, p2, T3B, p1.
10th row: As 2nd row.
11th row: [P2, T3F] twice, [T3B, p2] twice.
12th row: K3, p2, k3, p4, k3, p2, k3.
Rep these 12 rows.

Disappearing Cable

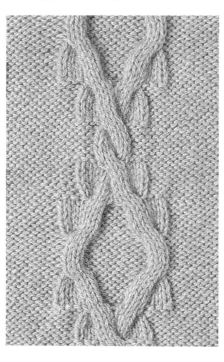

Worked over 18 sts on a background of reversed st st.
1st row (right side): P6, k6, p6.
2nd row: K6, p6, k6.
3rd row: P3, k3, C6F, k3, p3.
4th row: K3, p12, k3.
5th row: P3, k12, p3.
Work 4th and 5th rows once more, then 4th row again.
9th row: K3, T6B, T6F, k3.
10th row: P6, k6, p6.
11th row: K6, p6, k6.
Work 10th and 11th rows once more then 10th row again.
15th row: T6B, p6, T6F.
16th row: P3, k12, p3.
17th row: K3, p12, k3.
Work 16th and 17th rows once more then 16th row again.
21st row: C6F, p6, C6B.
Work 10th and 11th rows twice then 10th row again.
27th row: P3, C6F, C6B, p3.
Work 4th and 5th rows twice then 4th row again.
33rd row: P6, C6F, p6.

34th row: As 2nd row.
35th row: As 1st row.
36th row: As 2nd row.
Rep these 36 rows.

Open and Closed Cable

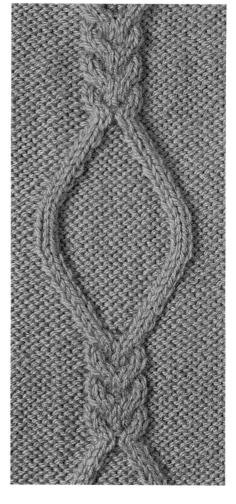

Worked over 18 sts on a background of reversed st st.
1st row (right side): P5, C4B, C4F, p5.
2nd row: K5, p2, k4, p2, k5.
3rd row: P4, T3B, p4, T3F, p4.
4th row: K4, p2, k6, p2, k4.
5th row: P3, T3B, p6, T3F, p3.
6th row: K3, p2, k8, p2, k3.
7th row: P2, T3B, p8, T3F, p2.
8th row: K2, p2, k10, p2, k2.
9th row: P1, T3B, p10, T3F, p1.
10th row: K1, p2, k12, p2, k1.
11th row: T3B, p12, T3F.
12th row: P2, k14, p2.
13th row: K2, p14, k2.
Work 12th and 13th rows once more, then 12th row again.
17th row: T3F, p12, T3B.
18th row: As 10th row.
19th row: P1, T3F, p10, T3B, p1.
20th row: As 8th row.
21st row: P2, T3F, p8, T3B, p2.
22nd row: As 6th row.

23rd row: P3, T3F, p6, T3B, p3.
24th row: As 4th row.
25th row: P4, T3F, p4, T3B, p4.
26th row: As 2nd row.
27th row: P5, C4F, C4B, p5.
28th row: K5, p8, k5.
29th row: P5, C4B, C4F, p5.
30th row: As 28th row.
31st row: P5, k8, p5.
Rep the last 4 rows twice more.
40th row: As 28th row.
Rep these 40 rows.

Framed Moss Stitch

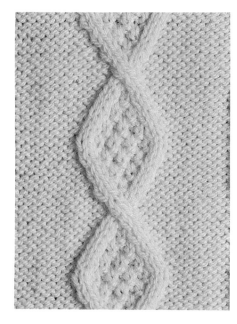

Worked over 13 sts on a background of reversed st st.

1st row (right side): P4, C5F, p4.
2nd row: K4, p2, k1, p2, k4.
3rd row: P3, T3B, k1, T3F, p3.
4th row: K3, p2, k1, p1, k1, p2, k3.
5th row: P2, T3B, k1, p1, k1, T3F, p2.
6th row: K2, p2, [k1, p1] twice, k1, p2, k2.
7th row: P1, T3B, [k1, p1] twice, k1, T3F, p1.
8th row: K1, p2, [k1, p1] 3 times, k1, p2, k1.
9th row: T3B, [k1, p1] 3 times, k1, T3F.
10th row: P2, [k1, p1] 4 times, k1, p2.
11th row: T3F, [p1, k1] 3 times, p1, T3B.
12th row: K1, p2, [k1, p1] 3 times, k1, p2, k1.
13th row: P1, T3F [p1, k1] twice, p1, T3B, p1.
14th row: K2, p2, [k1, p1] twice, k1, p2, k2.
15th row: P2, T3F, p1, k1, p1, T3B, p2.
16th row: K3, p2, k1, p1, k1, p2, k3.
17th row: P3, T3F, p1, T3B, p3.
18th row: K4, p2, k1, p2, k4.
Rep these 18 rows.
The cable as given above twists to the left. To work the cable twisted to the right, work C5B instead of C5F in the 1st row.

Double Cable and Moss

Worked over 17 sts on a background of reversed st st.

1st row (right side): P4, T4R, p1, T4L, p4.
2nd row: K4, p2, [k1, p1] twice, k1, p2, k4.
3rd row: P3, T3B, [k1, p1] twice, k1, T3F, p3.
4th row: K3, p2, [k1, p1] 3 times, k1, p2, k3.
5th row: P2, T3B, [k1, p1] 3 times, k1, T3F, p2.
6th row: K2, p2, [k1, p1] 4 times, k1, p2, k2.
7th row: P1, T3B, [k1, p1] 4 times, k1, T3F, p1.
8th row: K1, p2, [k1, p1] 5 times, k1, p2, k1.
9th row: T3B, [k1, p1] 5 times, k1, T3F.
10th row: P2, [k1, p1] 6 times, k1, p2.
11th row: T3F, [p1, k1] 5 times, p1, T3B.
12th row: As 8th row.
13th row: P1, T3F, [p1, k1] 4 times, p1, T3B, p1.
14th row: As 6th row.
15th row: P2, T3F, [p1, k1] 3 times, p1, T3B, p2.
16th row: As 4th row.
17th row: P3, T3F, [p1, k1] twice, p1, T3B, p3.
18th row: As 2nd row.
19th row: P4, C4F, p1, C4B, p4.

20th row: K4, p4, k1, p4, k4.
21st row: P4, C4B, p1, C4F, p4.
22nd row: As 20th row.
23rd row: P4, k4, p1, k4, p4.
Rep the last 4 rows once more.
28th row: As 20th row.
Rep these 28 rows.

Moss Stitch Hearts

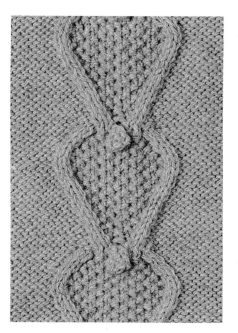

Worked over 19 sts.

1st row (right side): P6, T3B, k1, T3F, p6.
2nd row: K6, p3, k1, p3, k6.
3rd row: P5, C3B, p1, k1, p1, C3F, p5.
4th row: K5, p2, [k1, p1] twice, k1, p2, k5.
5th row: P4, T3B, [k1, p1] twice, k1, T3F, p4.
6th row: K4, p3, [k1, p1] twice, k1, p3, k4.
7th row: P3, C3B, [p1, k1] 3 times, p1, C3F, p3.
8th row: K3, p2, [k1, p1] 4 times, k1, p2, k3.
9th row: P2, T3B, [k1, p1] 4 times, k1, T3F, p2.
10th row: K2, p3, [k1, p1] 4 times, k1, p3, k2.
11th row: P1, C3B, [p1, k1] 5 times, p1, C3F, p1.
12th row: K1, p2, [k1, p1] 6 times, k1, p2, k1.
13th row: T3B, [k1, p1] 6 times, k1, T3F.
14th row: P3, [k1, p1] 6 times, k1, p3.
15th row: K2, [p1, k1] 7 times, p1, k2.
16th row: As 14th row.
17th row: T4F, [p1, k1] 5 times, p1, T4B.
18th row: K2, p3, [k1, p1] 4 times, k1, p3, k2.
19th row: P2, T4F, [p1, k1] 3 times, p1, T4B, p2.
20th row: K7, p2, K1, p2, K7.
Rep these 20 rows.
Bobbles may be knitted into this pattern by working the 19th row as follows:— P2, T4F, p1, k1, p1, MB, p1, k1, p1, T4B, p2.

Cables

Bobbles and Waves

Worked over 26 sts on a background of reversed st st.

1st row (right side): P2, T3B, p5, C6B, p5, T3F, p2.

2nd row: K2, p2, k6, p6, k6, p2, k2.

3rd row: P1, T3B, p4, T5B, T5F, p4, T3F, p1.

4th row: K1, p2, k5, p3, k4, p3, k5, p2, k1.

5th row: T3B, p3, T5B, p4, T5F, p3, T3F.

6th row: P2, k1, make bobble as follows:— knit into front, back and front of next st, [turn and knit these 3 sts] 3 times, then turn and sl 1, k2tog, psso (bobble completed), k2, p3, k8, p3, k2, make bobble as before, k1, p2.

7th row: T3F, p3, k3, p8, k3, p3, T3B.

8th row: K1, p2, k3, p3, k8, p3, k3, p2, k1.

9th row: P1, T3F, p2, T5F, p4, T5B, p2, T3B, p1.

10th row: K2, p2, [k4, p3] twice, k4, p2, k2.

11th row: P2, T3F, p3, T5F, T5B, p3, T3B, p2.

12th row: K1, make bobble as before, k1, p2, k5, p6, k5, p2, k1, make bobble, k1.
Rep these 12 rows.

Twist And Bobble

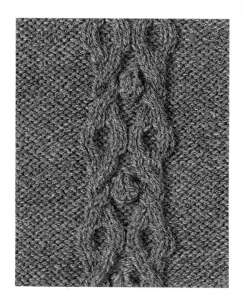

Worked over 16 sts on a background of reversed st st.

1st row (right side): P2, k4, p4, k4, p2.

2nd row: K2, p4, k4, p4, k2.

3rd row: P2, C4F, p4, C4B, p2.

4th row: As 2nd row.

5th row: P2, k4, p1, make bobble as follows:— [k1, p1, k1] into each of the next 2 sts, turn and p6, turn and k1, sl 1, k1, psso, k2tog, k1, turn, [p2tog] twice, turn, k2 (bobble completed), p1, k4, p2.

6th row: As 2nd row.

7th row: As 3rd row.

8th row: As 2nd row.

9th row: As 1st row.

10th row: As 2nd row.

11th row: [T4B, T4F] twice.

12th row: P2, k4, p4, k4, p2.

13th row: As 2nd row.

14th row: As 12th row.

15th row: [T4F, T4B] twice.

16th row: As 2nd row.
Rep these 16 rows.

Framed Cable

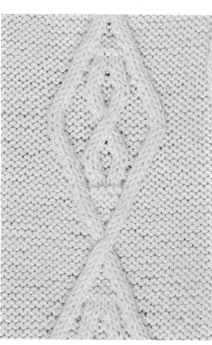

Worked over 20 sts on a background of reversed st st.

1st row (wrong side): K8, p4, k8.

2nd row: P8, C4B, p8.

3rd row: As 1st row.

4th row: P7, T3B, T3F, p7.

5th row: K7, p2, k2, p2, k7.

6th row: P6, T3B, p2, T3F, p6.

7th row: K6, p2, k4, p2, k6.

8th row: P5, T3B, p4, T3F, p5.

9th row: K5, p2, k6, p2, k5.

10th row: P4, T3B, p1, k4, p1, T3F, p4.

11th row: K4, p2, k2, p4, k2, p2, k4.

12th row: P3, T3B, p1, T3B, T3F, p1, T3F, p3.

13th row: K3, p2, [k2, p2] 3 times, k3.

14th row: P2, T3B, p1, T3B, p2, T3F, p1, T3F, p2.

15th row: [k2, p2] twice, k4, [p2, k2] twice.

16th row: P1, T3B, p2, T3F, p2, T3B, p2, T3F, p1.

17th row: K1, p2, k4, p2, k2, p2, k4, p2, k1.

18th row: [T3B, p4, T3F] twice.

19th row: P2, k6, p4, k6, p2.

20th row: K2, p6, C4B, p6, k2.

21st row: P2, k6, p4, k6, p2.

22nd row: [T3F, p4, T3B] twice.

23rd row: As 17th row.

24th row: P1, T3F, p2, T3B, p2, T3F, p2, T3B, p1.

25th row: As 15th row.

26th row: P2, T3F, p1, T3F, p2, T3B, p1, T3B, p2.

27th row: As 13th row.

28th row: P3, T3F, p1, T3F, T3B, p1, T3B, p3.

29th row: As 11th row.

30th row: P4, T3F, p6, T3B, p4.

31st row: As 9th row.

32nd row: P5, T3F, p4, T3B, p5.

33rd row: As 7th row.

34th row: P6, T3F, p2, T3B, p6.

35th row: As 5th row.

36th row: P7, T3F, T3B, p7.
Rep these 36 rows.

Garter Stitch Cable

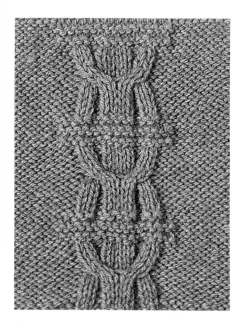

Worked over 16 sts on a background of reversed st st.

1st row (right side): P2, k2, p2, k4, p2, k2, p2.

2nd row: K2, p2, k2, p4, k2, p2, k2.
Rep these 2 rows twice more.

7th row: P2, T6R, T6L, p2.

8th row: As 2nd row.

9th row: As 1st row.

10th row: As 2nd row.

11th row: As 1st row.

12th, 13th, 14th, 15th and 16th rows: Knit.
Rep these 16 rows.

Woven Cable

Worked over a multiple of 8 + 4 sts on a background of reversed st st (minimum 20 sts). The example shown is worked over 28 sts.

1st row (right side): Knit.

2nd and every alt row: K2, purl to 2 sts before end of panel, k2.

3rd row: Knit.

5th row: K2, *C8B; rep from * to 2 sts before end of panel, k2.

7th row: Knit.

9th row: Knit.

11th row: K6, *C8F; rep from * to 6 sts before end of panel, k6.

12th row: As 2nd row.

Rep these 12 rows.

Lantern Rib

Worked over 20 sts on a background of reversed st st.

1st row (right side): P8, C2B, C2F, p8.

2nd row: K7, T2F, p2, T2B, k7.

3rd row: P6, T2B, C2B, C2F, T2F, p6.

4th row: K5, T2F, k1, p4, k1, T2B, k5.

5th row: P4, T2B, p1, T2B, k2, T2F, p1, T2F, p4.

6th row: K3, T2F, k2, p1, k1, p2, k1, p1, k2, T2B, k3.

7th row: P2, T2B, p2, T2B, p1, k2, p1, T2F, p2, T2F, p2.

8th row: K2, p1, k3, p1, k2, p2, k2, p1, k3, p1, k2.

9th row: P1, T2B, p2, T2B, p2, k2, p2, T2F, p2, T2F, p1.

10th row: K1, [p1, k3] twice, p2, [k3, p1] twice, k1.

11th row: T2B, [p2, T2B] twice, [T2F, p2] twice, T2F.

12th row: P1, [k3, p1] twice, k2, [p1, k3] twice, p1.

13th row: [K1, p3] twice, k1, p2, [k1, p3] twice, k1.

14th row: As 12th row.

15th row: T2F, [p2, T2F] twice, [T2B, p2] twice, T2B.

16th row: As 10th row.

17th row: P1, [T2F, p2] twice, k2, [p2, T2B] twice, p1.

18th row: As 8th row.

19th row: [P2, T2F] twice, p1, k2, p1, [T2B, p2] twice.

20th row: K3, T2B, k2, p1, k1, p2, k1, p1, k2, T2F, k3.

21st row: P4, T2F, p1, T2F, k2, T2B, p1, T2B, p4.

22nd row: K5, T2B, k1, p4, k1, T2F, k5.

23rd row: P6, [T2F] twice, [T2B] twice, p6.

24th row: K7, T2B, p2, T2F, k7.

25th row: P8, T2F, T2B, p8.

26th row: K9, p2, k9.

27th row: P9, k2, p9.

28th row: As 26th row.

Rep these 28 rows.

Inserted Cable

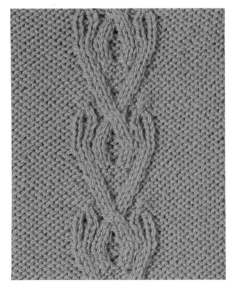

Worked over 14 sts on a background of reversed st st.

1st row (wrong side): K5, p4, k5.

2nd row: P5, C4F, p5.

3rd row: K5, p4, k5.

4th row: P4, T3B, T3F, p4.

5th row: K4, p2, k2, p2, k4.

6th row: P3, T3B, p2, T3F, p3.

7th row: K3, p2, k4, p2, k3.

8th row: P2, T3B, p4, T3F, p2.

9th row: K2, p2, k6, p2, k2.

10th row: P1, [T3B] twice, [T3F] twice, p1.

11th row: [K1, p2] twice, k2, [p2, k1] twice.

12th row: [T3B] twice, p2, [T3F] twice.

13th row: P2, k1, p2, k4, p2, k1, p2.

14th row: K1, T2F, T3F, p2, T3B, T2B, k1.

15th row: [P1, k1] twice, p2, k2, p2, [k1, p1] twice.

16th row: K1, p1, T2F, T3F, T3B, T2B, p1, k1.

17th row: P1, k2, p1, k1, p4, k1, p1, k2, p1.

18th row: T2F, T2B, p1, C4F, p1, T2F, T2B.

19th row: K1, C2B, k2, p4, k2, C2F, k1.

Rep from 4th row.

Bell Cable

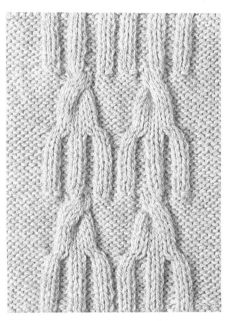

Worked over 26 sts on a background of reversed st st.

1st row (right side): K2, [p3, k2] twice, p2, [k2, p3] twice, k2.

2nd row: P2, [k3, p2] twice, k2, p2, [k3, p2] twice.

Rep these 2 rows 4 times more.

11th row: T5FL, k2, T5BR, p2, T5FL, k2, T5BR.

12th row: K3, p6, k8, p6, k3.

13th row: P3, k6, p8, k6, p3.

Rep these last 2 rows twice more, then the 12th row again.

19th row: P3, C6F, p8, C6B, p3.

20th row: K3, p6, k8, p6, k3.

Rep these 20 rows.

Cables

Wide Cable Panel

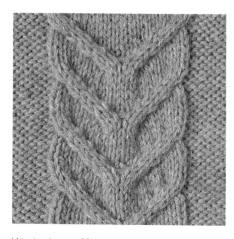

Worked over 20 sts on a background of reversed st st.

1st and every alt row (wrong side): Purl.
2nd row: K6, C4B, C4F, k6.
4th row: K4, C4B, k4, C4F, k4.
6th row: K2, C4B, k8, C4F, k2.
8th row: C4B, k12, C4F.
Rep these 8 rows.

Double Waves

Worked over 16 sts on a background of reversed st st.

1st row (right side): K2, p3, k2, p2, k2, p3, k2.
2nd row: P2, k3, p2, k2, p2, k3, p2.
3rd row: T3F, p2, T3F, T3B, p2, T3B.
4th row: K1, p2, k3, p4, k3, p2, k1.
5th row: P1, T3F, p2, C4F, p2, T3B, p1.
6th row: K2, p2, k2, p4, k2, p2, k2.
7th row: P2, [T3F, T3B] twice, p2.
8th row: K3, p4, k2, p4, k3.
9th row: P3, C4F, p2, C4F, p3.
10th row: K3, p4, k2, p4, k3.
11th row: P2, [T3B, T3F] twice, p2.
12th row: K2, p2, k2, p4, k2, p2, k2.
13th row: P1, T3B, p2, C4F, p2, T3F, p1.
14th row: K1, p2, k3, p4, k3, p2, k1.
15th row: T3B, p2, T3B, T3F, p2, T3F.
16th row: P2, k3, p2, k2, p2, k3, p2.
17th-32nd rows: Rep rows 1-16 inclusive but working C4B instead of C4F in the 5th, 9th and 13th rows.
Rep these 32 rows.

Framed Leaves

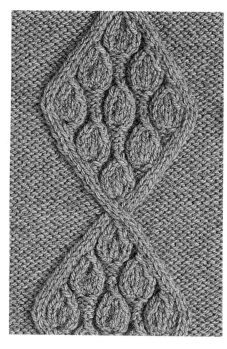

Worked over 21 sts on a background of reversed st st.

Note: Sts should only be counted after the 1st, 2nd, 33rd and 34th rows of this pattern.

1st row (right side): P8, T5L, p8.
2nd row: K8, p2, k1, p2, k8.
3rd row: P7, T3B, M5 (knit into front, back, front, back and front of next st), T3F, p7.
4th row: K7, p2, k1, p5, k1, p2, k7.
5th row: P6, T3B, p1, k5, p1, T3F, p6.
6th row: K6, p2, k2, p5, k2, p2, k6.
7th row: P5, T3B, p2, k2tog tbl, k1, k2tog, p2, T3F, p5.
8th row: K5, p2, k3, p3, k3, p2, k5.
9th row: P4, T3B, M5, p2, sl 1, k2tog, psso, p2, M5, T3F, p4.
10th row: K4, p2, k1, p5, k2, p1, k2, p5, k1, p2, k4.

11th row: P3, T3B, p1, k5, p5, k5, p1, T3F, p3.
12th row: K3, p2, k2, p5, k5, p5, k2, p2, k3.
13th row: P2, T3B, p2, k2tog tbl, k1, k2tog, p5, k2tog tbl, k1, k2tog, p2, T3F, p2.
14th row: K2, p2, k3, p3, k5, p3, k3, p2, k2.
15th row: P1, T3B, [M5, p2, sl 1, k2tog, psso, p2] twice, M5, T3F, p1.
16th row: K1, p2, k1, [p5, k2, p1, k2] twice, p5, k1, p2, k1.
17th row: T3B, p1, [k5, p5] twice, k5, p1, T3F.
18th row: P2, k2, [p5, k5] twice, p5, k2, p2.
19th row: T3F, p1, [k2tog tbl, k1, k2tog, p5] twice, k2tog tbl, k1, k2tog, p1, T3B.
20th row: K1, p2, k1, [p3, k5] twice, p3, k1, p2, k1.
21st row: P1, T3F, [sl 1, k2tog, psso, p2, M5, p2] twice, sl 1, k2tog, psso, T3B, p1.
22nd row: K2, p3, k2, p5, k2, p1, k2, p5, k2, p3, k2.
23rd row: P2, T3F, p2, k5, p5, k5, p2, T3B, p2.
24th row: K3, p2, k2, p5, k5, p5, k2, p2, k3.
25th row: P3, T3F, p1, k2tog tbl, k1, k2tog, p5, k2tog tbl, k1, k2tog, p1, T3B, p3.
26th row: K4, p2, k1, p3, k5, p3, k1, p2, k4.
27th row: P4, T3F, sl 1, k2tog, psso, p2, M5, p2, sl 1, k2tog, psso, T3B, p4.
28th row: K5, p3, k2, p5, k2, p3, k5.
29th row: P5, T3F, p2, k5, p2, T3B, p5.
30th row: K6, p2, k2, p5, k2, p2, k6.
31st row: P6, T3F, p1, k2tog tbl, k1, k2tog, p1, T3B, p6.
32nd row: K7, p2, k1, p3, k1, p2, k7.
33rd row: P7, T3F, sl 1, k2tog, psso, T3B, p7.
34th row: K8, p5, k8.

Rep these 34 rows.

Cupped Cable

Worked over 15 sts on a background of reversed st st.

1st row (right side): P5, T5L, p5.

88

2nd row: K5, p2, k1, p2, k5.
3rd row: P4, T3B, k1, T3F, p4.
4th row: K4, p2, k1, p1, k1, p2, k4.
5th row: P3, T3B, k1, p1, k1, T3F, p3.
6th row: K3, p2, [k1, p1] twice, k1, p2, k3.
7th row: P2, T3B, [k1, p1] twice, k1, T3F, p2.
8th row: K2, p2, [k1, p1] 3 times, k1, p2, k2.
9th row: P1, T3B, [k1, p1] 3 times, k1, T3F, p1.
10th row: K1, p2, [k1, p1] 4 times, k1, p2, k1.
11th row: T3B, [k1, p1] 4 times, k1, T3F.
12th row: P2, [k1, p1] 5 times, k1, p2.
Rep these 12 rows.

Big and Little Cable

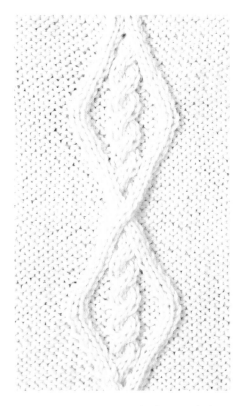

Worked over 16 sts on a background of reversed st st.
1st row (right side): P6, C4B, p6.
2nd row: K6, p4, k6.
3rd row: P5, C3B, C3F, p5.
4th row: K5, p6, k5.
5th row: P4, C3B, k2, C3F, p4.
6th row: K4, p8, k4.
7th row: P3, T3B, C4B, T3F, p3.
8th row: K3, p2, k1, p4, k1, p2, k3.
9th row: P2, T3B, p1, k4, p1, T3F, p2.
10th row: K2, p2, k2, p4, k2, p2, k2.
11th row: P1, T3B, p2, C4B, p2, T3F, p1.
12th row: K1, p2, k3, p4, k3, p2, k1.
13th row: T3B, p3, k4, p3, T3F.
14th row: P2, k4, p4, k4, p2.
15th row: K2, p4, C4B, p4, k2.
16th row: As 14th row.

17th row: T3F, p3, k4, p3, T3B.
18th row: As 12th row.
19th row: P1, T3F, p2, C4B, p2, T3B, p1.
20th row: As 10th row.
21st row: P2, T3F, p1, k4, p1, T3B, p2.
22nd row: As 8th row.
23rd row: P3, T3F, C4B, T3B, p3.
24th row: As 6th row.
25th row: P4, T3F, k2, T3B, p4.
26th row: As 4th row.
27th row: P5, T3F, T3B, p5.
28th row: As 2nd row.
Rep these 28 rows.

Twisted and Crossed Cable

Worked over 16 sts on a background of reversed st st.
1st row (right side): P2, C4B, p4, C4F, p2.
2nd row: K2, p4, k4, p4, k2.
3rd row: P1, T3B, T3F, p2, T3B, T3F, p1.
4th row: K1, [p2, k2] 3 times, p2, k1.
5th row: [T3B, p2, T3F] twice.
6th row: P2, k4, p4, k4, p2.
7th row: K2, p4, C4B, p4, k2.
8th row: As 6th row.
9th row: K2, p4, k4, p4, k2.
10th row: As 6th row.
11th row: As 7th row.
12th row: As 6th row.
13th row: [T3F, p2, T3B] twice.
14th row: As 4th row.
15th row: P1, T3F, T3B, p2, T3F, T3B, p1.
16th row: As 2nd row.
17th row: As 1st row.
18th row: As 2nd row.

19th row: As 3rd row.
20th row: As 4th row.
21st row: P1, [k2, p2] twice, k2, slip last 6 sts worked onto cable needle and wrap yarn 4 times anti-clockwise round these 6 sts, then slip the 6 sts back onto right hand needle, p2, k2, p1.
22nd row: As 4th row.
23rd row: As 15th row.
24th row: As 2nd row.
Rep these 24 rows.

Tramline Cable

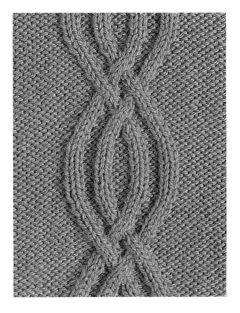

Worked over 18 sts on a background of reversed st st.
1st row (right side): K2, p3, k2, p4, k2, p3, k2.
2nd row: P2, k3, p2, k4, p2, k3, p2.
3rd row: As 1st row.
4th row: As 2nd row.
5th row: [T3F, p2] twice, T3B, p2, T3B.
6th row: K1, p2, k3, p2, k2, p2, k3, p2, k1.
7th row: P1, T3F, p2, T3F, T3B, p2, T3B, p1.
8th row: K2, p2, k3, p4, k3, p2, k2.
9th row: P2, T3F, p2, C4B, p2, T3B, p2.
10th row: K3, p2, k2, p4, k2, p2, k3.
11th row: P3, [T3F, T3B] twice, p3.
12th row: K4, p4, k2, p4, k4.
13th row: P4, C4F, p2, C4F, p4.
14th row: K4, p4, k2, p4, k4.
15th row: P3, [T3B, T3F] twice, p3.
16th row: K3, p2, k2, p4, k2, p2, k3.
17th row: P2, T3B, p2, C4B, p2, T3F, p2.
18th row: K2, p2, k3, p4, k3, p2, k2.
19th row: P1, T3B, p2, T3B, T3F, p2, T3F, p1.
20th row: K1, p2, k3, p2, k2, p2, k3, p2, k1.
21st row: [T3B, p2] twice, T3F, p2, T3F.
22nd row: As 2nd row.
23rd row: As 1st row.
Rep the last 2 rows once more then first of these rows again.
Rep these 26 rows.

Cables

Celtic Plait

Worked over a multiple of 10 + 5 (minimum 25). The example shown is worked over 25 stitches.

1st Foundation row (right side): K3, *p4, k6, rep from * to last 2 sts, p2.

2nd Foundation row: K2, *p6, k4; rep from * to last 3 sts, p3.

1st row: K3, *p4, C6F; rep from * to last 2 sts, p2.

2nd row: K2, *p6, k4; rep from * to last 3 sts, p3.

3rd row: *T5F, T5B; rep from * to last 5 sts, T5F.

4th row: P3, *k4, p6; rep from * to last 2 sts, k2.

5th row: P2, *C6B, p4, rep from * to last 3 sts, k3.

6th row: As 4th row.

7th row: *T5B, T5F; rep from * to last 5 sts, T5B.

8th row: As 2nd row.
Rep these 8 rows.

Lattice Pattern

Worked over a multiple of 16 + 1 (minimum 33) on a background of reversed st st. The example shown is worked over 33 sts.

1st row (right side): K1, *yf, k2, sl 1, k1, psso, p7, k2tog, k2, yf, k1; rep from * to end.

2nd row: P5, *k7, p9; rep from * to last 12 sts, k7, p5.

3rd row: K2, *yf, k2, sl 1, k1, psso, p5, k2tog, k2, yf, k2tog, yf, k1; rep from * to last 15 sts, yf, k2, sl 1, k1, psso, p5, k2tog, k2, yf, k2.

4th row: P6, *k5, p11; rep from * to last

11 sts, k5, p6.

5th row: *K2tog, yf, k1, yf, k2, sl 1, k1, psso, p3, k2tog, k2, yf, k2tog, yf; rep from * to last st, k1.

6th row: P7, *k3, p13; rep from * to last 10 sts, k3, p7.

7th row: K1, *k2tog, yf, k1, yf, k2, sl 1, k1, psso, p1, k2tog, k2, yf, [k2tog, yf] twice; rep from * to last 16 sts, k2tog, yf, k1, yf, k2, sl 1, k1, psso, p1, k2tog, k2, yf, k2tog, yf, k2.

8th row: P8, *k1, p15; rep from * to last 9 sts, k1, p8.

9th row: P5, *C7B, p9; rep from * to last 12 sts, C7B, p5.

10th row: K5, *p3, k1, p3, k9; rep from * to last 12 sts, p3, k1, p3, k5.

11th row: P4, *k2tog, k2, yf, k1, yf, k2, sl 1, k1, psso, p7; rep from * to last 13 sts, k2tog, k2, yf, k1, yf, k2, sl 1, k1, psso, p4.

12th row: K4, *p9, k7; rep from * to last 13 sts, p9, k4.

13th row: P3, *k2tog, k2, yf, k2tog, yf, k1, yf, k2, sl 1, k1, psso, p5; rep from * to last 14 sts, k2tog, k2, yf, k2tog, yf, k1, yf, k2, sl 1, k1, psso, p3.

14th row: K3, *p11, k5; rep from * to last 14 sts, p11, k3.

15th row: P2, *k2tog, k2, yf, [k2tog, yf] twice, k1, yf, k2, sl 1, k1, psso, p3; rep from * to last 15 sts, k2tog, k2, yf, [k2tog, yf] twice, k1, yf, k2, sl 1, k1, psso, p2.

16th row: K2, *p13, k3; rep from * to last 15 sts, p13, k2.

17th row: P1, *k2tog, k2, yf, [k2tog, yf] 3 times, k1, yf, k2, sl 1, k1, psso, p1; rep from * to end.

18th row: K1, *p15, k1; rep from * to end.

19th row: P1, k3, *p9, C7F; rep from * to last 13 sts, p9, k3, p1.

20th row: K1, p3, *k9, p3, k1, p3; rep from * to last 13 sts, k9, p3, k1.
Rep these 20 rows.

Hourglass

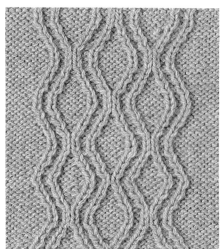

Worked over a multiple of 14 + 2 sts on a background of reversed st st. The example shown is worked over 30 sts.

1st row (wrong side): K1, p1, *k2, p1, k6, p1, k2, p2; rep from * to last 14 sts, k2, p1,

k6, p1, k2, p1, k1.

2nd row: P1, *T2F, p1, T2F, p4, T2B, p1, T2B; rep from * to last st, p1.

3rd row: [K2, p1] twice, *k4, [p1, k2] 3 times, p1; rep from * to last 10 sts, k4, [p1, k2] twice.

4th row: P2, *T2F, p1, T2F, p2, T2B, p1, T2B, p2; rep from * to end.

5th row: K3,*[p1, k2] 3 times, p1, k4; rep from * to last 13 sts, [p1, k2] 3 times, p1, k3.

6th row: P3, *T2F, p1, T2F, T2B, p1, T2B, p4; rep from * to last 13 sts, T2F, p1, T2F, T2B, p1, T2B, p3.

7th row: K4, *p1, k2, p2, k2, p1, k6; rep from * to last 12 sts, p1, k2, p2, k2, p1, k4.

8th row: P4, *k1, p2, k2, p2, k1 p6; rep from * to last 12 sts, k1, p2, k2, p2, k1, p4.

9th row: As 7th row.

10th row: P3, *T2B, p1, T2B, T2F, p1, T2F, p4; rep from * to last 13 sts, T2B, p1, T2B, T2F, p1, T2F, p3.

11th row: As 5th row.

12th row: P2, *T2B, p1, T2B, p2, T2F, p1, T2F, p2; rep from * to end.

13th row: As 3rd row.

14th row: P1, *T2B, p1, T2B, p4, T2F, p1, T2F; rep from * to last st, p1.

15th row: As 1st row.

16th row: P1, k1, *p2, k1, p6, k1, p2, k2; rep from * to last 14sts, p2, k1, p6, k1, p2, k1, p1.
Rep these 16 rows.

Four Dot Cable

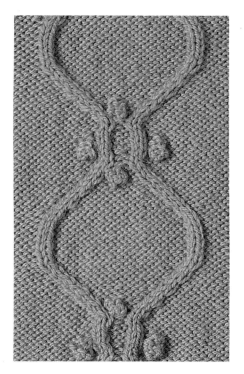

Worked over 25 sts on a background of reversed st st.

1st row (right side): P6, T4F, p2, MB (make bobble) as follows: knit into front, back and front of next st, [turn, k3] 3 times, turn, sl 1, k2tog, psso (bobble completed), p2, T4B,p6.

2nd row: K8, p2, k5, p2, k8.
3rd row: P8, T4F, p1, T4B, p8.
4th row: K10, p2, k1, p2, k10.
5th row: P8, T4B, p1, T4F, p8.
6th row: K6, MB, k1, p2, k5, p2, k1, MB, k6.
7th row: P8, k2, p5, k2, p8.
8th row: As 2nd row.
9th row: As 3rd row.
10th row: As 4th row.
11th row: P8, T4B, MB, T4F, p8.
12th row: As 2nd row.
13th row: P6, T4B, p5, T4F, p6.
14th row: K6, p2, k9, p2, k6.
15th row: P4, T4B, p9, T4F, p4.
16th row: K4, p2, k13, p2, k4.
17th row: P2, T4B, p13, T4F, p2.
18th row: K2, p2, k17, p2, k2.
19th row: T4B, p17, T4F.
20th row: P2, k21, p2.
21st row: K2, p21, k2.
Rep the last 2 rows twice more, then the 20th row again.
27th row: T4F, p17, T4B.
28th row: As 18th row.
29th row: P2, T4F, p13, T4B, p2.
30th row: As 16th row.
31st row: P4, T4F, p9, T4B, p4.
32nd row: As 14th row.
Rep these 32 rows.

Vine and Twist

Worked over 17 sts on a background of reversed st st.
1st row (right side): P6, C5, p6.
2nd row: K6, p5, k6.

3rd row: P5, T3B, k1, T3F, p5.
4th row: K5, p2, k1, p1, k1, p2, k5.
5th row: P4, T3B, p1, k1, p1, T3F, p4.
6th row: K4, p2, k2, p1, k2, p2, k4.
7th row: P3, k2tog, k1, p2, yon, k1, yfrn, p2, k1, sl 1, k1, psso, p3.
8th row: K3, p2, k2, p3, k2, p2, k3.
9th row: P2, k2tog, k1, p2, [k1, yf] twice, k1, p2, k1, sl 1, k1, psso, p2.
10th row: K2, p2, k2, p5, k2, p2, k2.
11th row: P1, k2tog, k1, p2, k2, yf, k1, yf, k2, p2, k1, sl 1, k1, psso, p1.
12th row: K1, p2, k2, p7, k2, p2, k1.
13th row: ·Purl into front and back of next st (called inc 1), k2, p2, k2, insert needle into next 2 sts on left-hand needle as if to k2tog, then slip both sts onto right-hand needle without knitting them (called sl 2tog knitwise), k1, pass 2 slipped sts over (called p2sso), k2, p2, k2, inc 1.
14th row: As 10th row.
15th row: P1, inc 1, k2, p2, k1, sl 2tog knitwise, k1, p2sso, k1, p2, k2, inc 1, p1.
16th row: As 8th row.
17th row: P2, inc 1, k2, p2, sl 2tog knitwise, k1, p2sso, p2, k2, inc 1, p2.
18th row: As 6th row.
19th row: P4, T3F, p1, k1, p1, T3B, p4.
20th row: As 4th row.
21st row: P5, T3F, k1, T3B, p5.
22nd row: As 2nd row.
23rd row: As 1st row.
24th row: As 2nd row.
25th row: P6, k5, p6.
26th row: As 2nd row.
Rep these 26 rows.

Twisted Ladder Cable

Work over 12 sts on a background of reversed st st.
1st row (right side): T3F, p2, T3B, T3F, p1.

2nd row: K1, [yfrn, p2, pass yfrn over the 2 purled sts, k2] twice, yfrn, p2, pass yfrn over 2 purled sts, k1.
3rd row: P1, T3F, T3B, p2, T3F.
4th row: *Yfrn, p2, pass yfrn over the 2 purled sts*, k4; rep from * to * once more, yrn, p2, pass yrn over 2 purled sts, k2.
5th row: P2, C4B, p4, k2.
6th row: As 4th row.
7th row: P1, T3B, T3F, p2, T3B.
8th row: As 2nd row.
9th row: T3B, p2, T3F, T3B, p1.
10th row: K2, *yfrn, p2, pass yfrn over 2 purled sts*, yrn, p2, pass yrn over 2 purled sts, k4, rep from * to * once more.
11th row: K2, p4, C4F, p2.
12th row: As 10th row.
Rep these 12 rows.

Two and Three Cross

Worked over 18 sts on a background of reversed st st.
1st row (right side): P1, [T2B, T2F, p2] twice, T2B, T2F, p1.
2nd row: K1, [p1, k2] 5 times, p1, k1.
3rd row: P1, [T2F, T2B, p2] twice, T2F, T2B, p1.
4th row: K2, [C2P, k4] twice, C2P, k2.
5th row: As 1st row.
6th row: As 2nd row.
7th row: [T2B, p2, T2F] 3 times.
8th row: P1, [k4, C2P] twice, k4, p1.
9th row: K1, p3, T2B, T2F, p2, T2B, T2F, p3, k1.
10th row: P1, k3, [p1, k2] 3 times, p1, k3, p1.
11th row: K1, p3, T2F, T2B, p2, T2F, T2B, p3, k1.
12th row: As 8th row.
13th row: [T2F, p2, T2B] 3 times.
14th row: As 2nd row.
15th row: As 3rd row.
16th row: As 4th row.
Rep these 16 rows.

Cables

Lattice Cross

Worked over 32 sts on a background of reversed st st.

1st row (right side): *[T2L] twice, p2, T2R, T2L, p2, [T2R] twice; rep from * once more.

2nd row: [K1,PB1] twice, [k2, PB1] 3 times, [k1, PB1, k2, PB1] twice, [k2, PB1] twice, k1, PB1, k1.

3rd row: P1, *[T2L] twice, T2R, p2, T2L, [T2R] twice*, p2 ; rep from * to * once more, p1.

4th row: K2, *PB1, k1, [PB1] twice, k4, [PB1] twice, k1, PB1*, k4, rep from * to * once more, k2.

5th row: P2, [T2L] twice, p4, [T2R] twice, p4, [T2L] twice, p4, [T2R] twice, p2.

6th row: K3, PB1, k1, PB1, k4, PB1, k1, [PB1] twice, k4, [PB1] twice, k1, PB1, k4, PB1, k1, PB1, k3.

7th row: P3, [T2L] twice, p2, [T2R] twice, T2L, p2, T2R, [T2L] twice, p2, [T2R] twice, p3.

8th row: K4, [PB1, k1, PB1, k2] twice, PB1, k2,PB1 [k2, PB1, k1, PB1] twice, k4.

9th row: P4, [T2L] twice, [T2R] twice, p2, T2L, T2R, p2, [T2L] twice, [T2R] twice, p4.

10th row: K5, *PB1, k1, T2, k1, PB1*, k4, T2, k4;rep from * to * once more, k5.

11th row: P4, [T2R] twice, [T2L] twice, p2, T2R, T2L, p2, [T2R] twice, [T2L] twice, p4.

12th row: As 8th row.

13th row: P3, [T2R] twice, p2, [T2L] twice, T2R, p2, T2L, [T2R] twice, p2, [T2L] twice, p3.

14th row: As 6th row.

15th row: P2, [T2R] twice, p4, [T2L] twice, p4, [T2R] twice, p4, [T2L] twice, p2.

16th row: As 4th row.

17th row: P1, *[T2R] twice, T2L, p2, T2R, [T2L] twice*, p2; rep from * to * once more, p1.

18th row: As 2nd row.

19th row: *[T2R] twice, p2, T2L, T2R, p2, [T2L] twice; rep from * once more.

20th row: PB1, k1, PB1, k4, T2, k4, PB1, k1, T2, k1, PB1, k4, T2, k4, PB1, k1, PB1.

Rep these 20 rows.

Bobble Tree

Worked over 12 sts.

1st row (wrong side): K5, p2, k5.

2nd row: P4, C2B, C2F, p4.

3rd row: K3, T2F, p2, T2B, k3.

4th row: P2, T2B, C2B, C2F, T2F, p2.

5th row: K1, T2F, k1, p4, k1, T2B, k1.

6th row: T2B, p1, T2B, k2, T2F, p1, T2F.

7th row: P1, k2, p1, k1, p2, k1, p1, k2, p1.

8th row: MB, p1, T2B, p1, k2, p1, T2F, p1, MB.

9th row: K2, p1, k2, p2, k2, p1, k2.

10th row: P2, MB, p2, k2, p2, MB, p2.

Rep these 10 rows.

Triple Criss Cross Cable

Worked over 26 sts on a background of reversed st st.

1st row (right side): P5, [C4F, p2] twice, C4F, p5.

2nd row: K5, [p4, k2] twice, p4, k5.

3rd row: P4, [T3B, T3F] 3 times, p4.

4th row: K4, p2, [k2, p4] twice, k2, p2, k4.

5th row: P3, T3B, [p2, C4B] twice, p2, T3F, p3.

6th row: K3, p2, k3, p4, k2, p4, k3, p2, k3.

7th row: P2, T3B, p2, [T3B, T3F] twice, p2, T3F, p2.

8th row: K2, p2, k3, p2, k2, p4, k2, p2, k3, p2, k2.

9th row: P1, [T3B, p2] twice, C4F, [p2, T3F] twice, p1.

10th row: K1, [p2, k3] twice, p4, [k3, p2] twice, k1.

11th row: [T3B, p2] twice, T3B, [T3F, p2] twice, T3F.

12th row: [P2, k3] twice, p2, k2, [p2, k3] twice, p2.

13th row: [K2, p3] twice, k2, p2, [k2, p3] twice, k2.

14th row: As 12th row.

15th row: [T3F, p2] twice, T3F, [T3B, p2] twice, T3B.

16th row: As 10th row.

17th row: P1, [T3F, p2] twice, C4F, [p2, T3B] twice, p1.

18th row: As 8th row.

19th row: [P2, T3F] twice, T3B, T3F, [T3B, p2] twice.

20th row: As 6th row.

21st row: P3, T3F, [p2, C4B] twice, p2, T3B, p3.

22nd row: As 4th row.

23rd row: P4, [T3F, T3B] 3 times, p4.

24th row: As 2nd row.

Rep these 24 rows.

Double Cross

Worked over 24 sts on a background of reversed st st.

1st row (right side): K4, p4, k8, p4, k4.

92

2nd row: P4, k4, p8, k4, p4.
3rd row: K4, p4, C8B, p4, k4.
4th row: As 2nd row.
5th row: C5L, p2, C5R, C5L, p2, C5R.
6th row: K1, p4, [k2, p4] 3 times, k1.
7th row: P1, C5L, C5R, p2, C5L, C5R, p1.
8th row: K2, p8, k4, p8, k2.
9th row: P2, C8B, p4, C8B, p2.
10th row: As 8th row.
11th row: P2, k8, p4, k8, p2.
12th row: As 8th row.
13th row: As 9th row.
14th row: As 8th row.
15th row: P1, C5R, C5L, p2, C5R, C5L, p1.
16th row: As 6th row.
17th row: C5R, p2, C5L, C5R, p2, C5L.
18th row: As 2nd row.
19th row: As 3rd row.
20th row: As 2nd row.
21st row: As 1st row.
22nd row: As 2nd row.
Rep these 22 rows.

Interrupted Weave

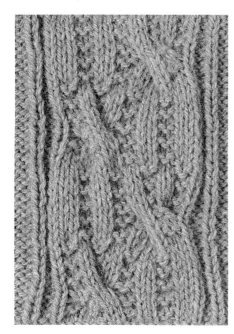

Worked over 24 sts on a background of reversed st st.
1st row (right side): K1, p2, k3, p2, k2, p2, k9, p2, k1.
2nd row: [P1, k2] twice, p2, k2, p11, k2, p1.
Rep the last 2 rows once more.
5th row: K1, p2, k3, p2, k2, p2, C8F, k1, p2, k1.
6th row: As 2nd row.
Now work 1st and 2nd rows twice more.
11th row: K1, p2, k9, p2, k2, p2, k3, p2, k1.
12th row: P1, k2, p11, k2, p2, [k2, p1] twice.
Rep the last 2 rows once more.
15th row: K1, p2, k1, C8F, p2, k2, p2, k3, p2, k1.

16th row: As 12th row.
Now work 11th and 12th rows twice more.
Rep these 20 rows.

Narrow Cross and Twist

Worked over 12 sts on a background of reversed st st.
1st row (right side): C4F, p4, C4B.
2nd row: P4, k4, p4.
3rd row: K2, T3F, p2, T3B, k2.
4th row: P2, k1, p2, k2, p2, k1, p2.
5th row: K2, p1, T3F, T3B, p1, k2.
6th row: P2, k2, p4, k2, p2.
7th row: K2, p2, C4B, p2, k2.
8th row: As 6th row.
9th row: K2, p1, T3B, T3F, p1, k2.
10th row: As 4th row.
11th row: K2, T3B, p2, T3F, k2.
12th row: As 2nd row.
Rep these 12 rows.

Wide Cross and Twist

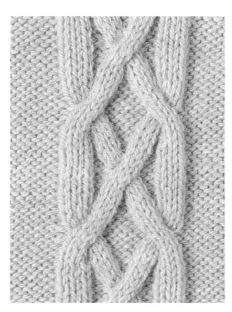

Worked over 18 sts on a background of reversed st st.
Special Abbreviations
T4BP (Twist 4 Back Purl) = slip next st onto cable needle and hold at back of work, knit next 3 sts from left-hand needle, then purl st from cable needle.
T4FK (Twist 4 Front Knit) = slip next 3 sts onto cable needle and hold at front of work, purl next st from left-hand needle, then knit sts from cable needle.
1st row (right side): C6F, p6, C6B.
2nd row: P6, k6, p6.
3rd row: K3, T4FK, p4, T4BP, k3.
4th row: P3, k1, p3, k4, p3, k1, p3.
5th row: K3, p1, T4FK, p2, T4BP, p1, k3.
6th row: P3, [k2, p3] 3 times.
7th row: K3, p2, T4FK, T4BP, p2, k3.
8th row: P3, k3, p6, k3, p3.
9th row: K3, p3, C6B, p3, k3.
10th row: P3, k3, p6, k3, p3.
11th row: K3, p2, T4BP, T4FK, p2, k3.
12th row: As 6th row.
13th row: K3, p1, T4BP, p2, T4FK, p1, k3.
14th row: P3, k1, p3, k4, p3, k1, p3.
15th row: K3, T4BP, p4, T4FK, k3.
16th row: As 2nd row.
Rep these 16 rows.

Ladder Cross

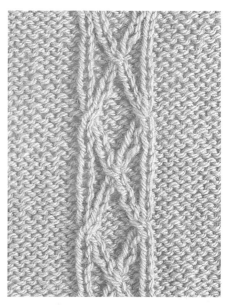

Worked over 8 sts on a background of reversed st st.
1st row (right side): C2L, p4, C2R.
2nd row: P2, k4, p2.
3rd row: K1, T2F, p2, T2B, k1.
4th row: P1, k1, p1, k2, p1, k1, p1.
5th row: K1, p1, T2F, T2B, p1, k1.
6th row: P1, k2, p2, k2, p1.
7th row: K1, p2, C2B, p2, k1.
8th row: As 6th row.
9th row: K1, p1, T2B, T2F, p1, k1.
10th row: As 4th row.
11th row: K1, T2B, p2, T2F, k1.
12th row: As 2nd row.
Rep these 12 rows.

Cables

Serpent Panel

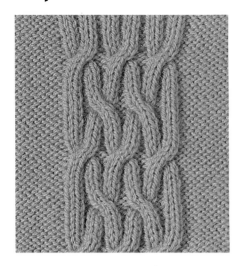

Worked over a multiple of 8 + 6 sts on a background of reversed st st. The example shown is worked over 22 sts.

Special Abbreviation

Twist 6 Back (or Front) = slip next 4 sts onto cable needle and hold at back (or front) of work, knit next 2 sts from left-hand needle, slip the 2 purl sts from cable needle back to left-hand needle and purl them, then k2 sts from cable needle.

1st row (right side): K2, *p2, k2; rep from * to end.
2nd row: P2, *k2, p2; rep from * to end.
3rd row: *Twist 6 Back (see Special Abbreviation), p2; rep from * to last 6 sts, Twist 6 Back.
4th row: As 2nd row.
5th row: As 1st row.
Rep the last 2 rows twice more, then the first of these rows again.
11th row: K2, *p2, Twist 6 Front; rep from * to last 4 sts, p2, k2.
12th row: As 2nd row.
13th row: As 1st row.
Rep the last 2 rows once more, then the first of these rows again.
Rep these 16 rows.

Twisted Tree

Worked over 9 sts.
1st row (right side): P3, [KB1] 3 times, p3.
2nd row: K3, [PB1] 3 times, k3.
3rd row: P2, T2R, KB1, T2L, p2.
4th row: K2, [PB1, k1] twice, PB1, k2.
5th row: P1, T2R, p1, KB1, p1, T2L, p1.
6th row: K1, [PB1, k2] twice, PB1, k1.
7th row: T2R, p1, [KB1] 3 times, p1, T2L.
8th row: PB1, k2, [PB1] 3 times, k2, PB1.
Rep these 8 rows.

Branched Cable I

Worked over 10 sts on a background of reversed st st.
1st row (right side): P3, C4F, p3.
2nd row: K3, p4, k3.
3rd row: P2, C3B, C3F, p2.
4th row: K2, p6, k2.
5th row: P1, C3B, k2, C3F, p1.
6th row: K1, p8, k1.
7th row: C3B, k4, C3F.
8th row: Purl.
Rep these 8 rows.

The cable as given above crosses to the left. To work the cable crossed to the right, work C4B instead of C4F in the 1st row.

Branched Cable II

Worked over 10 sts on a background of reversed st st.
1st row (right side): P3, C4B, p3.
2nd row: K3, p4, k3.
3rd row: P2, T3B, T3F, p2.
4th row: [K2, p2] twice, k2.
5th row: P1, T3B, p2, T3F, p1.
6th row: K1, p2, k4, p2, k1.
7th row: T3B, p4, T3F.
8th row: P2, k6, p2.
Rep these 8 rows.

The cable as given above crosses to the right. To work the cable crossed to the left, work C4F instead of C4B in the 1st row.

Interlocking Twist

Worked over 27 sts.
1st row (right side): K5, p1, k6, p3, k6, p1, k5.
2nd row: P5, k1, p6, k3, p6, k1, p5.
3rd row: K5, p1, C6B, p3, C6F, p1, k5.
4th row: As 2nd row.
Rep the last 4 rows once more, then 1st and 2nd rows again.
11th row: C12F, p3, C12B.
12th row: P6, k1, p5, k3, p5, k1, p6.
13th row: K6, p1, k5, p3, k5, p1, k6.
14th row: As 12th row.
15th row: C6F, p1, k5, p3, k5, p1, C6B.
16th row: As 12th row.
Rep the last 4 rows 3 times more, then 13th and 14th rows again.
31st row: C12B, p3, C12F.
32nd row: As 2nd row.
33rd–36th rows: As 1st–4th rows inclusive.
Rep these 4 rows once more.
Rep these 40 rows.

Moss and Faggot

Worked lengthways over 17 sts.
Note: Sts should only be counted after the 12th row.
1st row (right side): K2, yf, k3, yf, k2tog, [p1, k1] 5 times.
2nd row: Yf (to make 1 st), k2tog, [k1, p1,] 3 times, k1, k2tog, yf, k5, yf, k2.
3rd row: K2, yf, k1, k2tog, yf, k1, yf, k2tog, k1, yf, k2tog, [p1, k1] 4 times.
4th row: Yf (to make 1 st), k2tog, [k1, p1] twice, k1, [k2tog, yf, k1] twice, k2, yf, k2tog, k1, yf, k2.
5th row: K2, yf, k1, k2tog, yf, k5, yf, k2tog, k1, yf, k2tog, [p1, k1] 3 times.
6th row: Yf (to make 1 st), k2tog, k1, p1, k1, [k2tog, yf, k1] twice, k6, yf, k2tog, k1, yf, k2.
7th row: [K2tog, k1, yf] twice, k2tog, k3, [k2tog, yf, k1] twice, [p1, k1] 3 times.
8th row: Yf (to make 1 st), k2tog, [k1, p1] 3 times, yon, k2tog, k1, yf, k2tog, [k1, k2tog, yf] twice, k1, k2tog.
9th row: [K2tog, k1, yf] twice, k3tog, yf, k1, k2tog, yf, [k1, p1] 4 times, k1.
10th row: Yf (to make 1 st), k2tog, [k1, p1] 4 times, yon, k2tog, k3, k2tog, yf, k1, k2tog.
11th row: K2tog, k1, yf, k2tog, k1, k2tog, yf, [k1, p1] 5 times, k1.
12th row: Yf (to make 1 st), k2tog, [k1, p1] 5 times, yon, k3tog, yf, k1, k2tog.
Rep these 12 rows.

Wavy Border

Worked lengthways over 13 sts.
Note: Stitches should only be counted after the 1st, 4th, 5th or 14th rows.
1st and every alt row (wrong side): K2, purl to last 2 sts, k2.
2nd row: Sl 1, k3, yf, k5, yf, k2tog, yf, k2.

4th row: Sl 1, k4, sl 1, k2tog, psso, k2, [yf, k2tog] twice, k1.
6th row: Sl 1, k3, sl 1, k1, psso, k2, [yf, k2tog] twice, k1.
8th row: Sl 1, k2, sl 1, k1, psso, k2, [yf, k2tog] twice, k1.
10th row: Sl 1, k1, sl 1, k1, psso, k2, [yf, k2tog] twice, k1.
12th row: K1, sl 1, k1, psso, k2, yf, k1, yf, k2tog, yf, k2.
14th row: Sl 1, [k3, yf] twice, k2tog, yf, k2.
Rep these 14 rows.

Scallop Edging

Multiple of 13 + 2
1st row (right side): K3, *sl 1, k1, psso, sl 2, k3tog, p2sso, k2tog, k4; rep from * to last 12 sts, sl 1, k1, psso, sl 2, k3tog, p2sso, k2tog, k3.
2nd row: P4, *yrn, p1, yrn, p6; rep from * to last 5 sts, yrn, p1, yrn, p4.
3rd row: K1, yf, *k2, sl·1, k1, psso, k1, k2tog, k2, yf; rep from * to last st, k1.
4th row: P2, *yrn, p2, yrn, p3, yrn, p2, yrn, p1; rep from * to last st, p1.
5th row: K2, yf, k1, *yf, sl 1, k1, psso, k1, sl 1, k2tog, psso, k1, k2tog, [yf, k1] 3 times; rep from * to last 12 sts, yf, sl 1, k1, psso, sl 1, k2tog, psso, k1, k2tog, yf, k1, yf, k2.
6th row: Purl.
7th row: K5, *yf, sl 2, k3tog, p2sso, yf, k7; rep from * to last 10 sts, yf, sl 2, k3tog, p2sso, yf, k5.
Work 4 rows in garter st (every row knit).

Diagonal Rib and Scallop

Worked lengthways over 8 sts.

1st Foundation row (right side): K6, knit into front and back of next st, yf, sl 1 purlwise. 9 sts.
2nd Foundation row: KB1, k1, [yf, sl 1, k1, psso, k1] twice, yf, sl 1 purlwise. 9 sts.
1st row: KB1, knit to last st, knit into front and back of last st, turn and cast on 2 sts. 12 sts.
2nd row: K1, knit into front and back of next st, k2, [yf, sl 1, k1, psso, k1] twice, yf, k1, yf, sl 1 purlwise. 14 sts.
3rd row: KB1, knit to last 2 sts, knit into front and back of next st, yf, sl 1 purlwise. 15 sts.
4th row: KB1, knit into front and back of next st, k2, [yf, sl 1, k1, psso, k1] 3 times, k1, yf, sl 1 purlwise. 16 sts.
5th row: KB1, knit to last 2 sts, k2tog. 15 sts.
6th row: Sl 1 purlwise, k1, psso, sl 1, k1, psso, k4, [yf, sl 1, k1, psso, k1] twice, yf, sl 1 purlwise. 13 sts.
7th row: KB1, knit to last 2 sts, k2tog. 12 sts.
8th row: Cast off 3 sts (1 st on right-hand needle), k2, yf, sl 1, k1, psso, k1, yf, sl 1, k1, psso, yf, sl 1 purlwise. 9 sts.
Rep these 8 rows.

Fan Edging

Worked lengthways over 14 sts.
Note: Sts should only be counted after the 19th or 20th rows.
1st row (wrong side): K2, yf, k2tog, k5, yf, k2tog, yf, k3.
2nd and every alt row: K1, yf, k2tog, knit to end.
3rd row: K2, yf, k2tog, k4, [yf, k2tog] twice, yf, k3.
5th row: K2, yf, k2tog, k3, [yf, k2tog] 3 times, yf, k3.
7th row: K2, yf, k2tog, k2, [yf, k2tog] 4 times, yf, k3.
9th row: K2, yf, k2tog, k1, [yf, k2tog] 5 times, yf, k3.
11th row: K2, yf, k2tog, k1, k2tog, [yf, k2tog] 5 times, k2.
13th row: K2, yf, k2tog, k2, k2tog, [yf, k2tog] 4 times, k2.
15th row: K2, yf, k2tog, k3, k2tog, [yf, k2tog] 3 times, k2.
17th row: K2, yf, k2tog, k4, k2tog, [yf, k2tog] twice, k2.
19th row: K2, yf, k2tog, k5, k2tog, yf, k2tog, k2.
20th row: K1, yf, k2tog, knit to end.
Rep these 20 rows.

Double Diamond Edging

Worked lengthways over 9 sts.
Note: Sts should only be counted after the 1st or 12th rows.
1st and every alt row (right side): Knit.
2nd row: K3, k2tog, yf, k2tog, [yf, k1] twice.
4th row: K2, [k2tog, yf] twice, k3, yf, k1.
6th row: K1, [k2tog, yf] twice, k5, yf, k1.
8th row: K3, [yf, k2tog] twice, k1, k2tog, yf, k2tog.
10th row: K4, yf, k2tog, yf, k3tog, yf, k2tog.
12th row: K5, yf, k3tog, yf, k2tog.
Rep these 12 rows.

Leaf Edging

Worked lengthways over 8 sts.
Note: Stitches should only be counted after the 18th row.
1st row (right side): K5, yf, k1, yf, k2.
2nd row: P6, inc in next st by knitting into front and back of it, k3.
3rd row: K4, p1, k2, yf, k1, yf, k3.
4th row: P8, inc in next st, k4.
5th row: K4, p2, k3, yf, k1, yf, k4.
6th row: P10, inc in next st, k5.
7th row: K4, p3, k4, yf, k1, yf, k5.
8th row: P12, inc in next st, k6.
9th row: K4, p4, yb, sl 1, k1, psso, k7, k2tog, k1.
10th row: P10, inc in next st, k7.
11th row: K4, p5, yb, sl 1, k1, psso, k5, k2tog, k1.
12th row: P8, inc in next st, k2, p1, k5.
13th row: K4, p1, k1, p4, yb, sl 1, k1, psso, k3, k2tog, k1.
14th row: P6, inc in next st, k3, p1, k5.
15th row: K4, p1, k1, p5, yb, sl 1, k1, psso, k1, k2tog, k1

Garter Stitch Edging

16th row: P4, inc in next st, k4, p1, k5.
17th row: K4, p1, k1, p6, yb, sl 1, k2tog, psso, k1.
18th row: P2tog, cast off 5 sts using p2tog as first of these sts (1 st on right-hand needle), k1, p1, k5.
Rep these 18 rows.

Worked lengthways over 10 sts.
Note: Sts should only be counted after the 8th row.
1st row (right side): K3, [yf, k2tog] twice, [yf] twice, k2tog, k1.
2nd row: K3, p1, k2, [yf, k2tog] twice, k1.
3rd row: K3, [yf, k2tog] twice, k1, [yf] twice, k2tog, k1.
4th row: K3, p1, k3, [yf, k2tog] twice, k1.
5th row: K3, [yf, k2tog] twice, k2, [yf] twice, k2tog, k1.
6th row: K3, p1, k4, [yf, k2tog] twice, k1.
7th row: K3, [yf, k2tog] twice, k6.
8th row: Cast off 3 sts, k4 (not including st already on needle after casting off), [yf, k2tog] twice, k1.
Rep these 8 rows.

Birds Eye Edging

Worked lengthways over 7 sts.
Note: Sts should only be counted after the 4th row.
1st row (right side): K1, k2tog, [yf] twice, k2tog, [yf] twice, k2.
2nd row: K3, [p1, k2] twice.
3rd row: K1, k2tog, [yf] twice, k2tog, k4.
4th row: Cast off 2 sts, k3 (not including st already on needle after casting off), p1, k2.
Rep these 4 rows.

Diamond Edge

Worked lengthways over 12 sts.
Note: Stitches should only be counted after the 1st or 12th rows.
1st and every alt row (right side): K1, yfrn, p2tog, knit to end.
2nd row: K2, yf, k3, yf, sl 1, k1, psso, k2, yfrn, p2tog, k1.
4th row: K2, yf, k5, yf, sl 1, k1, psso, k1, yfrn, p2tog, k1.
6th row: K2, yf, k3, yf, sl 1, k1, psso, k2, yf, sl 1, k1, psso, yfrn, p2tog, k1.
8th row: K1, k2tog, yf, sl 1, k1, psso, k3, k2tog, yf, k2, yfrn, p2tog, k1.
10th row: K1, k2tog, yf, sl 1, k1, psso, k1, k2tog, yf, k3, yfrn, p2tog, k1.
12th row: K1, k2tog, yf, sl 1, k1, k2tog, psso, yf, k4, yfrn, p2tog, k1.
Rep these 12 rows.

Willow Edging

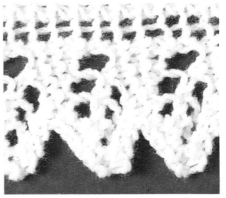

Worked over 10 sts.
Note: Stitches should only be counted after the 8th row.
1st row (right side): Sl 1, k2, yf, k2tog, *[yf] twice, k2tog; rep from * once more, k1.
2nd row: K3, [p1, k2] twice, yf, k2tog, k1.
3rd row: Sl 1, k2, yf, k2tog, k2, *[yf] twice, k2tog; rep from * once more, k1.
4th row: K3, p1, k2, p1, k4, yf, k2tog, k1.
5th row: Sl 1, k2, yf, k2tog, k4, *[yf] twice, k2tog; rep from * once more, k1.
6th row: K3, p1, k2, p1, k6, yf, k2tog, k1.
7th row: Sl 1, k2, yf, k2tog, k11.
8th row: Cast off 6 sts, k6 (not including st already on needle after casting off), yf, k2tog, k1.
Rep these 8 rows.